Contract Hazards

Contract Hazards

Lawyers and Their Landmines

STEPHEN J. CHOI
MITU GULATI
ROBERT E. SCOTT

OXFORD
UNIVERSITY PRESS

OXFORD
UNIVERSITY PRESS

Oxford University Press is a department of the University of Oxford. It furthers the University's objective of excellence in research, scholarship, and education by publishing worldwide. Oxford is a registered trade mark of Oxford University Press in the UK and in certain other countries.

Published in the United States of America by Oxford University Press
198 Madison Avenue, New York, NY 10016, United States of America.

Library of Congress Cataloging-in-Publication Data
Names: Choi, Stephen Jung, 1966– author | Gulati, Mitu author | Scott, Robert E., 1944– author
Title: Contract hazards : lawyers and their landmines / Stephen J. Choi,
Mitu Gulati, Robert E. Scott.
Description: New York : Oxford University Press, 2025. |
Includes bibliographical references and index.
Identifiers: LCCN 2025037582 (print) | LCCN 2025037583 (ebook) |
ISBN 9780197821749 hardback | ISBN 9780197821763 updf | ISBN 9780197821756 epub |
ISBN 9780197821770 online
Subjects: LCSH: Contracts | Commercial law | LCGFT: Law materials
Classification: LCC K1024 .C46 2026 (print) | LCC K1024 (ebook) |
DDC 346.07—dc23/eng/20250813
LC record available at https://lccn.loc.gov/2025037582
LC ebook record available at https://lccn.loc.gov/2025037583

DOI: 10.1093/9780197821770.001.0001

The manufacturer's authorized representative in the EU for product safety is Oxford University Press España S.A. of Parque Empresarial San Fernando de Henares, Avenida de Castilla, 2 – 28830 Madrid (www.oup.es/en or product.safety@oup.com). OUP España S.A. also acts as importer into Spain of products made by the manufacturer.

Note to Readers

This publication is designed to provide accurate and authoritative information in regard to the subject matter covered. It is based upon sources believed to be accurate and reliable and is intended to be current as of the time it was written. It is sold with the understanding that the publisher is not engaged in rendering legal, accounting, or other professional services. If legal advice or other expert assistance is required, the services of a competent professional person should be sought. Also, to confirm that the information has not been affected or changed by recent developments, traditional legal research techniques should be used, including checking primary sources where appropriate.

(Based on the Declaration of Principles jointly adopted by a Committee of the American Bar Association and a Committee of Publishers and Associations.)

Contents

PART II. GURUS AND NOVICES: BUILDING A THEORY

PART III. OTHER ARTIFACTS: LAWYERS, LEGAL CULTURE, AND LANDMINES

Acknowledgments

Too many people made this book possible for us to thank everyone here. The heart of the book is the hundreds of interviews with lawyers. Having promised them that nothing they said will be for attribution, we cannot thank them by name. But we hope they will find that we have been faithful to their core narratives.

Then there are our academic colleagues, many of whom have joined us on various parts of this project as we borrowed their knowledge and insights to look into domains that were initially foreign to us. We will fail to thank them all adequately because this journey has been a long one and so many have helped us along the way. We apologize in advance. And we know, even as we complete this manuscript, that there is much left unexplored.

A question that we've asked ourselves more than a few times along the way is how we came to see this project as a book. It started as *Contractual Landmines*, an article about systematic contractual hazards in sovereign bond contracts, aimed at an academic audience. The article described the prevalence of numerous anomalies in the wording of supposedly standard sovereign bond contracts that went unrecognized when the contract was executed but then were subsequently exploited when the sovereigns in question attempted to restructure their debts. That's where the project would have ended but for a set of three academic workshops that each of us had separately scheduled. *Contractual Landmines* was the paper we had in draft. Unusual for us, we decided that we would present that paper together at these workshops. Thanks to COVID, we had not seen each other in person in two years or more. This was an opportunity to connect again. We were excited about our *Landmines* paper and thought others might be as well.

At the outset, the workshops were not wildly successful. The first question at the first of the three workshops provided a hint of the skepticism that was to follow.

> *I'm reading your so-called landmine example on page three. And the clause makes perfect sense to me. I don't understand what you mean by landmines. I don't understand the point of the project.*

It turned out, the colleague who offered this comment had only read the first few pages of the paper where we showed a standard clause followed thereafter by the landmine version that omitted several key words. Those missing words, that the contract drafters had not noticed, inverted the intended meaning of the clause. The colleague had read the normal version, found it made sense, and stopped reading: he found the premise of our project that landmines could exist so implausible that there was no need to read further. Thankfully, we had a slide showing both the normal version and the landmine version. With a bit of glee, we put up both versions so that everyone in the audience could see the landmine. But if we thought it was to be smooth sailing from thereon, we were wrong.

Another comment followed:

> *This would never happen in an M&A practice. The motto of the firm I worked at was that no contract would go out the door unless we could fully explain every clause to a client.*

On to the next workshop:

> *If you are right, none of these law firms should be in business. They'd be sued and go bankrupt. And that's not happening. So . . .*

And,

> *I recently read a paper by [X] who studied a market not too dissimilar from yours and he finds that errors such as these are corrected by the market, just as theory would predict.*

Then, the last workshop and the coup de grâce for one of us:

> *Doesn't what you say contradict much of your prior work, including the Contracts casebook that I've been using for years?*

After the third workshop, we were grousing about our inability to persuade some readers that we had found something truly important. An old friend, Paul Stephan, had invited us for cocktails after the workshop. Paul was a sympathetic reader, but he had also witnessed the skepticism from both theorists and empiricists. He responded with characteristic candor to our complaints: "You are basically asking people to believe in unicorns. Not one unicorn, but a herd of unicorns. You need more evidence. And not just about sovereign bonds."

The book was born.

It was one thing for us to decide to write a book. But then the question was how to show others what we believed was a new perspective on contract theory. An initial thought was to identify as many aberrant contractual terms that subsequently blew up without warning that we could find. And we did go down that path initially. We assembled a file of seventeen of these landmines. In each case, we described the standard clause that people in the market thought they had contracted for, and then showed the slight variations in language in a subset of clauses that arguably supported a meaning 180 degrees from the market understanding. The problem, however, was that asking a reader to wade through pages of clause after clause was, well, torturous.

Here, we owe a debt to Ron Gilson. As background, Ron's classic piece from forty years ago on the role that deal lawyers play as "transaction cost engineers" has been foundational to our thinking.[1] Ron had attended one of our meetings with lawyers where they were discussing these landmines, and he advised:

> *Think of it as a story of your journey into these various corners of legal practice. The core of your project is the stories these lawyers have told you. Some of them have a folk tale aspect, but they don't come out of nowhere. They tell similar stories for a reason—they capture a core truth about the practice. If you can use data and theory to unpack and enhance their stories, you will have your book.*

We are not sure we have lived up to Ron's high standards. But we followed his advice. This book is our story, built from a combination of the stories we were told, the data we collected to test aspects of the stories, and the theory that helped us make sense of it all. Many of the lawyers who told their stories spoke to us on multiple occasions and at much greater length than it was reasonable for us to expect. Others read and commented on early drafts. They are authors of this book just as much as we are.

[1] Ronald G. Gilson, *Value Creation by Business Lawyers: Legal Skills and Asset Pricing*, 1973 YALE L. J. 239 (1984).

The many friends and colleagues who, with generosity and patience, read drafts, shared insights, helped us garner interviews, and contributed to our many stories include Tracy Alloway, Rob Anderson, Douglas Baird, Omri Ben Shahar, Patrick Bolton, Jamie Boyle, Caroline Bradley, Michael Bradley, Vince Buccola, Lee Buchheit, Lachlan Burn, Melissa Butler, Tara Chowdhury, Faith Chudkowski, Joseph Cotterill, John Coyle, Eva Davis, Elisabeth De Fontenay, Amanda Dixon, Keegan Drake, Reid Feldman, Ian Feng, Merritt Fox, Anna Gelpern, Tracey George, Ron Gilson, Victor Goldberg, Joel Greenberg, Henry Hansmann, David Hoffman, Cathy Hwang, Matt Jennejohn, Emily Johnson, Marcel Kahan, Kimberly Krawiec, Jody Kraus, Peter Lyons, David Leinwand, Dimitrios Lyratzakis, Yannis Manuelides, Florencia Marotta-Wurgler, Rodrigo Olivares-Caminal, Nate Oman, Ugo Panizza, Samir Parikh, Un Kyung Park, Graham Penn, Cecil Quillen, Bob Rasmussen, Barak Richman, Chuck Sabel, Felix Salmon, Melissa Sawyer, Alan Schwartz, Elizabeth Scott, Madison Sherill, Paul Stephan, Mark Stumpf, Anna Szymanski, Hadar Tanne, Jeremy Telman, George Triantis, Jena Watson, Mark Weidemaier, Glenn West, Robin Wigglesworth, Tess Wilkinson-Ryan, Albert Yoon, and Jeromin Zettelmeyer. Every one of their comments has contributed to this book. It goes without saying that errors are ours.

A special thanks to Julia Nielsen for the cover design and to Elizabeth Scott for suggesting the title and to our editors at Oxford, Rachel Mullaby and Jacqueline Ridberg Larabee, for their faith in our project and patience with our idiosyncrasies.

Steve, Bob, & Mitu

Introduction

The Contract Production Paradox

There is a hole in our understanding of contract law and theory. Much of the thinking about contracts literally starts with "assume this contract" and then proceeds without considering the production process for that contract. But the method of production matters to the output; to understanding why we have the output that we do.

There are consequences to this myopia about contract production. While we know a good deal about how to design the contractual rights and obligations that motivate parties to invest optimally in their relationship, we know little about how best to formulate the contract's terms and conditions, the actual language that implements their contract design. This is unfortunate because contract production considerations often will undermine the parties' design goals.

This book is a step toward filling the foregoing gap in our understanding of contract; one that we hope to persuade our readers is vital if we are to understand why commercial contracts often are seriously flawed even among the most sophisticated of parties.

There is a paradox in the process of producing contracts: the factors that generate efficiencies in production—standardization and economies of scale—are the same factors that produce significant inefficiencies in design—standardized contracts that do not accurately embody the terms that the market participants believed were in the contract at the time it was executed. Several adverse consequences follow from a production process that relies (of necessity) on standardized contracting. First among them is the practice, common to all commercial markets, of assigning a preeminent status to those provisions that have been successfully deployed over many generations of contracts. The quite plausible assumption is that experience shows that these historic terms are the best formulation of rights and duties for future contracts as well. The result is contract as artifact,[1] a singular package

[1] We are not the first to conceptualize contracts as artifacts. *See* Mark C. Suchman, *Contract as Social Artifact*, 37 Law & Soc. Rev. 91 (2003). Suchman's conceptualization, while related to our

Contract Hazards. Stephen J. Choi, Mitu Gulati, and Robert E. Scott, Oxford University Press.
 DOI: 10.1093/9780197821770.001.0001

of terms that have been molded over time into a form whose language is presumptively fixed and unchanging. This contract has a history, a core of embedded terms that are repurposed from contract to contract: it is far removed from the classical conception of contract as an instrument with no past and no future that exists only for the deal at hand.

The benefits to the parties in the market from packaging a contract in this way are obvious. Terms from prior contracts are adopted in order to exploit the market's experience with those terms. The core set of standardized terms then become solidified: in the language of many of our respondents, these provisions become "market." Once the contract is market, it can be transferred without the need for a costly and time-consuming examination of each of its constituent parts: the underlying asset together with its documentation can be sold as a unit. But packaging the contract in this way also leads to the practice of drafters failing to adapt the language in the document to the current transaction because the market assumes the contract documentation will be the same every time. The gravitational pull of the contract being "market" can be so significant that lawyers doing deals are reluctant to do anything more than tinker around the edges.

A recent and notorious example demonstrates the power of the "contract as artifact" perspective. In May 2007, the private equity firm Cerberus Capital entered into negotiations through a holding company to acquire the stock of United Rentals. The documentation used in previous deals of the same sort included a standard clause granting the seller the right to demand specific performance of the contract under specified conditions. But Cerberus, perhaps recognizing that the market was softening, insisted on the right to step away from the deal upon payment of a stipulated fee. After extended negotiations between highly compensated lawyers, an explicit provision was included providing that Cerberus could walk away by paying the termination fee.

The fly in the buttermilk, however, was that the lawyers for Cerberus did not remove the clause granting the seller the right to demand specific performance. Instead, they inserted language providing that the specific performance right was "subject to" the buyer's right to walk away. Then the market tanked and Cerberus sought to invoke its termination rights. Despite the "subject to" language, United Rentals invoked the specific performance

notion of an historical artifact, is one where contracts are embedded in the social context and function both to enable transactions and carry symbolic value.

clause. In the end, even though much evidence in the contract showed that Cerberus had bargained for the termination fee, they were forced into costly litigation before eventually prevailing at the Delaware Supreme Court.[2]

In the course of our research, we talked to a number of senior lawyers who had followed the Cerberus drama and some who had been close to the deal. An eminent Delaware judge, a former litigator, was emphatic. This was a case of bad drafting on the part of Cerberus. The duty of a drafter, he opined, was to ensure that all the parts of the contract worked in conjunction with each other and seamlessly. Most judges and law professors (as well as the general public) would surely endorse this view. But the transactional lawyers we consulted had a quite different take. One experienced lawyer vividly invoked the contract as artifact perspective:

> The clients probably wanted the deal done quickly . . . If you want to avoid negotiation delays over wording, you stick close to the language of the prior form. The prior form is sacred—you sometimes hear lawyers say, in response to a perfectly good argument to revise a clause "But this is the Wachtell form . . . or this is the Skadden form." You mess with the standard form as little as possible.[3]

An apt metaphor to capture this different perspective is to imagine the standard form contract as a complex instrument with many parts. The deal lawyer who is using that instrument to transact a particular deal does not have the skill, time, or motivation to design a new or different instrument (nor will anyone pay her to do so). Rather, the deal lawyer views modifying a contract in the same way as a mechanic views fixing a car: she is competent to repair certain parts, but the mechanism will remain no more or less functional than when it was first assembled. This perspective is crucial to understanding the world of standardized contracting. Transactional lawyers see the contract through the lens of the production process. Here, the question whether the standard form is well designed is irrelevant. If there are problems, they can only be addressed marginally in ways that do not undermine the basic form

[2] *United Rentals, Inc. v. RAM Holdings, Inc.*, 937 A.2d 810 (2007).

[3] Another transactional lawyer agreed with this sentiment. If you want to put in a new provision, but don't want to delete a longstanding standard provision, include the phrase, "Notwithstanding anything to the contrary contained herein." Ideally, one would like a perfectly drafted contract that sets forth all the rights and obligations exactly. But clients want their deal lawyers to get their deal done. They don't care about what is going to happen in the next deal with this same form.

itself. The specific performance clause in the Cerberus contract was part of the core "market" terms, so the lawyers did not remove the clause but instead attempted a costly work-around. Contract design in this world is sharply constrained by the demands of contract production.

The Cerberus example shows how market standardization makes possible production efficiencies but at the cost of documentation that often contains loopholes, obsolete language, and puzzling permutations that appear to change meaning in dramatic ways. We characterize these and other anomalies in the standard form as "landmines," in that they can be and sometimes are used strategically by one of the parties to gain a litigation advantage when the transaction disintegrates. Indeed, not until the transaction subsequently blows up do careful litigators read the language of the standardized terms and discover–either to their delight or horror–that the standard form language has either been modified or has not been adapted to changed conditions and now contains words and phrases that can be used to dramatically affect the rights of the parties to the contract.[4]

Our book seeks to understand this phenomenon of time-tested standard form language that, because of its apparent uniformity of meaning, is ubiquitous in commercial contracts but yet contains these inexplicable anomalies. Some anomalies appear to have been embedded when the standard form first originated; others seem to appear suddenly in a particular contract and then remain as part of the standard language in subsequent contracts. To determine how and to what extent a market's standard form contract has these embedded landmines, we examine how contracts are produced in different markets, ranging from contract production in large, liquid markets such as sovereign debt and syndicated leveraged loans, to more integrated markets such as private equity mergers and acquisitions (M&A), and to one-off, bespoke transactions. In each of these environments, there are measurable differences in how contracts are produced and those differences help explain the number and persistence of landmines in the standardized terms.

We begin our story with the following claim: legal scholars, economists, many lawyers, and the public believe two things about commercial contracts and the deals that they facilitate that are largely, maybe completely, false.

First, when thinking of commercial contracts, most observers assume that the bespoke negotiated contract is the relevant paradigm for conceptual

[4] For a similar perspective, with examples, see Glenn D. West, *The Perils and Delights of Contractual Boilerplate*, ABA Bus. L. Today (Apr. 15, 2025).

analysis. An entire branch of economic and legal theory is devoted to a study of contract design that focusses almost exclusively on a single, isolated transaction where contract terms are individually negotiated, agreed upon, and then drafted *ab initio* by the parties. But as we have just illustrated, this is a concept with little foundation in reality. Today, in nearly all contracting environments, contract language is largely standardized and assembled in a particular form that is then repeated largely unchanged from contract to contract to contract. There will be negotiations over price and there may be negotiations over certain terms. But in markets with many transactions, where deals need to be done quickly, the product of the negotiation will be agreement on marginal changes to standardized documentation that is otherwise virtually unchanged from earlier deals. Even one-off commercial contracts that are not standardized across a market are still composed of blocks of uniform language taken from law firm precedents or "optimal" contract clauses sold by commercial firms. As a consequence, the language in virtually all commercial contracts is adopted by parties "off the rack" rather than customized.

The second conventional belief is that any inapt or obsolete formulations in standard commercial contracts will be scrubbed clean by successive generations of transactional lawyers who will remove errors, update language to accommodate changes in legal or economic conditions, fill gaps and clean up ambiguities. Finance professors Clifford Smith and Jerald Warner, famously asserted, "harmful heuristics like harmful mutations will die out."[5] That belief is false. Our examination of contracting in different markets, from the standard forms in sovereign bonds and leveraged loans to one-off commercial contracts, reveals numerous instances of harmful landmines that persist over generations of deals. Moreover, these mutations or loopholes in the standard form have similar effects in widely disparate environments. In both the sovereign debt and leveraged loan markets, for example, apparently purposeful changes to standard language are used by debtors to cram down a restructuring while activist creditors use other errors to hold up the same deal. Passive investors are the losers in both markets.

We set out to advance our understanding of these contractual landmines by looking into the archives of various commercial contracts. We ask: How do landmines first appear in a standard contract term? When do these

[5] *See* Clifford W. Smith & Jerald B. Warner, *On Financial Contracting*, 7 J. FIN. ECON. 117, 123 (1979).

irregularities begin to be exploited and which ones persist over time? Are landmines more prevalent in some markets than in others? And how, if ever, are landmines repaired once embedded in the boilerplate?

A reader might ask: Don't these questions imply that landmines have been embedded in contracts as long as there have been standard form contracts? And, if so, why haven't these problems surfaced in litigation much earlier? This is an interesting question in its own right, and our responses are necessarily tentative and speculative. What we do know is that there has been an enormous growth over the past thirty plus years in the volume and dollar significance of financial contracting in many markets, ranging from the multitrillion dollar sovereign debt market to the dramatic rise of private equity in M&A, to the financing of these deals with billion dollar leveraged loans. At the same time, as the financial stakes in each deal increase significantly, an activist litigation strategy has become correspondingly more cost-effective. Many have noted an apparent increase in contract litigation: activist creditors and their lawyers appear ready to scrutinize carefully the product of any deal that turns sour and to exploit long ignored hazards buried in standardized language. It is in this world that the landmines that may have always existed in standardized language become uniquely salient.

Perhaps in response to these developments, the major American law firms that specialize in handling commercial deals have grown dramatically in size as well as wealth. Today, for example, a young lawyer intent on maximizing her income over her career could readily choose big firm law practice over a career in finance.[6] As the volume of profitable business opportunities increases significantly, so does the burden on the transactional lawyer to promptly execute the task of negotiating and approving the necessary contract documentation in order to "do the deal" and turn to yet another one.

The increase in the economic value of each deal may also be responsible for what many lawyers report as a change in the culture that had previously shaped their behavior. Many of the lawyers we have interviewed report a decline in the norms of trust and reciprocity that historically bonded the lawyers who negotiate complex transactions under extreme time pressures.[7] These norms facilitated mutual agreement on the "intended" meaning of contract language notwithstanding the presence of words that may appear to alter that meaning. The norms supported a "reputation market" in

[6] *E.g.*, Cara Lombardo, *On Wall Street, Lawyers Make More Than Bankers Now*, Wall St. J. (June 22, 2023).

[7] Gilson, *supra* Acknowledgments note 1.

which landmines were bypassed so that deals could be concluded without the increased costs of a word-by-word review of the standardized language. But reputations are now more difficult to establish as markets have grown in size and economic value.[8] Contracting parties are more anonymous, and the greater stakes in any single deal increases the likelihood that parties may choose to sacrifice long-term reputations in order to profit from immediate returns. In the brave new world of financial contracting, the typical transactional lawyer is trapped between the pressure to conclude economically important transactions promptly and the consequences of having the landmines in those transactions subsequently exploited by market activists.

* * *

This book is structured as a version of a picaresque novel.[9] It describes our collective adventure starting from the time we first encountered landmines in a standard form sovereign debt contract through our discovery of more hazards in other contexts, to our efforts to use theory and data to explain the persistence of some and the repair of others. Armed with a theory that appeared to rationalize the world of sovereign debt, we turned to other markets to study the landmines embedded there and to test whether our theorizing about sovereign debt applied to environments as distant as bespoke commercial contracts, private equity M&A, and the liability management transactions that have roiled the burgeoning market in leveraged loans.

The book is organized in three parts. Part I, *A New Paradigm?*, begins with a story that shows how several innocuous changes in the words of a standard clause in a sovereign debt contract can transform that clause in the hands of an expert into a weapon that can be wielded in a subsequent restructuring of troubled debt. Additional stories taken from the world of sovereign debt persuaded us that we were seeing a different paradigm, one that required a more systematic inquiry into the landmines that each story revealed. As we were burrowing more deeply into sovereign debt, we learned of landmines in other markets, including the worlds of private equity M&A and syndicated leveraged loans. These stories suggested that the problem had a wider scope than we had first assumed. Each of the stories in this Part illustrate a different type of landmine, ranging from anomalies that favor debtors who are

[8] Alan Schwartz & Robert E. Scott, *Contract Theory and the Limits of Contract Law*, 113 Yale L. J. 541, 557 (2003).

[9] Apologies to Miguel Cervantes.

resisting repayment or seeking time to recover to those that are exploited by activist creditors looking to improve their position in a debt restructuring contest.

Part II, *Gurus and Novices: Building a Theory*, explains how we used our detailed investigations of sovereign debt to build a theory of how and when landmines arise and persist, and then test it with data. We began by interviewing experts in the sovereign bond market and found that the market for lawyers is sharply divided between experts (our gurus) who both draft contracts and advise in restructuring contests and novices who are only involved at the drafting stage. This leads to an asymmetry where lawyers representing sovereigns better reflect their clients' interests than lawyers representing dispersed creditors. We then turn to a conceptual problem: Can a standard form contract be understood as the market standard even if the language in the individual terms is not identical across the market? Here, we focused on the market's understanding that "standard" refers only broadly speaking to the language in a term and not to its precise wording. This analysis allowed us to harmonize the regnant theories purporting to explain the existence of these incomplete contracts. Thereafter, we developed empirical data to support our theory that the market for sovereign bond lawyers—divided between experts and novices with misaligned incentives—explains both the existence and persistence of landmines.

Part III, *Other Artifacts: Lawyers, Legal Culture, and Landmines*, looks to see how the theory in Part II works in other markets. We began by imagining the poles of a continuum formed by the relative thickness of the market in which contracting takes place. We asked whether landmines can be found across this contractual range from the thick liquid markets to the classic one-off or "bespoke" commercial contract. We first looked for evidence of standardization and of resulting landmines in the prototypical commercial contract. Thereafter, we turned to the market for private equity acquisitions, an environment that falls between the extremes of the large, liquid market and the bespoke transaction. We found evidence there that key actors can create a network that coordinates market-wide repairs to dangerous landmines. Finally we turned to leveraged loans, another large and liquid market where claims of creditor-on-creditor violence compete with liability management transactions that restructure contract rights in order to give some of the creditors priority over others. Here we see the main themes in the book fully realized: guru lawyers propose new ways of exploiting landmines in the standard contract while novice lawyers can only insert marginal provisions that fail to deter these efforts. In the absence of dramatic shocks to the market, deeply embedded terms in the artifact contract successfully repel major changes to the documentation.

We conclude by focusing on the core normative questions that underlie our project. Common law courts in the commercial centers of New York and Delaware have long held that courts should limit interpretive debates to the text of the written agreement, and that text is to be interpreted according to the plain meaning of the language used. Our project casts doubt on this interpretive doctrine. It is no longer fair to assume that the words used mean what the parties intended for them to mean, or to assume that if the parties have erred it's their responsibility to correct the error going forward. In a world in which production efficiencies impede the scrutiny of the language in standard form contracts at the drafting stage, there is a plausible argument for a "landmine exception" to the dominant textualist view. But implementing this exception under current contract doctrine is challenging. If contract interpretation doctrine remains resistant to reform, the landmine problem might also be addressed by stimulating networks of drafters to coordinate on removing mutations and historic anomalies from the standard form. While networks are being developed in some markets, achieving coordination in others remains a daunting challenge. Perhaps the best hope for solving the contract production paradox, therefore, is to continue to highlight the plight of the quotidian transactional lawyer so that the profession itself can be mobilized to create mechanisms for coordinating landmine removal.

PART I

A NEW PARADIGM?

Chapter One
A Visit from Gandalf

Greece 2010

In the world of sovereign debt, Spring of 2010 was a time of innocence when the markets assumed that sovereign debt crises only erupted in emerging markets, and then only rarely. Few thought that a debt crisis could infect a country in western Europe and certainly not a Euro area member such as Greece. Greek debts were risk free assets; almost equivalent to a German bond (maybe better, since they paid a bit more).

In late 2009, the Greek government revealed that the predecessor government had been doctoring the accounting numbers on their debt. As a result, the market temporarily shut Greece out from further loans. But market observers still assumed that this was only a temporary blip. After all, Greece was a Euro area nation with the European Central Bank and many wealthy industrialized countries serving as backstops sufficient to provide Greece with needed financing.

It was in this context that Lee Buchheit came to talk with a group of law students in an advanced Contracts class about the debt crisis in Greece.[1] For decades, Lee was the guru who heads of governments around the world would turn to when their nation was in debt distress.[2] During the European debt crisis of 2010–2013, when Lee had multiple countries calling him in desperate need, a number of financial journalists (and, as a result, our students) took to referring to him as Gandalf, the character from the *Lord of the Rings*, whose arrival is a sign of trouble in the offing. The joke was that knowing Lee's travel schedule was a way of predicting which countries were on the brink of a sovereign default.

[1] For background on the Greek crisis and Buchheit's involvement in its restructuring (which did not occur until more than a year after the events we describe in the text), *see* Patrick Bolton, Mitu Gulati, Xueven Fu, & Ugo Panizza, *The 2012 Greek Retrofit and Borrowing Costs in the European Periphery*, 1 J. L. & Empirical Anal. (2024, in preprint).

[2] *See* Joseph Cotterill, *It's Lee Buchheit's World: We Just Get to Live in It*, FT Alphaville (May 23, 2012).

Contract Hazards. Stephen J. Choi, Mitu Gulati, and Robert E. Scott, Oxford University Press.
 DOI: 10.1093/9780197821770.003.0001

To this point in the course, the students had been discussing historical debt crises. But, in this session with Lee, they were being asked to engage with actual contract provisions for a country that might soon need to restructure (despite vociferous claims by European politicians to the contrary). And Gandalf the Grey (aka Lee) was our guest.

There are few things more daunting for a law student than reading a 130-page single spaced indenture or agency agreement where entire paragraphs consist of a single sentence. To keep the students engaged, therefore, they were asked to read and react to the Greek debt contracts by adopting the role of advisers to the Greek government as it responded to the current crisis. Greece was in the early stages of its crisis and, as countries in crisis do, was denying that it needed to restructure its debts. This was but a temporary liquidity crisis, the government asserted. Moreover, no country in the Euro area needed to restructure its debt. Indeed, Greece was so confident about being able to weather the storm that it had not even hired counsel to advise it about the possibility of a restructuring.

But even if Greece was solvent and confident about surviving this crisis, why not prepare for the worst-case scenario? So, as Greece's counsel, the students were to assume that Greece had payments coming due on a set of its foreign-law-governed bonds and did not have the funds to make the payments. If so, what options did Greece have under the loan contracts? Among the options the students were to consider included: (1) granting a subset of creditors some assets as collateral in exchange for delaying the payments that were due to them; or (2) finding a subset of debts where it would not be unduly harmful to delay payment (e.g., if there were some bonds that had a lengthy grace period before the Event of Default clause was triggered).

We had asked Lee, our visiting expert, to evaluate and critique the student proposals. Each of the teams of students would have ten minutes to make their presentations and Lee was to play the role of Greece's attorney general who was choosing whose advice to take. His only request was to see in advance some of the contracts for the Greek bonds that the students would be using for their presentations.

The next day, the student groups made their presentations. They had worked hard to identify and analyze the relevant provisions and their conclusions were virtually the same. No, Greece could not grant any particular subset of bondholder's collateral in exchange for an extension of maturities because the bonds all had negative pledge clauses providing that if any one set of international creditors received a collateral enhancement, the others were to receive an equivalent enhancement. And, no, there were no particular bonds where Greece could afford to default without significant consequences: triggering the Events of Default clause on some bonds would in turn trigger the Cross Default clause in all the other bonds.

Lee took the floor next. He began by telling the audience of students and guests what they thought they already knew. The foreign law Greek bonds the students had examined did contain a negative pledge clause. And this clause required Greece equally and ratably to secure each of these bond issues if it ever created any form of security interest over its revenues, properties, or assets in order to secure an "External Indebtedness." That was all pretty standard.

Then Lee asked if anyone in the class, including the law professors teaching the course, had looked at the definition of External Indebtedness. The answer was no. Why not? Because in all the bond documents they had examined previously, the definition of External Indebtedness was virtually the same. It was a standard term that limited a country's obligations under its loan contracts to foreign currency debt obligations. And so it was with Greek bonds issued prior to January 1, 2000 when the Euro was adopted as the common currency of the European Union. After that date, however, the Euro became the "lawful currency" of Greece.

But Greece's form of negative pledge (and, crucially, the definition of External Indebtedness) *did not change for more than four years after the adoption of the Euro*; the "lawful currency" just quietly ceased being the Drachma and instead became the Euro. In practical terms, this meant that Greece's negative pledge clause in its foreign law bonds issued prior to 2004 would *only* be triggered by the creation of a lien to secure a non-Euro-denominated Greek debt. And since Greece had virtually no non-Euro-denominated debt, the negative pledge in that significant stock of Greek debt was toothless. Vis-à-vis the debt issued between 2000 and 2004, Greek assets could be pledged to new borrowing in Euros without having to give its older debt an equivalent pledge.

It took the room a few minutes to realize that Lee had unwound the negative pledge clause. Once they saw this, smiles broke out—this was fun! Greece was saved; at least in our hypothetical world.

Lee was not done, however. He next pointed to the Events of Default provision. Most of the Greek bonds that were part of the exercise had incorporated a standard set of "Events of Default." With a few small variations, these included:

- *failure to pay interest (with a 30-day grace period);*
- *other covenant defaults (with a 30-day grace period after written notice to the issuer);*
- *"External Indebtedness" is accelerated, or a payment is missed under such External Indebtedness and continues beyond the specified grace period;*
- *a general moratorium is declared on "External Indebtedness"; and*
- *any government order or decree preventing Greece from performing its obligations under the bonds.*

The point to note, Lee explained, was that the cross-acceleration, cross-default, and moratorium Events of Default in these bonds applied only to External Indebtedness; a term that in Greek bonds issued prior to 2004 excluded Euro-denominated obligations. Thus, these Events of Default in pre-2004 bonds could *only* be triggered by an event affecting the miniscule amount of Greek debt that was denominated in currencies other than Euros.[3] Stated differently, a payment default on a Greek Euro-denominated bond that had been issued between 2000 and 2004, or the acceleration of such an instrument, would not have cross-default consequences across much of the Greek debt stock.[4]

At the time, we assumed that Lee had just stumbled upon this blunder in the Greek contracts issued between 2000 and 2004. Surely, this was a rare occurrence. It is not surprising that occasional mistakes occur; after all these are dense, standardized contracts and contract drafters can be forgiven for failing to read each clause to ensure that it continues to embody their understanding of the transaction. But it was surprising that it took four years to correct the erroneous External Indebtedness clause in the Greek bonds. This is especially so when Lee showed us that the error was readily apparent once the contract was reviewed by an expert. To be sure, it did get corrected eventually. Yet, one might have imagined that among the many highly compensated lawyers drafting Greek foreign law bonds from 2000 to 2004, at

[3] These features of the Greek bonds are described in Lee C. Buchheit & Mitu Gulati, *How to Restructure Greek Debt*, Duke Law School Working Paper (2010).

[4] Starting in 2004, the definition of "External Indebtedness" in Greece's foreign law-governed bonds was changed. Under the new version of the definition, indebtedness for borrowed money is "External" if either (i) it is denominated in a currency other than Euros or (ii) borrowed from foreigners under a foreign law-governed contract.

least one would have noticed this failure to update a key clause and made the needed correction.

In the end, this particular blunder didn't make a difference: Greece's debt problems turned out to be much bigger than the class exercise. But the germ of an idea had been planted: It matters how contracts are produced. Conventional theory teaches that production mistakes will soon self-correct. Terms such as External Indebtedness can be rendered obsolete by changing circumstances, but theory tells us that parties are motivated to promptly revise an outdated term before it can infect subsequent transactions. And yet, this experience teaches otherwise. Before this contract term was repaired, millions of dollars of Greek bonds were issued with an outmoded clause that could have had significant monetary consequences for unsuspecting investors.

Moreover, there were other reasons to worry about the integrity of these contracts beyond the failure to adapt to changed conditions. It is common knowledge in the sovereign debt market that the debtors' lawyers are primarily responsible for producing the contract language: these lawyers might well be motivated to advance their clients' interests by altering boilerplate language in order to shift some of the default risk to the creditors who purchase the bonds. On the other side, the investment bankers, who nominally represent the interests of the largely anonymous creditors, are interested in efficiently marketing the bonds and not in pouring over boilerplate to find obscure changes in the contract's language. In short, in addition to explaining the failure to update an obsolete term that favored the debtor, this asymmetry may also explain why harmful modifications to standard language go unnoticed at the time the contract is drafted.

Our earlier work on contract stickiness led us to wonder whether a troublesome term in a contract might persist and eventually become embedded in the standard form. By opening a range of new interpretive possibilities, often years after a contract is executed, these embedded distortions of the market's understanding of the standard language could expose contracting parties to unexpected litigation risk. Realizing both that obsolescence or mutations can occur and that standardized contract terms are sticky and resistant to change, we began to examine more closely the ways that contracts are produced once the design of the contract has been agreed upon.

Production considerations loom large when markets are thick, and contract terms can be standardized across the market. Billions of dollars can be traded around the world using standard form contract terms that appear virtually identical in every contract. Standardization substantially reduces the transaction costs of producing (and learning about) the contract's terms. And the very uniformity of language contributes to norms of comity among negotiating lawyers who may rely on the unchanging character of standardized language to approve the documentation without undertaking the painstaking word-by-word review of every term in the contract. However, this standardization may also lead to inefficiencies: changing troublesome terms requires coordination among many diverse interests.

As the case of the Greek bonds illustrates, there is a trade-off in the production of standardized commercial contracts. The factors that generate efficiencies in the process of producing contracts can obscure the existence of changes in language or background conditions that alter the market's previous understanding of the transaction. Nevertheless, in many markets where more and more parties participate in the same or similar transactions, parties may still prefer standardization and the associated economies of scale even at the risk of documentation that doesn't align with their understanding of the transaction.[5] And so we wondered: Were there more of these errors or embedded anomalies? If so, how many and did they persist? And did their presence change anything?

To find answers to these questions, we began to investigate the existence, prevalence, and persistence of these linguistic anomalies in the liquid markets in which sovereign bonds are issued and traded. We then explored whether linguistic anomalies exist in other contexts—including the private equity mergers & acquisitions and the leveraged loan markets. In the following chapters, we report on what we found.

[5] A market is "thick" when many parties participate in the same or similar transactions and will benefit from coordinated responses to the contracting environment.

Chapter Two
Landmines

Introduction

The failure to fix the definition of External Indebtedness in Greek sovereign bonds was a blunder. It is unsurprising that blunders occur, even in billion dollar transactions done by white shoe law firms. One of us recalls, not with fondness, the experience as a junior attorney of updating a complex credit agreement at 2:00 am because some bankers wanted to seize a "market window." If the document seems incomprehensible, and no one is available to help, then the novice changes the names and dates from the prior transaction and says a prayer that predecessor drafters had a better grasp of what they were doing. There was a name for this: the "prayer method of drafting."

For users of the prayer method, mistakes and errors are predictable. But these documents supposedly passed the scrutiny of a senior partner before being submitted, and thus one might assume that any errors (deliberate or inadvertent) should eventually be corrected. As a test of that assumption, return to Chapter One, where Lee Bucheit (aka Gandalf) was pulling rabbits out of hats for the students. A student asked Lee, "Are there more of these out there?" He responded, "I hate to say this, given that I'm a member of this profession, but I can usually find a handful in each contract."

A handful? In every document? It's a different world than the one that Clifford Smith and Jerold Warner hypothesized in their classic article on bond covenants if dodgy features can be found in every transaction that goes sour, thereby inviting litigators to scour the contract looking for strategic leverage. This level of mistakes contradicts the conventional premise that an occasional error can be explained if we assume widespread use of the prayer method of drafting and if the senior partner, believing that standard boilerplate language never changes, only cursorily reviews the document. Moreover, perhaps these errors by the "handful" could spread. And perhaps some market intermediaries would develop a legal specialty of searching for and exploiting them.

Contract Hazards. Stephen J. Choi, Mitu Gulati, and Robert E. Scott, Oxford University Press.
 DOI: 10.1093/9780197821770.003.0002

A threshold question raised by Lee's story was whether these mistakes were ever exploited. There is certainly a widespread belief that, at least for lawyers of a generation ago, norms of comity deterred the exploitation of errors in the documentation. Reputation matters in markets with repeat transactors, such as may have existed in law firms of that era, and the fear of damaging ongoing relationships might have constrained parties from taking advantage of infelicitous drafting.[1] After all, the failure to revise the definition of External Indebtedness was never raised by Greece in 2010, even though the drafting omission did give it an advantage over some investors. It is possible that the investors holding those bonds never even knew about that flaw in the contract.

At this stage, therefore, we were intrigued, but we did not know whether we had a story, let alone how to chase it down. Lee Buchheit might be able readily to identify errors and mistakes in contracts, but he was atypical—he was, after all, the eminence of the sovereign debt bar.[2] We decided to put the project on the shelf and just observe. Perhaps we would find more of these anomalies. Beyond that, we were curious whether any of these drafting mistakes and anomalies would be used to gain an advantage in subsequent disputes despite the negative reputational impact of aggressive litigation. And, if so, were they then quickly corrected? Without those two elements, it was not clear we had a story worth telling.

In this chapter, we highlight the first four events that suggested that the manner in which these standardized contracts were produced might create significant legal peril well after the contract was concluded. Each event was described to us by a senior practitioner, sometimes years after the event in question. Collectively, these stories persuaded us that there was something in the way these contracts were produced that we did not yet fully understand and that required much deeper investigation.

Along the way, we began to call these drafting anomalies "landmines" because we realized that, collectively, they did in fact create genuine and

[1] Reputation works best to constrain misbehavior in smaller trading communities where everything that happens soon becomes common knowledge and boycotts of bad actors are easy to enforce. Whether the law firms of a generation ago fit that model is an open question; but reputations also are effective in markets that can establish trade associations, such as the corporate law committees of the ABA, Here the association becomes a form of collective memory regarding the contracting behavior of their members. For discussion, see Alan Schwartz & Robert E. Scott, *Contract Theory and the Limits of Contract Law*, 113 Yale L. J. 541, 557 (2003).

[2] On Lee Buchheit and his status in the sovereign debt world. *See* Robin Wigglesworth, *Lee Buchheit: The Crisis Veteran on the Sovereign Debt Frontline*, FT Alphaville (July 2, 2019); Jessica Pressler, *Debt Head*, New York Magazine (June 12, 2012).

unexpected litigation risk.[3] We also stopped describing them as errors or blunders. Some were, such as the one identified by Buchheit in the Greek bonds. But not all.

At the start of our project in 2011, we imagined that we might at most find a half dozen or so of these various landmines. Today, we have collected stories of over fifty exploded landmines and dozens more potential landmines that have yet to be exposed in sovereign bond contracts. The list keeps growing both because lawyers who know about our project send us new ones and because we have gotten better at digging for landmines ourselves. As the stories in Chapter Three illustrate, we've found landmines not just in the sovereign debt contracts but in corporate leveraged loan and private equity M&A agreements as well.

In the chapters that follow, we report on our theoretical and formal analyses of the landmine phenomenon. But the beating heart of our project began with these four stories told to us by the senior lawyers who not only draft these contracts but who are engaged when default looms and the debtor and their investors attempt to restructure the debt.[4] These four exemplars also illustrate a confounding fact: not all landmines are careless errors; there are different types.

Four Stories

Greece (2011)

Soon after the class session recounted in Chapter One, a landmine appeared that did blow up. Conditions in Greece had worsened enough

[3] The story of the Greek lawyers failing to update the definition of External Indebtedness after Greece joined the Euro shows that what we have found are a variety of anomalies, some are simple errors but others, like the Greek bonds, are the product of obsolescence. The original clause was intentionally drafted to cover all foreign debt. Then, as the world changed (i.e., the creation of the Euro), the original clause became obsolete. To the untutored eye, it still worked, albeit in a limited fashion. It was not a mistake in the sense of a phrase being inadvertently omitted or incorrectly inserted. Instead, the context changed but the clause remained the same. It was a blunder only in the context of knowing that Greece probably didn't intend to draft clauses with unusually narrow rights for investors in the bonds done between 2000 and 2004. This was like a landmine that lay buried and whose depth is unknown. But if discovered by the sovereign debtor in a crisis context, it could be detonated.

[4] One note before we describe these four key events. Over the years, we have done more than a dozen projects using interviews to better understand the legal phenomenon we were trying to study. Getting senior lawyers to talk to us is generally like pulling teeth. But with this project on contract landmines, almost every person we asked made time for us and often wanted to talk beyond the time we had scheduled. This may be hubris, but we'd like to think this was a clue to the significance of the project.

that, by mid-2011, restructuring counsel and bankers had been hired and conversations about relief from the IMF and an exchange with private creditors had begun.[5] But at that stage in mid-2011, it was just talk; the official Greek position remained that any restructuring, if at all, would be on a voluntary basis only. The goal was to give the creditors of Greece and those holding the debt of all the other vulnerable European nations as much reassurance as possible.

In the midst of all this, a missive landed on the desk of the Greek debt authorities. A creditor was claiming that the Event of Default provision in its bonds had been triggered, and it was considering accelerating its debt. The creditor stated, however, that it was prepared (under appropriate conditions) to stand down and not force the entire stock of Greek debt into default. Otherwise, the single creditor's action initiating an Event of Default would potentially trigger cross-default provisions across much of the rest of the Greek debt. And that would then cause mass accelerations, ratings downgrades, and an entire parade of horribles.

The typical Event of Default provision, reads something like this:

> The following shall each constitute an "Event of Default":
>
> (a) the Republic fails to pay interest on any Note before the day falling 30 days after the due date for such payment; or
>
> (b) the Republic is in default in the performance of any covenant, condition or provision in these Conditions and continues to be in default for 30 days after written notice thereof has been given to the Republic by any Holder; or
>
> . . .
>
> (c) any payment of principal in relation to any Relevant Indebtedness is not paid when due at maturity after giving effect to any applicable grace period or
>
> (d) the Republic declares a moratorium with respect to the Notes.[6]

Reading this clause, the Greek team must have thought the creditor's claim was frivolous since Greece was current on all its payments, had not violated

[5] These events are described in Patrick Bolton, Mitu Gulati, Xueven Fu, & Ugo Panizza, *The 2012 Greek Retrofit and Borrowing Costs in the European Periphery*, 1 J. L. & Empirical Anal. (2024, in preprint).

[6] *See* Hellenic Republic, Offering Circular, €2,500,000,000, 1.875%. Notes due 2026 (July 19, 2019).

any of the covenants, had not declared a moratorium, or done any of the things that would ordinarily trigger an Event of Default. What was going on?

From what we have heard, the creditor's letter explained that its bonds had a different and nonstandard Event of Default clause.[7] This clause provided that it was an Event of Default if the debtor:

> [By] reason of actual or anticipated financial difficulties, *commences negotiations with one or more of its creditors* . . . with a view to rescheduling any of its indebtedness.[8] (emphasis added)

The creditor's position was that Greece had, in fact, "commenced negotiations with one or more of its creditors," even if these conversations were about a purely voluntary exchange. Those conversations thus entitled this creditor to declare an Event of Default and potentially trigger a large number of cross defaults. Unless, that is, Greece agreed to buy back its bonds at a hefty premium.

We don't know how much the creditor settled for or whether it got paid at all. A part of what a sovereign obtains in return for paying off a creditor whose contract contains a novel contractual clause is the creditor's silence and the hope that other creditors with similar language in their contracts will not appear asking for payment in full. We suspect that the creditor received a recovery. After all, it had a good argument that an Event of Default had been triggered, and yet no formal claim was subsequently made by that creditor.

How did this clause get into the Greek bond contract? This language was often found in syndicated loans but never in bonds. We asked sovereign debt experts if they could explain why the clause was introduced into the Greek contract. Their best guess was that the clause had been inadvertently copied into a bond contract from an older syndicated loan document. Someone must have then determined the clause was problematic because it does not appear in later issues of Greek bonds. But as of the time of the Greek crisis in 2011 and 2012, no one—at least not on the Greek side—had been aware of this provision until this creditor and its lawyers found it and made the argument for special consideration.

[7] One of us heard this story from multiple sources in the context of research for Bolton et al., *supra* note 5.

[8] This type of Event of Default is described by the Loan Market Association in its description of standard provisions. *See Navigating Loan Documentation in Distressed or Pre-Distressed Scenarios*, Gibson Dunn (Jan. 31, 2018).

This story illustrates how a landmine can surface when standard terms in other instruments are casually and carelessly imported into the original source documents that form the current standard form debt contract. Most of these terms were embedded at a time when the lawyers participating in the transformation from syndicated loans to the sovereign bond template were novices in the new market, and so thoughtless importation from other corporate documents occurred before experience revealed the problem with the importation practice.

To be sure, drafting lawyers who write commercial contracts for multiple markets often borrow standard terms that are particularly useful in one market and, anticipating the same utility, use them in another, seemingly similar, market. This practice is particularly tempting for drafters who write debt contracts for syndicated loans as well as sovereign clients.[9] Syndicated loans and sovereign bonds share many similarities; they are issued in large, liquid markets with standardized terms principally designed to reduce the risk of the debtor's default. It may seem appropriate, therefore, to write into the contract of a sovereign debtor a "hair trigger" Event of Default clause that was found to efficiently reduce the default risk in the syndicated loan context. But as this story suggests, the importation of terms from other credit instruments into sovereign bonds can have unhappy consequences if the accepted meaning of the term does not translate meaningfully to the sovereign context. The result is a landmine—a term without any accepted meaning in the new environment.

Greece (2015)

Fast forward four years to 2015. Greece had completed a brutal restructuring of most of its sovereign debt in 2012, but the country was still struggling to get on its feet—a situation that was made worse by the Syriza government abandoning large portions of its IMF program.[10] The situation deteriorated to the point that in June 2015 Greece failed to make a required payment to the IMF. This led to an outcry in the press because defaults on the IMF are

[9] *See* Tal Kastner, *Systemic Risk of Contract*, 45 BYU L. Rev. 451 (2021) (describing the phenomenon as "modular drift"). For an empirical analysis of this borrowing phenomenon, and the problems it can cause in the context of M&A agreements, *see* Robert Anderson & Jeffrey Manns, *The Inefficient Evolution of Merger Agreements*, 85 Geo. Wash. L. Rev. 101 (2017).

[10] *See* Paul Thomsen, *The IMF and the Greek Crisis: Myths and Realities*, Speech at the IMF (Sept. 30, 2019).

highly unusual. As the *New York Times* reported, there are only a small group of countries that have ever defaulted on IMF obligations (Zimbabwe, Sudan, Somalia), and they are among the poorest and worst governed in the world.[11] Greece was publicly embarrassed. Nevertheless, Greece made it through those tough times. The arrears to the IMF were cured, and there were no other defaults on the restructured bonds from 2012 or on the obligations owed to other European nations.

In the midst of this drama, a landmine was nearly triggered. The source of the problem was an Event of Default provision in one of a small fraction of Greek bonds that were not restructured in 2012 when Greece had restructured the bulk of its debt. A handful of bonds, a combination of government-guaranteed and plain vanilla instruments under English law, had escaped the restructuring. A holder of one of these bonds had discovered a landmine in its Event of Default clause and attempted to use it to extract an extra recovery.

To begin, it helps to recall what the standard Event of Default provision provides: if a specified set of events occurs and is continuing, such as a failure to make an interest payment on the required day, and that failure is not cured within a specified amount of time (e.g., thirty days), the creditor is entitled to demand that all of the payments owed to it on future dates be accelerated. One of the stipulated events of default that is often found in the bonds of emerging market nations is the sovereign's failure to retain the membership of the IMF or to be eligible to use its resources.

For example, Zambia's 2015 bond has a standard IMF Event of Default clause that reads:

> *If any of the following events occurs and is continuing* [then the creditors may accelerate the debt]

[One such event is]:

> *[T]he Issuer ceases to be a member of the International Monetary Fund (the "IMF"), or ceases to be eligible to use the general resources of the IMF.*[12]

[11] Jim Yardley, James Kanter, & Jack Ewing, *Greece, Missing IMF Payment, Is Effectively Called in Default*, N.Y. Times (June 30, 2015).

[12] *See* Republic of Zambia, $1,250,000,000, 8.970%. Amortizing Notes due 2027 (Offering Circular, July 28, 2015); *See also* Republic of Turkey, $1,500,000,000, 4.875%. Notes due Apr. 16, 2043 (Prospectus Supplement, Jan. 13, 2015).

Tajikistan in 2017 has a slightly different version that states:

> *If any of the following events occur and is continuing* [then the creditors may accelerate the debt]

[And one of the events is]:

> *[T]he Republic fails to maintain its membership in, and eligibility to use the general resources of, the IMF.*[13]

It is important to note that in both the listed clauses, the event in question has to occur and be *continuing* in order to trigger an Event of Default. Creditors cannot declare a default once the disabling event has been cured. After all, the debtor has now fixed the problem that had caused the creditor to be insecure about receiving prompt payment.

Greece, however, was in default to the IMF, and one might ask whether that default violated the condition in the Events of Default clause requiring the debtor to maintain "eligibility to use the general resources of the IMF." Fortunately for Greece, the IMF had a broad concept of eligibility to use general resources and had been careful not to say anything publicly about Greece being ineligible. Indeed, the IMF stayed clear of even using the term "default," saying only that Greece was in arrears. So, one might think that the IMF clause, even if it were in the bond contracts, would not create any problems for Greece. But there was one bond, a Greek railroad bond issued in 2002 (maturing in 2017), that permitted the creditor to demand accelerated payment:

> ***if at any point [Greece] ceases to be a member in good standing*** *of the International Monetary Fund or ceases to be fully eligible to utilize the resources of the International Monetary Fund[.]* (emphasis added)

The holders of this bond and its lawyers realized that this version of the IMF Event of Default clause differed from the standard form term in two crucial respects. First, there was no requirement that the defaulting event had to be "continuing," as was the case in the Zambian and Tajik clauses. Once the

[13] *See* Republic of Tajikistan, $500,000,00, 7.125%. Notes due 2027 (Listing Prospectus, Sept. 14, 2017); *see also* Republic of Ghana, Global Medium Term Notes Program (Mar. 24, 2021).

event occurred, regardless of whether it was subsequently cured, the creditor had a continuous put option until the maturity date. Second, there was an additional requirement in this clause: the country had to be "in good standing" with the IMF. And while there was a general understanding of what it meant to be "eligible to use the general resources" of the IMF, there was no understanding about what it meant to be "in good standing."

Given this departure from the standard term, the creditor claimed that this provision gave it the option to declare a default. We were told that a distinguished Queen's Counsel was recruited to write an opinion supporting that position.[14] Armed with the QC's opinion, the creditor informed the Greek authorities that it was willing to refrain from declaring a default and causing the entire house of cards to fall (due to the triggering of cross-default clauses in Greece's other bonds) if Greece were to buy back the bonds held by this investor at a premium. We don't know the details of what happened next. Maybe that creditor got a hefty settlement, or maybe Greece was able to persuade the creditor that its legal claim would not prevail. In any event, no default was called. Today, none of Greece's bonds have an IMF "member in good standing" clause.

How did the "in good standing" language ever get included in the Greek bond? The "in good standing" language creates a risk that all of the sovereign's external debt could be accelerated immediately because of a single court's interpretation of language that had no understood meaning in the market. This is not an outcome that either party would intentionally agree to ex ante. Any strategic advantage from such overly broad events of default language would likely accrue to activist creditors who might wish to exploit this anomaly in forthcoming restructuring negotiations. But activist creditors are not present at the contract drafting stage, and thus an ambiguous clause that permits a unilateral claim of default based on lack of "good standing" is unlikely to be the product of purposeful bargaining at the drafting stage.

We surmised instead that the "in good standing" landmine was a mistake—the product of human error. Lawyers motivated to limit their time investment in drafting efforts or facing constraints due to market pressures are rarely motivated to ask for new provisions that alter the contract's allocation of risks. Such a request necessarily requires additional time and cost

[14] One of us learned of this story in the context of research and interviews for Bolton et al., *supra* note 5.

in negotiating an appropriate quid pro quo. And yet, drafting lawyers under time pressure may make errors. Accounts from drafting lawyers who issue these contracts and scholars who study their efforts suggest that these linguistic irregularities that offer activist creditors strategic opportunities result from such inattention and inadvertence.[15]

In theory, there should be a balance between such errors arising periodically and experienced lawyers recognizing the problem and eventually stamping them out. This equilibrium might result in more frequent errors in the early stages of the standard form sovereign debt contract when attorneys were beginning to develop expertise and less frequent errors occurring once the standard form was more established in the market.

Our first two stories involved creditors trying to extract disproportionate payments by threatening to call an early default, either by exploiting a term that was unfamiliar to the sovereign market or by taking advantage of a randomly occurring mistake. Next, we turn to stories of sovereign debtors threatening the use of landmines to stop creditors from litigating.

Venezuela/Argentina (2020)

In 2020, the Republic of Venezuela, mired in default since 2017, informed incredulous creditors that their claims for interest payments might be void. Venezuela then offered to enter into a tolling agreement with the creditors in exchange for their agreement to refrain from seizing Venezuelan assets in court. The assertion that claims on interest were void came as a shock to the investors who believed they had six years after default to bring claims under New York's statute of limitations. The Maduro administration in Venezuela asserted, however, that its debt contracts had "prescription" clauses that contractually reduced the six-year statute of limitations provided by state law to three years.[16]

[15] *See, e.g.*, Stephen J. Choi, Mitu Gulati, & Robert E. Scott, *Evolution or Intelligent Design? The Variation in Pari Passu Clauses*, 20 Am. L. & Econ. Rev. 1 (2018).

[16] For a discussion, see Mark Weidemaier & Mitu Gulati, *The Sideshow About Venezuela's Prescription Agreement*, Creditslips.org (Sept. 29, 2020). For the PDVSA tolling agreement offered in 2020, see http://www.pdvsa.com/images/DocumentosOficiales/comunicados/TOLLING_AGREEMENT_9_10_2020.pdf. In the recent past, Argentina has also attempted to use the prescription clause argument. *See* Ape Grp. SPA v. Republic of Argentina, 2022 WL 463309, at *2-3 (S.D.N.Y. Feb. 15, 2022); *see also* Anna Szymanski, *Argentina Borrows From the Elliott Playbook*, Reuters BreakingViews (Jan. 8, 2021).

Was this plausible? As described to us by industry veterans, the prescription clause in earlier times had little to do with the statute of limitations. Instead, the standard clause specified the number of years that the fiscal agent is required to wait for investors to appear and collect their funds *once the agent has received the funds from the sovereign debtor.*[17] Thus understood, the prescription clause functioned for the convenience of the fiscal agent: it did not have to hold the funds indefinitely. Once the prescription period is over, the creditor then has to go to Caracas, Buenos Aires, or some other sovereign capital, to chase payment. In its traditional formulation, the prescription clause did not exhaust the obligation to pay; it only shifted the location. The clause made sense in the days when investors brought physical coupons into the bank to get paid. In the modern era, however, where payments are made directly into bank accounts of the noteholders, it is not clear what function these clauses serve. Prescription clauses nonetheless remain in many sovereign bond contracts, and their formulations have changed in ways that sometimes surprise investors.

The standard modern prescription clause provides the following:

> *Claims in respect of principal and interest will become void unless presentation for payment is made within a period of ten years in the case of principal and three years in the case of interest* ***from the Relevant Date.*** (emphasis added)

The reader is then referred to the definition of "Relevant Date," which states that:

> *"Relevant Date" means whichever is the* **later of** *(i) the date on which any such payment first becomes due and (ii) if the full amount payable has not been received by the Fiscal Agent on or prior to such due date, the date on which, the full amount having been so received, notice to that effect shall have been given to the Bondholders.*[18]

[17] The debtor would still be liable to the noteholders conditional on the state's statute of limitations, but in any event, the fiscal agent's duty would have been discharged.

[18] For discussions of the variations in these clauses and their implications, see Mark Weidemaier & Mitu Gulati, *Venezuela's Weird and Possibly Mythical Prescription Clause*, creditslips.org (Feb. 1, 2020); Mark Weidemaier & Mitu Gulati, *The Sideshow About Venezuela's Prescription Clause*, creditslips.org (Sept. 29, 2020); Mark Weidemaier & Mitu Gulati, *Investors in Province of Buenos Aires Bonds Might Want to Look at Their Prescription Clauses*, American Bankruptcy Institute Blog (abi.org).

But in some cases, this standard clause has been revised to delete the reference to the Relevant Date, providing instead:

> *Claims in respect of principal and interest will become void unless presentation for payment is made within a period of ten years in the case of principal and three years in the case of interest ~~from the **Relevant Date**~~.*[19]

This change in the standard form term has a potentially dramatic effect on the obligations of the sovereign debtor. On its face, the revised clause makes claims "void" after a certain period of time irrespective of the relevant statute of limitations.

Similar revised terms have appeared in other bonds. For example, the clause in Russia's 2017 bond reads:

> *Claims against the Russian Federation in respect of principal and interest* ***shall become void unless made within a period of three years from the date following the Maturity Date or a relevant Interest Payment Date, as applicable.***[20]

As it turned out, despite the claims of the Maduro government, the Venezuelan bonds had the standard version of the clause, and so their attempt to pressure investors by threatening the expiry of the prescription period failed. But investors who fail to pay attention to the prescription clause in the Russian bonds are in for a rude surprise if Russia, having gone into default in April 2022, continues in that state beyond mid-2025. If investors do not appreciate the nonstandard formulation of the Russian prescription clauses, their claims for interest and principal will begin to evaporate.

In the course of talking to industry insiders about how the prescription clauses had evolved in cases such as Russia, we learned that for a number of years Argentinian bonds had an even more potent revision to the standard version of the clause.

Starting at least in 2005, Argentina's prescription clause read:

> *Claims against the Republic for the payment of principal, interest, if any, or other amounts due on the Bonds will be prescribed unless made within five*

[19] Weidemaier & Gulati, *Venezuela/s Weird Prescription Clause*, *supra* note 18 (discussing various prescription clauses).

[20] Russian Federation, $2,500,000,000, 5.25%. Bonds due 2047 (Offering Circular, Sept. 22, 2017).

> *years, with respect to principal,* ***and two years,*** *with respect to interest, premium, if any, or other amounts due on the Bonds, in each case from the date on which such payment first became due,* ***or a shorter period if provided by Argentine law.***[21]

As in the Russian clause, there is no mention of "Relevant Date." The clause thus appears to permit Argentina to reduce the prescription period unilaterally by passing a law. This change to the standard form term must have been introduced in the course of one of the many Argentine defaults and restructurings between 2005 and 2020. And, anecdotally, we have heard that Argentina might have used this weapon in negotiations with non-cooperating creditors.[22] In any event, at some point someone on the creditor side did object to this language, and the aberrant language giving Argentina the power to shorten the prescription period unilaterally was removed from Argentina's 2020 bonds and thereafter.

The standard practice for drafting new bond issues suggests a different source of the linguistic variations to the standard prescription clause. In addition to careless mistakes or the unthinking importation of terms from syndicated loan or corporate bond contracts, landmines may also result from *purposeful* actions to introduce or retain anomalies in the standard form contract language. A random error can favor either party to the contract, but the risk of an ambiguity favoring sovereign debtors is acute in liquid markets that follow the standard drafting practice. Since the debtor's lawyers are primarily responsible for producing the contract language, they are both motivated and positioned to advance the interests of their clients by shifting some of the default risk from the debtor to the creditors who purchase the bonds.

These purposeful insertions are not necessarily opportunistic efforts to seek advantage. Vagueness may be introduced when there is a negotiating impasse between the investors' interest in holding the sovereign to strict repayment terms and the sovereign's interest in carving out reasonable exceptions to those duties. But whatever the motivation for the departure from the standard term, the divergent incentives of issuers and underwriters during the drafting process increase the likelihood of purposeful additions or omissions that enhance a sovereign's post-default position. Consider, for

21 Republic of Argentina, Exchange Offer (Prospectus Supplement, Jan. 10, 2005).

22 We heard this in the course of our interviews. But there is no public confirmation of that strategy being used.

example, the sovereign's typical obligation to waive sovereign immunity unconditionally. The sovereign's interests are enhanced if thereafter a change in the waiver term introduces vagueness, such as a clause that we have found in a number of bonds providing that the waiver is subject to "applicable law," a term that is undefined and, therefore, could arguably be a reference to the sovereign's domestic law.

Sri Lanka (2023)/Argentina (2005)

Sri Lanka went into default in April 2022. Most creditors refrained from bringing suit, as they generally do with sovereigns (where typically there are no ready assets to seize). Wanting to see how things played out while accumulating interest on the unpaid amounts, the creditors instead waited to see whether Sri Lanka could get aid from the IMF or China or elsewhere and pull itself out of the doldrums. Hamilton Bank, a fund based in St. Kitts and Nevis, decided, however, to jump the queue and filed suit, perhaps hoping that recovering a judgment might give it a strategic advantage.[23]

Sri Lanka wasn't making any payments that it owed to creditors, so one might think that this was as simple as these cases go. Presumably, any creditor could declare default, accelerate the debt, and recover the balance of the loan owed to them. Sri Lanka thought otherwise. Defending against Hamilton Bank's request for a judgment, it explained to the court that Hamilton Bank, being only a "beneficial owner" of the bonds, was not entitled to sue. As per the contract, only the "registered holder" was entitled to sue.[24] So, who was the "holder"? As is typical for most publicly traded sovereign bonds today, an administrative intermediary, Cede & Co., formally holds the bonds as the registered holder, while investors such as Hamilton Bank retain a beneficial ownership interest in the bonds indirectly through Cede & Co. This ownership structure facilitates low-cost and rapid transactions in the underlying bonds.

Can it possibly be that the beneficial owners of the Sri Lankan bonds were not entitled to sue after there is a default? Could it be that litigation was only permitted by the registered holder, Cede & Co., who had no interest in the

[23] See Mark Weidemaier & Mitu Gulati, *Raise a Glass to Freedom . . . From Debt Restructurings*, FT ALPHAVILLE (Apr. 23, 2023).

[24] *See* Hamilton Reserve Bank Ltd., v. The Democratic Socialist Republic of Sri Lanka, 2023 WL 2632199 (S.D.N.Y.).

litigation? Here are the key clauses that Sri Lanka's lawyers pointed to in their brief asking for outright dismissal of the creditor's claim.[25]

First, there is the general provision as to who gets rights:

> *Nothing in this Indenture . . . shall give to any Person, other than the parties hereto and their successors hereunder and the Holders of Securities, any benefit or any legal or equitable right, remedy or claim under this Indenture.*

And "beneficial owners," such as Hamilton Bank are not parties to the indenture.

Further, and more specifically, the indenture provides:

> *[T]he Holder of any Security shall have the right, which is absolute and unconditional . . . to institute suit for the enforcement of any such payment, and such rights shall not be impaired without the consent of such Holder.*

Given that the indenture neither gives rights to institute suit to anyone but the registered holder nor provides any mechanism for Cede & Co. to delegate its power, Sri Lanka appeared to have a powerful argument. To rub salt in the wound, Sri Lanka pointed out that it had only agreed to "a limited waiver of sovereign immunity" as to proceedings "brought by any Holder of a Bond."[26] And, once again, the "Holder" is defined as "Cede & Co."

Sri Lanka might have won the case if the court had interpreted the contract terms literally with no consideration of context. As it turned out, the New York court did not accept the Sri Lankan argument. The federal judge found it impossible to believe that the parties intentionally delegated the exclusive right to sue to an administrator such as Cede & Co., who was unlikely to have any interest in bringing suit.[27] Indeed, industry experts had predicted that Sri Lanka would not prevail on their claim because a similar argument had been previously unsuccessful in litigation before the Second Circuit Court of Appeals.[28] What was surprising, however, was that in the

[25] Defendant's Memo in Support of its Motion to Dismiss, Hamilton Reserve Bank Ltd., v. The Democratic Republic of Sri Lanka, No. 22. Civ. 5199 (DLC) (S.D.N.Y. Nov. 4, 2022).

[26] *Id.*

[27] *Id.*

[28] One of the Argentine provinces had tried to advance such an argument eighteen years earlier in order to disrupt creditor litigation, and that case had had enough legs to go up to the Second Circuit Court of Appeals before it was resolved. Applestein v. Province of Buenos Aires, 415 F.3d 242 (2d Cir. 2005). In *Applestein*, the documentation for the bonds explicitly permitted the registered holder to

wake of that previous litigation, the Sri Lankan bonds, as well as other sovereign contracts, still had not been revised.[29]

One might ask here, given the Second Circuit decision years before, whether Sri Lanka had wasted resources making an argument that was likely to lose. But experts explained to us that Sri Lanka was looking to delay the creditor obtaining a judgment for nonpayment. Making a plausible claim that required counsel to write briefs and present arguments and the court to write an opinion gave Sri Lanka the time to conduct its restructuring: if the debtor obtained consent from enough creditors, it could cram down Hamilton Bank before any judgment was rendered.

But how had this provision ever become part of the standard form? One sovereign debt expert offered the following explanation:

> My suspicion is this: In the very early days of the Eurobond market (1960s and 70s), the securities were in bearer form and traded through delivery of physical script. So, in those days, a "Holder" was whoever showed up clutching the bond. In 1982, the US Congress passed the Tax Equity and Fiscal Responsibility Act (TEFRA) that outlawed the issuance of bearer bonds in the USA. So, the market shifted to the present structure—the issuance of a single registered "global" bond to be held by a "common depository" like Cede & Co. That common depository, then, has as its clients the clearing agencies like Euroclear and Clearstream. The clearing agencies, in turn, have accounts for institutional customers like HSBC—nominees who in turn open accounts for the ultimate beneficial owners. When a payment is made on the bond it flows down this waterfall and ends up in the accounts of the beneficial owners.
>
> When that switch to global bonds occurred, the bond drafters did not adjust the definition of "Holder" to reflect the fact that the registered holder—the common depository—had no economic interest in the bond and was not holding itself out to perform trustee-type functions for the beneficial owners. [G]iven that New York courts generally . . . interpret [contracts] literally, the [defendant sovereign] would have had a pretty good argument.

give permission to sue to others, such as the beneficial owners. There was no such express permission in this case, which Sri Lanka argued distinguished the cases. The New York district court, however, held that it was implicit, under an extension of the logic of *Applestein*, that the registered holder could grant such permission. Hamilton Bank, 2023 WL 2632199, *2.

[29] The Argentine indentures have been remedied on this point, but few others appear to have been updated.

The landmine in this last story is different from the first three exemplars. Here the standard form contract has not been revised erroneously or changed in order to pursue a strategic advantage. Nor has a term that was useful in earlier documentation been imported unthinkingly into the quite different context of the sovereign bond market: the standard form has remained unchanged. What has changed are the underlying economic and legal facts that have rendered the standard definition of a "holder" obsolete, and contract drafters have failed to effect the needed changes in language that would repair the resulting anomaly.

In contract theory, it is generally assumed that contracts between private parties do not contain such obsolete terms. If a term in a prior contract becomes inapt, parties will not include the term in their current contract. This view implicitly assumes, however, that parties' contracting choices are not affected by the choices of other market actors. This assumption does not hold in large liquid markets where parties trade using a standard form contract. Here, a contracting party will retain an obsolete term in the standard form contract if the market would punish a supplier of a new or revised term for departing from the market standard.[30] In such cases, innovation requires parties to *coordinate* with other market actors on a new term for the market. This condition may well describe sovereign bond contracts, as well as many other market types, where parties may continue to issue contracts that contain an obsolete term despite the risk of strategic behavior.

In short, there may be a plausible explanation for the persistence of obsolescence in sovereign bonds and other similar standard form contracts. Continuing to use a contract with obsolete terms would be an inexplicable response when contracting parties are autarkic but may be a possible best response when parties are interdependent. Thus, when contracts are standardized across a market, a party's best response to its strategic situation may be to choose not to amend the terms of a sovereign bond contract even though the obsolete terms may generate mistaken judicial interpretations.

[30] *See* Alan Schwartz & Robert E. Scott, *Obsolescence: The Intractable Production Problem in Contract Law*, 121 Colum. L. Rev.1659, 1688–1689 (2021). Individual parties in these markets cannot use the option of creating a substitute term to replace the obsolete standard term. Because of the additional costs of learning about the new term, they would then be offering a more expensive contract than others in the market who continue to use the standard term. Their only choice is either to retain the obsolete term or attempt to coordinate with other market actors on an apt term.

Divergent Roles of the Debtor's and Creditor's Lawyers

In each of these stories, either the debtor or a set of creditors advanced during litigation an unexpected meaning for a term that had a well-understood "standard" meaning for the lawyers who drafted the contract. In the patois of the transactional lawyers doing these deals, everyone involved thought they had contract terms that were "market." And they were "market" until a crisis occurred and litigation counsel found a new divergent meaning in the clause that varied unexpectedly from "market." That's the sense in which we call these contract landmines.

Contract landmines have two elements. First, the parties initially believe they have contracted for a standard "market" set of provisions; provisions essential to the standard form that mirror the purposes of the underlying transaction. Second, when a debt crisis looms, restructuring or litigation counsel for one side or the other searches for a linguistic anomaly allowing it to argue for a meaning that gives their client an unexpected advantage in their efforts to resolve the crisis. But for this strategy to succeed, there have to be landmines in the first place. The premise of our book is that there are lots of landmines in contracts, many more than theory assumes.[31]

A background fact is that there are no lawyers who are representing the interests of the creditors during the contract negotiations; at least there are no lawyers with an interest in revising a term in order to aid the creditors in the event things blow up in the future. The creditors' lawyers at the deal-making stage in a typical bond contract (sovereign, corporate, municipal, or otherwise) are those who work for the underwriters. It is standard practice that they are hired and paid by the debtor—partly because at the deal stage there are as yet no creditors.[32] Actual creditors only appear after the

[31] We use two methods to identify these linguistic anomalies that result in a potential unexpected and (costly) litigation advantage for a contracting party when the debtor nears or is in financial distress. First, we look to expert lawyers—"guides" who identify potential landmines in contracts within their areas of expertise. Second, we look for a linguistic anomaly that unexpectedly "blew up" in a debt restructuring, leading one party to threaten potentially costly litigation over the meaning of the linguistic anomaly.

[32] This is a phenomenon known as "designation" and is widespread in the sovereign bond contracting world. *See* Michael Bradley, Irving De Lira Salvatierra & Mitu Gulati, *Lawyers: Gatekeepers of the Sovereign Debt Market*, 38 Int'l Rev. L. & Econ. 150 (2014). The fact that the counsel for the underwriters are selected by and paid by the issuers will strike at least some as problematic on its face (it did us). We do not explore the legal ethics of this practice. For a treatment of this issue in the leveraged loan context, see Trevor Clark, Financial Markets and the Ethics

deal is done and the underwriter sells the securities. And if the debt goes into distress in the future, creditors then hire specialist litigators, not the lawyers who were the original underwriter's counsel. Thus, there is little incentive for the underwriter's counsel to negotiate for contract provisions that may advantage the creditors at some later date. Indeed, given this structure and the underwriter's overwhelming interest in getting the deal done quickly, there is no incentive for the lawyers who nominally represent the creditors to make any changes to the standard market document.

On the debtor's side, things are different. The drafting begins when the underwriter's lawyers provide an unrevised standardized precedent to the sovereign's lawyers for their review. The sovereign's lawyers are primarily responsible for proposing *any and all* redline changes to the standard form contract. Suggested revisions and changes to standard language are then reviewed by the underwriter's lawyers. The underwriter's strongest motivation is to resist any changes in the standard form that might raise concerns in the market and thereby reduce the price for the bond issue or otherwise cause the issue to miss a propitious market window.

This entrenched drafting practice suggests that the most significant changes in the standard form contract will result from language drafted by the debtor's counsel. Otherwise, there is little incentive for either party to tinker with the standardized terms of the contract.[33]

WHERE DO THE STORIES LEAD?

The first thing that strikes us about the four stories is that the landmines they describe differ from each other. One story centered on apparently

OF LEGAL PRACTICE (Oxford University Press, forthcoming 2025); Cathy Hwang & Andrew Tuch, *Lend Me Your Counsel*, S. CAL. L. REV. (forthcoming 2025).

[33] There is a further asymmetry in the process of drafting sovereign bond contracts. The firm that prepares the original offering document might well be the same firm asked to assist during a restructuring. However, the particular lawyers who are asked to step in during a restructuring are likely to be restructuring specialists rather than the drafting lawyers who prepared the initial contract documentation. Nevertheless, because of the linkage within the firm between the drafting lawyers and the restructuring specialists there may be an incentive for the debtor's lawyers to insert a landmine at the front end to aid in a future restructuring effort. But we would not expect too much. In over two decades of studying sovereign restructurings, we've never heard any restructuring lawyer, when they find an unexpected contract feature that helps their side, speak admiringly of the drafter who inserted the landmine, let alone want to suggest to the law firm management or client that this person had done an especially good job.

purposeful changes to a standard term that gave the debtor leverage when attempting to avoid the effects of a default. But juxtaposed against the seemingly deliberate addition of language that appeared to impair the creditors' rights, another landmine was the result of an apparently inadvertent drafting error. This random error provided an opportunity for an activist creditor to negotiate for favorable treatment. A third exemplar revealed the effects of incorporating terms borrowed from earlier syndicated loan documentation into the standard form when the modern sovereign bond debt contract was created in the early 1990s.[34] Here, landmines result from the failure to recognize the critical differences between syndicated loans and sovereign bonds. Finally, the fourth story illustrates another danger of standard form contracting: difficulties in coordination may prevent the standard terms from being updated to reflect changes in current practices, leading to obsolete terms.

Once we had an even larger set of contemporary landmines that we could analyze with data, we could develop categories of landmines with common characteristics to see whether there are differences in the frequency and durability of the aberrant terms that map on to the categories. The landmine stories so far gave us some clues. Combining background realities about the way sovereign debt contracts are generated in the real world added content to those clues and enabled us to construct the categories. Beginning with our surmise that these four stories were prototypes, we did some categorization.

Historical Holdovers

Some terms in the standard form sovereign loan contract have no contemporary purpose. Recall our first story of Greece's difficulties in 2011, where the Events of Default included the additional phrase "*commences negotiations with one of its creditors*." Here, the term appears to have been carried over from documentation involving syndicated loans, where it may have functioned appropriately. But terms such as this manage to survive after

[34] The sovereign bond market has had multiple incarnations. In the post-World War II era, there was initially a thin market in the period from 1960 to 1990 where the only issuers tended to be highly rated sovereigns doing small issuances. Then, after the Latin American debt crisis of the 1980s, syndicated loans were converted to "Brady" bonds and this set the basis for the modern bond market. For a description of the history, see Michael Bradley, Elisabeth de Fontenay, Irving de Lira Salvatierra & Mitu Gulati, *Pricing Sovereign Debt: Foreign Versus Local Parameters*, 24 Eur. Fin. Mgt. 261 (2018).

the market fundamentally changed and moved from syndicated loans to bonds. They continued as part of the standard form contract, carried over from deal to deal. Others may have migrated into the standard form contract from corporate bond instruments that served as a drafting template. These historical holdovers survive, it seems, simply because they have survived so long. No one quite knows what the term means in the current context, but most market actors assume they are harmless, and no one has a sufficient incentive to remove them. Nevertheless, holdovers from prior documentation are empty vessels that function as landmines when litigators assert an unexpected meaning for the term.

Our fourth story also illustrates the historical holdover in the form that we suspect is its most common manifestation—obsolescence. Here, legislation eliminating bearer bonds and designating a central depository for the contract caused the standard definition of a "holder" to be obsolete. A failure to update the standard form contract to accommodate changing technology created the resulting landmine. Obsolete terms such as this are a cousin of the historical holdover: these terms become landmines when changes in the law or the economic environment cause the standard clause to no longer fit the current context. More troubling, a now inapt clause may be susceptible to a new meaning that impairs the interests of the party the clause was initially designed to protect.[35]

Random Error

Now return to Greece in 2015, where the phrase "*ceases to be a member in good standing of the International Monetary Fund*" was added to a standard term regarding membership in the IMF and the key word "*continuing*" was deleted from the Events of Default provision. Notwithstanding the possibility of a purposeful change designed to create new strategic opportunities

[35] Drafting guru, Ken Adams, writes of the "successors and assigns" clause, in responding to an attempt by another drafting guru, Tina Stark, to find some justification for its persistent use, despite a seeming lack of utility and general confusion about its meaning:

> [A simple explanation for the continued use of this clauses] is that it's a useless provision that survives because drafters are unsure what function it serves and so are loath to get rid of it. And it's sufficiently obscure that one can project onto it all sorts of unlikely meanings.

Kenneth A. Adams, *It's Time to Get Rid of the "Successors and Assigns" Provision*, The Advocate 30 (June/July 2013).

in the future, landmines such as this are likely blunders. In the sovereign debt context, errors result from the need to satisfy client demand that a deal be taken to market quickly and from a lack of expertise of the sovereign context on the part of the drafting lawyers. To be sure, lawyers, particularly inexpert ones, will generally have an incentive to leave existing documentation alone. But on occasion, there will be no choice but to update the documentation. Here the combination of inexperience and deal time pressure can produce errors. In the sovereign debt market, for example, there was pressure in the early 2000s to shift from unanimity action clauses to collective action clauses requiring less than unanimous creditor approval to modify contract terms. Then in the 2010s, sovereigns moved to update the infamous *pari passu* clause to make clear that the clause did not require ratable payments to creditors.[36] A few years later, there was a widespread shift from the use of fiscal agency structures to trust structures. When inexpert attorneys are required to redraft to incorporate a design change, this moment of "opening the hood" to make what appears on its face to be a simple modification may lead to errors.

Subversive Accretion

Here, recall our third story, where both Venezuela and Argentina in 2020 had prescription clauses in their contracts that departed significantly from the standard form contract by omitting the key phrase "*from the Relevant Date*" and, in the latter case, adding language suggesting the prescriptive period could be further reduced by Argentine law. There are a number of landmines such as this where a standardized and well-understood term is changed by the addition (or omission) of a new phrase or clause. Notable here is that these changes inevitably favor the debtor's interests and impede the rights of the creditors. It is tempting to think of these terms that systematically favor the debtor as simply further illustrations of human error: a modification introduced by drafting lawyers who do not fully understand the function of the original standard term. But the effect of these changes is subversive to the extent that in every case they invite the debtor, who is primarily responsible for making revisions to the contract, to escape liability under the revised conditions.

[36] We describe in detail the ongoing saga of *pari passu* in Chapter 4.

In such situations, a plausible inference is that a knowledgeable drafter has added words or phrases that turn a bright-line obligation of the debtor into a more imprecise or vague standard. By thereby granting the debtor discretion in the exercise of a duty, the subversive accretion provides a litigation advantage should a default risk materialize. A dynamic relationship may also exist between errors and subversive accretions. Debtors' lawyers may correct errors over time that disfavor their client while leaving in place errors that cut the other way. The underwriters' lawyers, on the other hand, do not have the same incentive to search for and correct errors.

* * *

The stories not only suggest that landmines exist, but also that some market actors will invest in close reading of the standard form contract to discover them and then act to exploit them. And it isn't just the oft-reviled activist creditors who are exploiting the errors in the standard form. As we've seen with both Argentina and Venezuela, sovereigns also try to exploit these advantages. The result is disruption and wasteful expenditures on lawyers' fees regardless of the ultimate resolution of the dispute. Landmines, in short, function as a deadweight cost, a tax on the market, negatively affecting price and return for all participants.

The landmines exemplified by the four stories in this chapter, together with the other examples we discovered subsequently, provoke a further question: Do these landmines exist in markets other than the relatively unique conditions characterized by sovereign debt? We turn to this question in Chapter Three, where we discuss landmines in two different markets that we learned about as we were pursuing the trail in sovereign bonds. First, we look at a landmine that has recently roiled the market for syndicated leveraged loans: modifications to the standard contract have recently led to cries of unfairness and have generated a new and controversial mechanism for pre-bankruptcy restructuring of distressed firms. The second story provides evidence of what we have called a random error. A landmine resulted from apparent inexperience: a drafter's failure to understand and modify the standard terms of an M&A purchase agreement that is then exploited strategically by a more expert counterparty.

Chapter Three
Beyond Sovereigns

Introduction

Our search for landmines in sovereign bond contracts began as a natural outgrowth of a decade-long collaboration on sovereign debt research. The knowledge and experience we gained of the sovereign debt market gave us a unique opportunity to study the landmine puzzle that had intrigued us ever since Lee Buchheit visited our class in 2011 and told his story of the External Indebtedness clause in the Greek bonds.

But then we asked: Are there landmines in other markets? Or is the sovereign bond market a uniquely fertile ground for landmines? To answer these questions, we needed a guide to help us uncover landmines in other markets. We found our initial sherpa in Bob's former student at Columbia Law, Matt Jennejohn. Matt, a law professor at Brigham Young, started out in practice as an M&A lawyer and now does research on M&A contracts. We asked him whether he had come across any landmine-like provisions in M&A deal documents. A few months later, we received an email from him with a link to a post on a law firm's blog by an eminent M&A lawyer, Glenn West. Matt's email came with the caption, "M&A Landmine?"

Matt's email explained that Glenn West was an unusual character. Matt had met him when Glenn had invited Matt to present an empirical paper on M&A drafting practices at an ABA annual meeting. He seemed to have an encyclopedic knowledge of the case law from multiple jurisdictions. Glenn also seemed to have an interest in both documenting and trying to change the way many M&A lawyers drafted contract language in apparent ignorance of developments in the case law. Most important, Glenn shared our interest in identifying contract landmines.[1] We reached out to Glenn, who was generous in pointing us toward new markets and documents we could mine.

[1] *See* Glenn D. West, *The Perils and Delights of Contractual Boilerplate*, ABA Bus. L. Today (Apr. 15, 2025).

Contract Hazards. Stephen J. Choi, Mitu Gulati, and Robert E. Scott, Oxford University Press.
 DOI: 10.1093/9780197821770.003.0003

Glenn's blog post, that Matt had pointed us to, described a widespread and unthinking use of various clauses in M&A agreements.[2] These clauses, Glenn wrote, had become the equivalent of brainless sea squirts. Sea squirts, he explained, are creatures who begin life with a brain and a tail. They use their brain and tail to find a rock to attach themselves. But once attached, they consume their brain and tail and remain attached to the rock—living out life as a brainless water filter. According to Glenn, there were many contract provisions like this in the M&A world.[3] There might have been initial reasons for drafters to use some of these clauses (or phrasings in clauses), but the language had been repeated so many times that the reasons had been lost. Many of the lawyers routinely putting these clauses in their agreements had little idea of their purpose beyond the fact that the clauses in question were "market." There was a lesson for fellow lawyers: Using clauses whose rationale one doesn't understand can be perilous because the clause sometimes has effects on contract rights quite different from what one expects.

Glenn cautioned us not to assume that the presence of some contract landmines in the M&A context means that all the dynamics from the sovereign bond context would translate. In both, the "standard form" exerted considerable power on future contracting. But both the reasons for the importance of the "form" and the dynamics of repairing the landmines were different in the two settings. As a result, so were the outcomes. Glenn wrote:

> Merger and acquisition agreements differ significantly from sovereign bonds. While I have criticized the stubborn persistence of harmful or ineffective boilerplate in the M&A deal world, this persistence does not stem from a desire for uniformity or blind adherence to a sacred form. The dynamics involved in negotiating merger and acquisition agreements often dictate that comments on a form agreement be kept to a minimum, making the improvement of the form a secondary goal. Moreover, what one party considers bad boilerplate may be seen as beneficial by another. . . . But one

[2] Glenn West, *Avoiding the Mindless Use of the Brainless MAC Clause*, Weil Private Equity Blog (Aug. 17, 2017).

[3] We subsequently found slides from a Continuing Legal Education (CLE) presentation that Glenn had made at the University of Texas, where he had a list of brainless variants of clauses in M&A agreements that he provided as warnings to the lawyers attending the session. *See* Glenn West, *Revenge of the Sea Squirts: More Encrusted Boilerplate*, 15th Annual Mergers and Acquisitions Institute (Oct. 11, 2019). *See also* Glenn West, *Do You Really Know What "Consequential Damages" Means?* (May 18, 2020).

> conclusion [holds across both settings]—the tug of form and market is strong indeed.[4]

Not long after we read Glenn's posts, we saw an article by Reid Feldman, a Paris-based M&A specialist, who had engaged with some of our prior work.[5] Feldman was interested in the reasons why similar anomalies persisted in M&A contracts. Feldman explained that clients in the M&A context had strong incentives to pay close attention to terms and, therefore, so did their lawyers. Nevertheless, he noted, there were flawed terms that managed to persist in a nontrivial faction of M&A contracts, long after the flaws were well recognized in the industry.

The final article that pushed us out of our comfort zone in the sovereign space was by Trevor Clark, a partner at the UK-based firm, Linklaters, now turned law professor.[6] Clark had observed an increase in the number of ambiguities and loopholes in European leveraged loan contracts. He was intrigued by the increase because he thought it could not be explained by the pure market-based explanation that increased demand for these types of investments translated into looser investor protections. An increase in debtor bargaining power would result in more terms that were clearly debtor favorable. And there was some of that. But what he was seeing was an increase in ambiguities and loopholes that were then being exploited by aggressive debtor lawyers in a manner that surprised the creditors. Something beyond an increase in the debtors' bargaining power was going on.[7]

The observations by West, Feldman, and Clark pushed us to expand our project. In addition to sovereign bonds, we began to focus on M&A and leveraged loans, and particularly the subsets of those worlds where private equity dominated. As the stories in Chapter Two illustrated, litigation against sovereigns for breach of contract has become increasingly common over the past several decades, underscoring the importance of contract language in

[4] Glenn D. West, *The Form Doesn't Know Anything: A Response to Gulati, Chowdhury & Chudkowski*, 79 U. Miami L. Rev. 628 (2025).

[5] Reid Feldman, *Black Holes and Boilerplate in M&A Practice*, 19 Bus. L. Int'l 140 (2018).

[6] Trevor Clark, *The Pendulum Swing in Leveraged Finance Loan Terms: The Role of Designation*, 38 J.Int'l Bnk. L. Reg. 45 (2023).

[7] In his forthcoming book, Trevor uses interviews with lawyers to understand the shift in drafting practices. He finds two factors that may explain what has been occurring. First, the practice of the issuer/debtor side designating the counsel for the investors. And second, a loosening of ethical norms on the part of the lawyers doing the drafting work (partly driven by the influence of US style private equity norms). Designation was a feature that we also thought might be at play in explaining landmines in sovereign debt, and so we were intrigued. As we report in Chapter Thirteen, we are persuaded that Trevor is right about the relevance of the shift in norms as well.

that market. And now West, Feldman, and Clark claimed that landmines appear and persist in the much different environments of M&A and leveraged loan transactions; environments in which the parties clearly do care about the contract language. It seemed that the process by which these commercial contracts are produced in quite different markets could hold a key to the landmine puzzle.

But the puzzle remained: If contract language matters, what explains the presence of landmines in the M&A market, for example? Enter Peter Lyons. Pete, recently retired from M&A practice at a large international law firm, had begun teaching a course on corporate deals at the University of Virginia. Hoping for some insight on the assertions by Feldman, West, and Clark, we approached Pete. Turned out that he, too, was interested in contract landmines. He had worked on leveraged debt financings early in his career, and then moved to doing both public and private M&A deals. Pete volunteered to contact some of his former partners and colleagues at other firms to ask for examples of deals in their practice that had blown up. Pete's contacts responded enthusiastically. Each one sent us multiple deals from different markets that they thought were good examples of the landmine phenomenon. What we learned from these examples, along with the clues from Clark, West, and Feldman, form the basis for Part III of the book where we examine M&A contracts, the syndicated leveraged loan market, and bespoke commercial agreements. The dynamics of contract production are different, but landmines exist in all three environments. And sometimes they persist.

Two More Stories

As a precursor to what follows in Part III, we relate two stories that we learned from Pete Lyons and his friends in practice. Many of the same determinants that appeared in the sovereign context are apparent as well in these disparate markets: misplaced assumptions about the meaning of standard terms lead to drafters' failure to find (and repair) landmines that later explode.

Serta (2020)

In 2016, Serta Simmons, one of the largest mattress companies in the world, entered into a series of credit agreements with lenders. By 2019, the company was having difficulty meeting its obligations to these creditors. Advent International, serving as Serta's private equity sponsor, had acquired a majority stake in the parent company of Serta in 2012. Wanting to restructure Serta's debt, Advent turned to Evercore, a financial advisory firm, just in time for the pandemic in 2020 when things got worse still for Serta.[8]

Advent and Evercore contacted Serta's creditors, inviting them to come up with a plan. One group, including the heavyweight funds Apollo and Angelo Gordan, put together a proposal to help Serta by doing what is referred to as a dropdown transaction. This was a transaction that had been used infamously a few years earlier by J.Crew in which the company's intellectual property assets that J.Crew's creditors thought secured their debt were moved into an "unrestricted" subsidiary and thereby out of the creditors' package of collateral. The now dropped-down intellectual property assets were then used to finance additional loans to the company contrary to the interests of J.Crew's other secured creditors. (Unhappy creditors referred to the transaction as "J. Screwed."[9])

The scuttlebutt was that Advent believed that the proposal from the Apollo/Angelo Gordan group was the best they would get. So, Advent and Serta initially didn't respond to attempts by a competing creditor group to contact them. When Advent and Serta finally answered the competitors' call, they found that the alternate group and its lawyers were suggesting an even more attractive plan. In essence, the plan from the alternate group, which included the creditors Eaton Vance and Invesco as "participating" lenders, was to provide the company with additional "new" financing and also take a haircut on what was owed to them. In exchange, the participating lenders current lending was elevated in priority over the other "non participating" lenders, including Apollo and Angelo Gordan. To use the industry lingo, Serta would get a "longer runway" to try and get their metaphorical plane off the ground. In return for this longer runway, the participating lenders would fare much better if Serta were to declare bankruptcy than

[8] Among the numerous law firm practice notes, blog posts, and academic articles describing the Serta transaction are, *Serta's Chapter 11: Upholding the Up Tier*, Restructuring Interviews (July 14, 2023); Shana Elberg, Evan A. Hill, & Catrina A. Shea, *Uptier Exchange Transactions Remain in Vogue, Notwithstanding Litigation Risk*, Skadden Arps (Feb. 21, 2021); Evan A. Hill & Mason Walther, *Lessons From Recent Uptier Transaction Litigation*, 37 Turnarounds & Workarounds 1(Oct. 2023); Vincent S.J. Buccola & Greg Nini, *The Loan Market Response to Dropdown and Uptier Transactions* 53 J. Legal Studies 489 (2024); Vincent S.J. Buccola, *Efficacious Answers to the Non-Pro Rata Workout*, 171 U. Penn. L. Rev. 1859 (2023).

[9] There was even a National Public Radio *Planet Money* episode. *See* Mary Childs & Amanda Aronczyk, *J.Screwed*, NPR.org (May 22, 2020).

the non-participating lenders who were excluded from what was being described as an "Up Tier."

Supposedly, the Apollo-Angelo Gordan group had considered and dismissed this same strategy of "creditor-on-creditor" violence as too aggressive. The excluded creditors would be so disadvantaged if the firm did end up in bankruptcy that there was sure to be litigation. But Serta's sponsor was willing to roll the dice on litigation: if the equity was going to have shot at getting any value, it needed more runway.

Ordinarily, one would think that such a move would not be possible in a traditional syndicated loan structure. The obligation to share equally any payments received from the debtor has long been among the "sacred rights" of lenders in a syndicate. One might think, therefore, that a debtor colluding with a subset of creditors to create value for itself and its favored creditors by extracting value from other creditors would run afoul of the equal sharing clause.

But the traditional syndicated loan structure had been modified around the time of the financial crisis of 2008–2010. The severity of the crisis had produced the need for a number of lenders to exit their syndicates. For their part, debtors were trying to weather the crisis and didn't want lenders calling in Events of Default. So loan documents were modified to provide debtors with more flexibility during periods of distress. These "covenant-lite" agreements included "open market purchase" clauses, allowing debtors to purchase the interests of individual syndicate members on the "open market" without having to obtain the approval of the other members of the syndicate. They became standard in the market as creditors, holding too much liquidity, agreed to looser credit terms in order to "chase too few deals."

The Serta loan documents had this clause:

> *[A]ny Lender may, at any time, assign all or a portion of its rights and obligations under this Agreement [to the Debtor] (A) through Dutch Auctions open to all Lenders holding the relevant Term Loans on a pro rata basis or (B) through open market purchases.*

Formulated in terms of the rights of any lender to assign its rights and obligations under the Agreement, the clause provides that the debtor can buy the interests of any lender in two ways. Either (A) through a Dutch Auction that has to be open to all lenders on pro rata basis or (B) through an open market purchase. And here, the key is that option B, the open market purchase option, unlike option A (the Dutch Auction), *does not say that the purchase has to be offered to all lenders on a pro rata basis.*

In addition, the sharing clause in the Serta loan documents provided that the pro rata sharing obligation did not apply to "any payment obtained by any Lender as consideration for the assignment of or sale of a participation in any of its Loans to any permitted assignee or participant, including any payment made or deemed made in connection with [the open market purchase provision]."

Given that an "open market purchase" apparently could be done vis-à-vis specific lenders, Serta exchanged the loan participations of its favored lenders for new loan participations that would now have priority over the other, disfavored lenders who had not been made this offer. The lower face amount of these new, higher priority loan participations provided the company debt relief. The favored creditors, for their part, were elevated in priority, an invaluable right in the context of a company on the brink of bankruptcy. The disfavored lenders were left with debt obligations at a lower priority.

To quote one of the lawyers who discussed the Serta transaction, the open market clause and the modifications to the sharing clause "created a hole one could drive a truck through; it was just that at the time of including that provision, it is unlikely anyone was thinking it would be used that way. And it was not; not for almost a decade."

We interviewed close to fifty senior lawyers in the leveraged loan business and all but a few said that the particular way in which the "open market clause" was used was unexpected. Put differently, the goal behind including this clause—to allow debtors to remove troublesome creditors following the financial crisis of 2008–2010—was quite different from the creditor versus creditor arrangement in Serta. That said, most lawyers we interviewed agreed that the clause gave an aggressive private equity sponsor a plausible basis for the Serta type Up Tier. To quote one respondent close to the transaction, "they took that damn truck and drove it [through the ambiguity in the contract] like it was stolen."[10] Another said:

> Anyone who thought about [the open market clause] for two seconds would have seen the loophole. My guess . . . and I was a junior lawyer then; at the time this provision was put in [to the standard forms around 2008–2010], such a transaction would have been too big a violation of norms. But

[10] The reference may be to a song from the 2016 movie *Sing Street* titled "Drive it Like You Stole it."

> then the players changed, private equity guys came in, and Covid hit. The unthinkable became the obvious. If you look at 2020, this was not the only Up Tier, or even the most aggressive.

There are arguments for why the Up Tiering in Serta violated the terms of the loan contract. One is that the lien subordination was in fact a lien release and the latter required creditor approval. Another that is implicit in the meaning of an "open market transaction" is that the deal has to be offered to all on the open market (for cash perhaps). And, finally, there is the argument that the transaction violates the implicit duty of good faith and fair dealing or amounts to tortious interference with contract rights.

Thanks to Pete Lyons and his contacts, we were able to persuade two senior lawyers who had worked on implementing Serta type transactions to talk to our students. In describing the deals in class, the two lawyers spent the bulk of their time describing the transactional structures and the contract terms used in the Serta deal and two follow-on Up Tiers, debt restructurings involving Boardriders, an apparel and footwear company, and TriMark, a restaurant supply company. As class was coming to an end, one of the students challenged them: "Was there fallout? Were people in the industry reluctant to do business with the firms who had implemented these aggressive structures?"

We worried that our guests might take umbrage at the question, but they seemed eager to discuss it. One admitted that he had initially been concerned. He explained:

> Covid pushed us all to take these transactions seriously. There had been a few attempts before, . . . the trapdoor in J.Crew was one of them. The contracts had been loose for a while. They were "cov lite." It was a matter of time. The specific transaction [Up Tier] might not have been anticipated. But everyone knew the docs had gaps and debtors could use them. It was a matter of time before [Private Equity] firms, who were aggressive anyway, used them.

Our other guest followed up:

> I don't think, unless some court rules against this entire category of transactions, that this will stop. If the clients want to do these transactions, we know how to design them. It's that simple. Every big firm is trying to set

> up [Liability Management Transaction] departments these days. They are [recruiting away] our associates.

Whether these types of transactions will stop or not remains an open question as of this writing. Serta's efforts to stave off bankruptcy through its Up Tiering transaction ultimately failed. Serta filed for bankruptcy in Texas in January 2023, and the disadvantaged non-participating lenders challenged the transaction in the bankruptcy proceedings. The bankruptcy judge upheld the use of open market purchases as part of the Up Tier.[11] But on December 31, 2024, the Fifth Circuit Court of Appeals reversed the bankruptcy court. The appellate court held that the "open market purchase" provision does not allow "non pro rata" repurchases on the market, thereby throwing cold water on the use of this particular technique.[12] As multiple respondents pointed out, the Serta Up Tier was but one technique and it was no longer state of the art. There was now an entire industry of lawyers figuring out new ways to do these liability management transactions (LMTs). They didn't need this particular loophole; they had long since figured out a slew of new techniques.[13] But that story is for Chapter Thirteen.

Save Mart (2022)

Our second story involves a commercial acquisition—a market different from the syndicated leveraged loans. It concerns a 2022 sale of the Save Mart supermarket chain of stores to the private equity firm, Kingswood Capital. The story circulating in the legal community told of a drafting

[11] *Bankruptcy Court Rules That "Up Tier" Transaction in Serta Simmons Bedding Case Did Not Violate Implied Covenant of Good Faith and Fair Dealing*, Winston & Strawn (July 5, 2023).

[12] Alexander Gladstone, *Serta Simmons Debt Restructuring Struck Down by Appeals Court*, Wall St. J. (Dec. 31, 2024).

[13] Bankruptcy law professor, Adam Levitin, wrote in his blog post:

> Although the opinion is an important punctuation point, I don't think it will itself fundamentally change the use of liability management transactions; there's really little downside from pursuing them and potentially plenty of upside.
>
> . . .
>
> The 5th Circuit probably killed off "open-market purchase" Up Tier exchanges, but that's only one flavor of LMT. The opinion does not affect all of the other types of LMTs we've seen: drop-downs (like J.Crew or Chewy), Sale-Leasebacks (Windstream), Double Dips/Pari Plus (like At Home or Wheel Pros or Sabre), and Up Tiers that do not hinge on "open market repurchase" language (e.g., Robertshaw, Wesco/Incora, TriMark). We're going to continue to see fights over those types of transactions.
>
> Adam Levitin, *Serta Simmons UpTier, Implications*, Creditslips.org (Jan. 2, 2025)

blunder.[14] Boiled down by the *Financial Times*'s Sujeet Indap, this was a story of a California family learning the hard way how private equity firms play contract hardball.[15] Law firm memos, for their part, saw the story as an object lesson for lawyers: don't unthinkingly rely on standard terms.[16]

The main character in the story is the clause defining "Closing Date Indebtedness." The lawyers for Save Mart (owned by the Piccinini family) had used a standard form definition for "Closing Date Indebtedness." The problem was that they had not been accounting for the value of one of their subsidiaries in a fashion that matched the definition of "indebtedness" that was in the standard form. The end result of the drafters' failure to modify the standardized provision to match the specific transaction may have cost the Piccinini family over $100 million.

Here is what happened. For purchases of this type, there is a formula that is typically used to estimate the final price that will be paid for the company. There is the "Base Amount," which essentially is the sale price of the company based on an approximation of what the aggregate value is to the buyer before deducting, among other things, any indebtedness of the company that may be owing as of the closing and changes in working capital that may occur between signing and closing. In the case of Save Mart, this Base Amount was $245 million. At this stage, however, the buyer is an outsider. The buyer, therefore, contracts to pay an estimated price at the closing based on the amount the seller tells the buyer the deductions to the Base Price are as of the closing, but with the buyer having a right to make a final determination of the correct amount of the deductions after the closing and once it takes possession of the company and can more thoroughly determine what the indebtedness (and changes to working capital) was at closing.

Typically, no one expects large differences between the estimated price paid at closing and the final price once the buyer acquires the company and can fully evaluate the actual versus estimated deductions from the Base Amount. But here, there was a significant disconnect.

As is standard, Closing Date Indebtedness, one of the main deductions from the Base Amount for calculating the estimated and final price, was

[14] *$70 M Drafting Mistake Forces Save Mart to Pay Buyer*, Legal IO (May 16, 2024); John Kupiec, Matthew P. Salerno, & Brandon Welcome, *Raw Deal: Seller Ordered to Pay Buyer Over Twice the Purchase Price in Post-Closing Price Adjustment Dispute*, Cleary Gottlieb (Mar. 25, 2024).

[15] Sujeet Indap, *The Inequity Method of Accounting*, FT Alphaville (Apr. 11, 2024).

[16] *Drafting and Diligence Matter in M&A: Lessons from "Save Mart,"* Fasken (Sept. 13, 2024).

defined in the contract as "the aggregate amount of all Indebtedness of the Group Companies [as of the closing date]." The problem was that "Group Companies" was defined to include all of the company's wholly owned subsidiaries, as well as a significant but only partially owned joint venture called SSI. However, the SSI joint venture was accounted for as an unconsolidated subsidiary on the company's balance sheet using the equity method of accounting, meaning that SSI's debt was deducted from its total valuation and reflected as a net amount. In other words, SSI's debt was not listed as part of the aggregate debt of the company and its subsidiaries. Thus, when the seller provided the estimated closing date calculation, which the buyer then paid at the closing, the indebtedness of SSI was not included as a deduction from the Base Amount.

However, when the buyer later made the final calculation of the amount of debt of the Group Companies after closing, the buyer included the total amount of the SSI debt ($109 million), as the contract appeared to require, notwithstanding that the company had already accounted for that debt by netting it out of the value of SSI (resulting in a net investment in SSI for the company of $22.5 million).

While the seller believed its $22.5 million net investment in SSI fully accounted for the $109 million, the contract unfortunately defined the amount to be deducted from the Base Amount to include the aggregate amount of all indebtedness of the Group Companies (which included SSI).

To add to the drama, Kingswood appears to have understood that there was a problem in how SSI's value was being incorporated into the purchase price that the Piccinini's thought they were going to receive. Ordinarily, if a party sees that a counterparty believes they will receive a much higher price than the party plans to pay, that discrepancy would be flagged before the deal closes. To fail to do so, especially when the disparity in question is $109 million, is at a minimum, a recipe for litigation. But Kingswood did not alert Save Mart.

Here is what Kingswood's lead executive on the deal said:

> We were surprised that the seller didn't put any SSI debt in their definition of indebtedness as of the closing, and our view was, if that's what they believed and we raised it, we thought it would be a contentious topic . . .
>
> Again, we had had a draft purchase agreement from them dating back to, you know, December that clearly laid out the debt of operating subsidiaries, as well as debt guaranteed by Save Mart was, in fact, indebtedness for

> purposes of the transaction. Again, it's a very standard definition. So no, we assumed that they had read their own document that they drafted.

Ultimately, the $109 million post-closing adjustment in Kingswood favor was upheld in arbitration and confirmed by the Delaware Chancery Court. We could stop here. The story illustrates how blindly using a standard definition, without tailoring it to the deal characteristics at hand, can result in disaster. Again, as with the Serta Up Tier transaction, there was the question of acceptable norms and the potency of reputational constraints. One of our students explicitly asked: "Are Kingswood and its lawyers going to suffer a reputational penalty for doing what they did?"

Our guests for that day in class—two senior transactional lawyers and a judge—complimented the student for her question. But they were unclear about the answer. As a literal matter, Kingswood and its lawyers were asking that the contract terms be strictly followed (a contract that their *counterparties* had drafted). They were entitled to do that, and, indeed, an arbitrator and two appeals courts agreed. But how one behaves vis-à-vis such an advantage that results from the counterparty not understanding its own contract, is a matter of norms. Older lawyers that we have interviewed decry the loss of the "reputational market" that previously would have deterred aggressive actions like Kingswood's. It may be only a coincidence but the fraying of those norms appears to coincide with the landmine stories we have heard in transactions like Serta and Save Mart.[17]

Where Do The Stories Lead?

Serta and *Save Mart* tell two different landmine origin stories.

In *Serta*, the landmine is the product of an ambiguous clause, the open market purchase provision, inserted into the standard form in leveraged

[17] In his post describing the *Save Mart* drama, Glenn West wrote:

> This case raises some serious questions about dealmaking ethics depending on who understood what and when about the potential inclusion of the SSI debt as a deduction to the Purchase Price. During my career I was once faced with a client pursuing a course of action that I believed was legally correct, but morally wrong, and my response was to refuse to represent them in the resulting dispute. Typically, sharp business practices will catch up with you eventually.

Glenn D. West, *Post Closing Adjustments Gone Wrong*, Business Law Today (May 13, 2024).

loan transactions to deal with a single issue during a crisis, the desire to allow certain creditors to exit from the lender pool. Contracts with these "cov-lite" provisions became the standard in the wake of the financial crisis as lenders competed for business in a low interest rate economy. The clauses were not drafted in a way that excluded strategic behavior perhaps because drafters believed that market norms of comity constrained unfair actions against competitors. But as large and aggressive private investment funds, such as Apollo and Angelo Gordan, entered this previously staid market, norms began to decay resulting in what was decried after *Serta* as "creditor on creditor violence." In that new environment, the loosely drafted open market purchase clause created a vulnerability that was exploited at the expense of the minority of creditors who did not participate in the open market repurchase by the debtor.

How does the loophole in *Serta* fit with the landmine categories that we identified from the stories about sovereign debt? In one respect, the loose drafting was a drafting error, a failure to preclude actions that would potentially damage any creditor finding itself in the minority. The fact that this loophole could have been plugged at the outset is demonstrated by the significant number of contracts following *Serta* in which drafters inserted so-called "Serta-blockers" in an effort to deter similar Up Tier transactions.[18] But this is not the type of random error that we found in the standard form sovereign debt contract. Changes such as the use of the open market purchase clause were borrowed from bond contracts and have become embedded in the core of the contract: they remain there today even after their original purposes are no longer served. This loophole is best described as what we previously have called an historical holdover, terms in the contract that survive, it seems, simply because they have survived so long. No one quite knows what the terms means in the current context but no one has a sufficient incentive to remove them. Nevertheless, holdovers from prior documentation are empty vessels that function as landmines when litigators assert an unexpected meaning for the term.

Save Mart, in contrast, is an example of a *random error*, similar in effect if not in its nature to what we observed in sovereign debt contracts: the drafters of the Save Mart contract used a standard form provision without tailoring it to the particular requirements of the deal at hand. One can wonder why such an error occurred in the first place? Commercial acquisition contracts

[18] Buccola & Nini, *supra* note 8.

are artifacts, comprising long, complicated, boilerplate provisions that have historically been part of the documentation. Attorneys dealing with such contracts can fall prey to the assumption that the standard terms are fixed and unchanging: they may economize on their time by focusing on specific parts of the contract, such as the bottom line sales price, without adequately addressing components in the contract determining how this price is actually computed. This would include understanding the computation mechanism in the provision for Closing Date Indebtedness in the Save Mart contract. Not all lawyers have the same degree of experience and expertise in working with the detail of a complex contract. Put another way, *Save Mart* may be an example of a divide in the market for commercial lawyers: novice attorneys may make errors and more expert attorneys and their no-holds-barred private equity clients may take advantage.

* * *

The landmines exemplified by the stories in the preceding chapters, together with the many other examples we have subsequently discovered, provoke further questions: Do these landmines persist and evolve over time as the suspect language is repeated in subsequent contracts? Or, is the aberrant language once discovered then promptly revised to eliminate any future exploitation? The fact that drafting anomalies occur occasionally is not surprising, even with billion dollar contracts. But what if these different types of landmines persist and are prevalent in large numbers? The greater the number of landmines, the stronger the incentive for market actors to search for them in order to secure a litigation advantage.

We begin to answer the persistence puzzle by returning to the sovereign bond world and tracing the evolutionary story of the infamous *pari passu* landmine. Chapter Four tells that story.

Chapter Four
Pari Passu and the Evolution of a Landmine

Introduction

Thus far, we've told a set of stories. They are suggestive but do not by themselves tell us that there is a more systematic phenomenon. We turn to that next. If we take a single landmine and trace its evolution over time, what would we find? How does the landmine arise? Does the irregularity persist, appearing in subsequent documentation used by different parties? Can the market coordinate to eliminate the landmine from the standard form going forward? To make progress on answering these questions, we turn to the saga of the *pari passu* clause.

The *pari passu* provision is standard fare in cross-border sovereign bonds and its historical evolution has been extensively mined.[1] Our focus is on the landmines that arise and disappear in this single clause. Tracking the evolution of the clause from the beginning of the modern standard form sovereign bond contract in the early 1990s to today allows us to identify points at which the clause morphed and landmines were either created or eliminated. We don't pretend that the saga of the *pari passu* clause is representative. Our purpose here is to the mine the fossil record for clues as to how landmines arise, mutate, and disappear.

[1] *See* Marc Flandreau, *Pari Passu Lost and Found: The Origins of Sovereign Bankruptcy 1798–1873*, Institute for New Economic Thinking, Working Paper (2022); Ben Chabot & Mitu Gulati, *Santa Anna and His Black Eagle*, 9 Cap. Mkts. L. J. 216 (2014); Anna Gelpern, *Courts and Sovereigns in the Pari Passu Goldmines*, 11 Cap. Mkts. L. J. 251 (2016); Lee C. Buchheit & Jeremiah Pam, *The Pari Passu Clause in Sovereign Debt Instruments*, 53 Emory L. J. 869 (2004).

Contract Hazards. Stephen J. Choi, Mitu Gulati, and Robert E. Scott, Oxford University Press.
 DOI: 10.1093/9780197821770.003.0004

Origin Stories

The origins of the *pari passu* clause in unsecured sovereign debt are obscure. That has not prevented a number of different origin stories from emerging over time. Most of these stories conclude that the clause had a distinct purpose in transactions that predate the modern standard form sovereign bond contract but that those purposes no longer apply in the current context.[2] One of the origin stories, for example, draws on a possible connection to the days of gunboat diplomacy, when imperial powers sometimes deployed gunboats to take over the defaulting debtor's custom houses and force payments to creditors.[3] Here, the *pari passu* clause guaranteed that all creditors would have equal access to those payments. But that was over a century ago and those conditions are no longer apt. Another origin story traces the evolution of the *pari passu* clause to domestic statutes in certain civil law jurisdictions that in the past might have interfered with the creditors' priority; the statutes were no longer relevant, but the clause remained.[4] The clause might have been a staple in corporate debt transactions but, the story claims, it has no obvious function in modern sovereign instruments. Yet another story traces the clause to the London Stock Exchange rules and practices for sovereign restructurings of the early 20th century.[5]

To understand why the market concluded that the clause had no apparent meaning in a sovereign bond, consider the typical clause that provided:

> *The Notes rank, and will rank,* pari passu *with all unsecured External Indebtedness of the Republic.*

The notion of "rank" (the modifier to the term "pari passu" in most of the clauses) comes from bankruptcy law. Claims that rank pari passu (or equally) get paid pro rata in the event of a liquidation event. But sovereigns are never liquidated. So what purpose was the clause serving in a contract where the

[2] We take the background for this chapter from our prior work. Mitu Gulati & Robert E. Scott, The Three and a Half Minute Transaction: Boilerplate and the Limits of Contract Design (University of Chicago Press, 2013); Mark Weidemaier, Robert E. Scott, & Mitu Gulati, *Origin Myths, Contract, and the Hunt for Pari Passu*, 38 L. & Soc. Inquiry 72 (2013); Stephen J. Choi, Mitu Gulati, & Robert E. Scott, *Variation in Boilerplate: Rational Design or Random Mutation*, 20 Amer. L. & Econ. Rev. 1 (2018).

[3] Chabot & Gulati, *supra* note 1.

[4] Buchheit & Pam, *supra* note 1.

[5] Flandreau, *supra* note 1.

debtor was a sovereign state? The conventional answer was "None." In the common understanding, therefore, whatever its origin, the obsolete *pari passu* clause was an inconsequential clause in the agreement between the lender and each borrower, simply specifying how much the creditor would be repaid.

A veteran British lawyer speculated:

> Back in the days when people didn't have existing texts to work from they may well have looked to different markets for precedents. I would guess that in the UK the debenture stock market might have been the source used. This market involved corporate issuers and bonds secured on the issuer's assets by a floating charge, so very different context. It may be that this is where the pari passu condition crept in—relevant in the bankruptcy of a corporate issuer but not in the case of a sovereign (at least, not in the same way). Once in, it stayed in!

Despite the murky origins, and despite the conventional view in the market that the term carried no apparent meaning, by the 1970s, *pari passu* was a clause common in every sovereign syndicated loan. And here an entirely different origin story emerged that focuses on the period when the sovereign market shifted from syndicated loans to bonds in the mid-1980s and 1990s. In the course of restructuring the syndicated loans, smaller banks were pressured by their governments and by larger lending institutions to dramatically reduce their claims against defaulted borrowers. Determined not to endure similar write-downs in the future, the story goes, the smaller banks demanded that the new bonds include a package of terms, including a *pari passu* clause, that would protect them against restructuring requests. Armed with the *pari passu* clause, a bondholder could refuse to participate in a restructuring and then sue those who did participate for a ratable share of their payments.

The argument for this interpretation was advanced in 1984 by Brian Semkow, a professor of international finance and banking.[6] Semkow's

[6] Semkow argued that:

> In the event that the corporate laws governing the borrower will rank the unsecured claims, however, the [*pari passu* clause] will not prevent the lending banks from being discriminated against.... In the context of the sovereign borrower, the *pari passu* covenant has a different effect. This provision will prevent sovereign borrowers from discrimination against the lending banks in the payment of creditors out of general revenues or foreign currency reserves.

Brian W. Semkow, *Syndicating and Rescheduling International Financial Transactions: A Survey of the Legal Issues Encountered by Commercial Banks*, 18 INT'L LAW. 869, 899 (1984).

argument was that the clause was, in effect, an agreement *among* the creditors. As such, the agreement would be breached if some but not all creditors accepted the debtor's settlement offer. The creditors who objected thus could enjoin the other creditors from receiving any payment. This argument in short was that *pari passu* required a "pro rata" payment to the nonconsenting creditors.

Fast forward to the 1990s as the syndicated loan market was dissolving and the modern bond market emerged in its place. Lee Buchheit (remember Gandalf from Chapter One) wrote a series of short articles and later a book that tackled the *pari passu* question. Buchheit speculated that *pari passu*, like many other clauses, had migrated from a predecessor standard form. The clause was short, had some Latin (lawyers like that), and was probably harmless so long as it was never applied. But Buchheit also sounded a note of concern. In response to the Semkow argument, that the *pari passu* clause imposed an obligation among creditors to one another, he worried that some in the industry might claim that the clause *also* meant that the sovereign was obligated to pay all creditors on a pro rata basis. This claim, Buchheit explained, was false on its face. Sovereigns in distress always needed to pay certain creditors (e.g., trade creditors or the IMF that had provided emergency financing) before others. In the modern era of sovereign debt, that had been the way things had always worked, despite *pari passu* clauses being omnipresent. Pro rata payment could not possibly be what the clause meant.[7]

In any event, in the miasma that surrounded the decline of the syndicated loan market, the transformation of loans into Brady Bonds, and the emergence of a robust market in international sovereign debt, *pari passu* was imported as a standard term in the original standard form documentation supporting the new market. The result is a landmine—a term without any

[7] In his 1995 book, Buchheit wrote:

> [A] lender who remains unpaid at a time when other creditors are current on their loans may articulate his grievance in terms of liberty, equality or fraternity, but he should not invoke his *pari passu* covenant as the legal basis for his disappointment. This provision assures the creditor that its loan will not be subordinated to the claims of other creditors in the event of the borrower's bankruptcy, but it does not force the solvent borrower to make pro rata payments to all its creditors.

Supporting Buchheit's view, the eminent English lawyer, Philip Wood, wrote, in his treatise:

> It should also be observed that the *pari passu* clause has nothing to do with the time of payment of unsecured indebtedness since this depends upon contractual maturity. The *pari passu* undertaking is not broken merely because one creditor is paid before another.

See Kenneth Klee & Mitu Gulati, *Sovereign Piracy*, 56 Bus. Lawyer 635, n.49 (2000) (citing Buchheit and Wood).

understood meaning in the new environment that could and did lead to unexpected litigation.[8] As noted in Chapter Two, we call these one-time importation mistakes the "historical holdover" landmines. Because the historical holdover landmines are embedded in the original source standard form for the modern sovereign bond template, we might predict that once embedded these landmines are unlikely to disappear even over long periods of time. And, as the following evolutionary story makes clear, the initial *pari passu* landmine not only continues in deal after deal, but it mutates in ways that increase the number and severity of the litigation risks that it spawns.

Brussels (2001)

What Lee Buchheit feared, happened: a landmine had been planted in the documentation that comprised the standard form contract. Along the way in the life of the clause, a few words were added to a subset of *pari passu* clauses. The best evidence is that these modifications were the product of human error: lawyers with an inadequate understanding of the sovereign context tried to clarify the meaning of a clause that otherwise seemed to have no purpose. In any event, the words *"in right of payment"* were added to the standard clause, making it read:

> *The Notes rank, and will rank,* pari passu ***in right of payment*** *with all unsecured External Indebtedness of the Republic.*[9] (emphasis added)

Absent any knowledge of what people in the market have always done and assumed, what might the additional language mean? At a minimum, the initial *pari passu* landmine, which on its face was a meaningless historical holdover, was further weaponized by the addition of language that pointed to an enhanced right of an undetermined nature for the bondholder. Someone who found this latter version of the clause might well turn to those claiming that the clause was ambiguous and say: "Let me help remedy your confusion. This new version of the clause with the words "in right of payment" tells us

[8] Gulati & Scott, *supra* note 2 at 115–118.

[9] This story is told in detail in Gulati & Scott, *id.* The broader narrative of Argentina's default in 2001, attempts to restructure, and various legal battles (including *pari passu*) is told in GREGORY MAKOFF, DEFAULT: THE LANDMARK COURT BATTLE OVER ARGENTINA'S $100 BILLION DEBT RESTRUCTURING (Georgetown University Press, 2024).

exactly what it means to rank *pari passu* in the sovereign context: it means that creditors who rank equally get to be *paid* equally."

That is what happened. In the late 1990s, Peru had concluded one of the last of the Brady restructurings of 1980s debts. There was, however, a holdout who had refused the Peruvian deal. Believing that sovereign immunity protected it from creditors attaching its sovereign assets, Peru was paying the restructured Brady obligations and ignoring the holdouts.[10]

The holdout was Elliott Associates, a hedge fund determined to challenge the common practice of sovereigns securing consent to a restructuring by strong-arming nonconsenting creditors. Elliott had purchased Peruvian unrestructured debt with a face value of about $55 million for roughly $11 million. The discount reflected the market's prediction that bondholders would not be able to recover anything close to full face value.

The story we've been told is that the key players at Elliott began by luring several bright Ivy League graduates away from the tedium of big law. The plan was to turn the regnant copy and paste model of contract drafting to their advantage by reading clauses carefully and then doing contract arbitrage. Along the way, it was discovered that the *pari passu* clause in the Peruvian bond contract contained the tantalizing "in right of payment" additional language. The clause in Peru's debt instruments provided:

> *The obligations of [Peru] hereunder do rank and will rank at least* pari passu *in priority of payment with all other External Indebtedness of [Peru], and interest thereon.*[11]

The question for Elliott was how to use the fortuitous revision to force Peru to pay the bonds in full. That required refuting Buchheit's argument that whatever the clause meant, it did not entitle creditors to demand ratable payments. Elliott took Buchheit on directly: The key to its strategy was retaining Andreas Lowenfeld, an eminent New York University Law School professor who specialized in international matters.

Lowenfeld was not a sovereign debt scholar. But he was willing to assert, based on his experience in the international arena, that Buchheit was wrong.

[10] For discussions of what happened in the Elliott v. Peru part of the saga, see Rodrigo Olivares-Caminal, *The Pari Passu Interpretation in the Elliott Case: A Brilliant Strategy, but an (Awful) Outcome?*, 40 Hofstra L. Rev. 39 (2011); Kenneth Klee & Mitu Gulati, *Sovereign Piracy*, 56 Bus. Law. 235 (2001).

[11] Affidavit of Jay H. Newman in Support of Plaintiff's Motion for Summary Judgment, Elliott Assocs., L.P. v. Banco de la Nacion, 194 F.R.D. 116 (S.D.N.Y. 2000) (No. 96 Civ. 7916 (RWS)).

While Buchheit might have been unclear about the meaning of the *pari passu* clause, Lowenfeld had no problem discerning that the clause meant that all creditors ranking *pari passu* were entitled to be paid on an equal pro rata basis. Indeed, Lowenfeld opined, given the "in right of payment" language, what else could the clause possibly mean? And since the words in clauses negotiated by sophisticated commercial parties are presumed to have meaning, the court in Brussels gave Elliott an injunction against payments being made out of Euroclear (the Brussels clearinghouse) unless Elliott was paid in full.[12]

Elliott then either had a dollop of luck or was smart enough to time its litigation extraordinarily well. One story we have heard is that the Peruvian leader, Alberto Fujimori, was in political trouble at the time. Elections were approaching, one of his henchmen was caught on camera attempting a bribe, and Fujimori wanted to avoid a default on the recently concluded Brady restructuring. Another story is that Peru's economy was booming and that a default was seen as inimical to the progress that had been made since the Brady restructuring a few years before. Regardless, the instruction was given in late 2000 for Elliott to be paid in full; the final amount being $58.3 million, which gave Elliott roughly a gain of 400% from its original investment.[13]

One might surmise from this that Elliott was simply fortunate in buying bonds that happened to contain the enhanced landmine language. But in time even more dangerous modifications of the standard form clause surfaced with language yet worse for Buchheit's argument that no sovereign debtor in its right mind would agree to a ratable payment clause. For example, the clause in Italian bonds from around that period read:

> *The Notes rank, and will rank,* pari passu, *with all unsecured External Indebtedness [of the Republic] . . .* ***and shall be payable as such.***[14] (emphasis added)

[12] As we understand what happened from those who were closer to events—with the caveat that we've heard differing stories—Lowenfeld's opinion was submitted in the litigation in New York, where Elliott obtained its judgment. They then attempted to obtain injunctions in other jurisdictions including Brussels. And Lowenfeld's *pari passu* opinion provided a basis for their request for an injunction that was in fact granted in Brussels. See Olivares-Caminal, *supra* note 10 at 23 (quoting the reference in the grant of injunction in Brussels to the fact that the agreement had a *pari passu* clause).

[13] *Id.* at 45.

[14] For a discussion of the Italian clause, see Andrea E. Kropp, *Restructuring Italy's New York Law Bonds*, 15 Cap. Mkts. L. J. 139 (2020).

The words "and shall be payable as such" appeared to give the clause precisely the meaning that Buchheit was claiming was nonsensical and that Lowenfeld was claiming was the correct one. Thus, as the clause mutated, the risk to sovereigns increased proportionately. The original *pari passu* clause in the standard form sovereign bond contract had no contemporary function. This was the basic historical holdover landmine—risky perhaps, but thought by many to be relatively harmless. But adding language like that of Italy's to the standard market clause (together with at least some commentators supporting the ratable payments interpretation) and the landmine was primed to blow up. And it did.

Given the dominant role of the debtor's counsel in drafting a sovereign bond contract, the additional language that found its way into the Peruvian and Italian bonds cannot readily be explained as the product of a negotiation between the parties. After all, this landmine has the effect of increasing the ex post leverage of activist creditors seeking to undermine a proposed restructuring agreement, a result that the debtor's counsel would vigorously resist. Moreover, activist creditors only appear when the debtor nears default, they are not represented during the drafting process. Thus, it is difficult to characterize any of these mutations as "purposeful." Given the principal motivation of the drafting lawyers to conclude a deal quickly, the best evidence is that these mutations are errors, a misguided effort to clarify ambiguous language that results in increased litigation risk.

Post Brussels

The 2001 Brussels decision had the potential of opening the floodgates to holdout litigation. The Latin American debt crisis of the 1980s had resulted in over two dozen sovereigns having to restructure their obligations. And there were many debts that had not been tendered in the restructuring exchange offers. The holders of these unrestructured debts now were excited by the prospect of obtaining full payment using Elliott's *pari passu* strategy. Rumors of attractive settlements traveled through the market. But some creditors received an unwelcome surprise when they studied their clauses. Recall again, the standard *pari passu* clause:

> *The Notes rank, and will rank,* pari passu *with all unsecured External Indebtedness of the Republic.*

Some contracts, however, had clauses with five additional words. The clause in these contracts provided:

> *The Notes rank, and will rank,* pari passu *with all unsecured External Indebtedness of the Republic* ***except as provided by mandatory law.***[15] (emphasis added)

In the cross-border *corporate* context, the phrase "*except as provided by mandatory law*" has an understood meaning. The qualification makes sense because the mandatory law would be that of the local sovereign that likely specified that certain obligations of the corporate debtor that were owed to the government (e.g., taxes) have priority over other debt obligations. But in the sovereign bond context, could the lenders to a sovereign possibly have negotiated for the sovereign to be able to negate a creditor's *pari passu* rights simply by passing a law? That makes no sense.

How did this language make its way into the standard clause? There are two possibilities: Lawyer error or strategic lawyering.[16] The blunder or human error conjecture is that the deal lawyer in question largely handles corporate deals and only rarely drafts sovereign debt contracts. Constrained by time pressure, they might use documentation from a corporate deal as the template for the sovereign deal and fail to appreciate the very different sovereign context. Alternatively, perhaps a sovereign-side lawyer, recognizing that the creditors would demand a *pari passu* covenant, decided to add the "mandatory law" language to forestall the possibility that a holdout creditor might subsequently use *pari passu* against the debtor in the same way that Elliott Associates did against Peru. As we have noted, because of the short-term focus of underwriters, sovereign-side lawyers can more readily introduce terms that favor the sovereign. And here we see the addition of vague language that results in a pro-sovereign landmine.

It may not be necessary to decide whether this language resulted from human error or a subversive accretion. When the errors favor the sovereign, the debtors' lawyers may simply choose not to correct the errors, leading to the persistence of pro-sovereign errors. Thus, we can group these

[15] *See* Khaled Fayyad & Dimitrios Lyratzakis, *Restructuring Venezuela's Debt Using Pari Passu*, 28 Duke J. Int'l & Comp. L. 185 (2017).

[16] This is not to say that there aren't others who see these provisions as intentionally bargained for, as Semkow, *supra* note 6, did. *See* Robert Cohen, "*Sometimes a Cigar Is Just a Cigar*": *The Simple Story of Pari Passu*, 40 Hofstra L. Rev. 11 (2011).

pro-sovereign errors together with other purposeful changes in favor of the sovereign in the "subversive accretion" category. In any event, whether the problematic language is the product of a deliberate addition to the standard form clause or, alternatively, a pro-sovereign error that sovereign's counsel have little incentive to remove, the effect is the same: sovereigns are handed a landmine to exploit should the deal turn sour.

New York (2011)

One might think that after Peru's modified *pari passu* clause blew up in Brussels in 2000, subsequent contracts would have been revised immediately. That did not happen. The same clause with the enhanced landmine risk persisted for over a decade after *Peru v. Elliott* with few efforts to negate the ratable payment interpretation.[17] We conducted a study involving more than a hundred interviews with practitioners who explained that there was no need to address what was clearly an aberrant decision by the court in Brussels: no court in New York or England, they repeatedly proclaimed, would interpret *pari passu* as had the Brussels court.

But the unthinkable did happen. In 2011, a decade after that Brussels decision, holdout creditors persuaded a New York federal district court to grant them a ratable payments injunction. That decision was appealed. But the Second Circuit Court of Appeals affirmed the trial court, while offering the following advice to the litigating lawyers:

> The particular language of the *pari passu* clause dictated a certain result in this case, but going forward, sovereigns and lenders are free to . . . draft different *pari passu* clauses that support the goal of avoiding holdout creditors.[18]

[17] One might argue that the addition of the "except as provided by mandatory law" language was an attempt to indirectly preclude the ratable payments interpretation.

[18] NML Capital, Inc. v. Republic of Argentina, 727 F.3d 230, 248 (2d Cir. 2013). We should note that although the *pari passu* clause was seen then as crucial in granting the injunction, the Second Circuit also suggested that there were other reasons, such as Argentina's bad behavior, that justified the injunction. For contemporary accounts, see, e.g., *Second Circuit Construes Pari Passu Clause in Argentine Bond Issuance*, Weil Restructuring Blog (Dec. 13, 2012). More recently, as other attempts to use the *pari passu* argument in support of an injunction have been rejected by New York courts, it is unclear now whether *pari passu* alone can justify the injunction, or whether bad behavior by the debtor is also required. *See* James M. Blakemore & Michael J. Lockman, *Pari Passu Undone: Game Changing Decisions for Sovereigns in Distress*, 3 Emerging Markets Restructuring J. 1 (Spring 2017).

The financial cost of having ignored that advice was staggering. The recovery in the Peru case was $55 million on debt purchased at a price of around $11 million. In the case of Argentina, bonds purchased for around $250 million yielded over $2 billion.

The legal disaster with Argentina finally awakened the sovereign market community. Yet, the diversity of parties and the intense resistance to changing "market" terms in the standard form contract, made it difficult for the parties in this large, liquid market to coordinate around a method of defusing the *pari passu* landmine. Three years went by—and trillions of dollars of bonds were issued—without any meaningful changes in the wording of the standard *pari passu* clause. Finally, after all appeals (including to the US Supreme Court) were exhausted, the International Monetary Fund (IMF) and the International Capital Markets Association (ICMA) agreed on a way to repair the landmine embedded in the *pari passu* clause. And so, starting around 2014, a newly revised standard clause began being used by sovereign issuers.

Unfortunately, the chosen corrective endorsed by the coordinating groups failed to address the central problem: *pari passu* still has no apparent purpose in a sovereign debt contract. One might have thought that the easiest and safest course of action would be to eliminate the clause entirely. After all, whatever language was chosen to address the ratable payment problem, litigation risk was inherent in using vague terminology amenable to multiple meanings, especially where the clause served no discernable purpose. But not a single sovereign issuer elected to just delete the useless and dangerous clause. To be sure, some modifications were made. Clauses were scrubbed clean of the added words "in right of payment" and "except as provided by mandatory law" that altered litigation risk. And in some cases, the Latin "*pari passu*" was replaced with "equally." But rather than address the underlying question of what purpose the clause serves, the agreed upon solution was to limit the corrective to refuting the ratable payments interpretation. Mexico's 2014 revised version of the *pari passu* clause typified the new standard form:

> *The debt securities rank and will rank . . . equally ~~in right of payment~~ with all other public external indebtedness of Mexico.* ***It is understood that this provision shall not be construed so as to require Mexico to make payments under the debt securities ratably with payments being made under any other public external indebtedness.***[19] (emphasis added)

19 United Mexican States, $1,000,000,000, 3.6%. Global Notes Due 2025 (Pricing Supplement, Jan. 12, 2015 to Prospectus Supplement, Nov. 17, 2014).

Because this modified clause retains the core *pari passu* obligation, it remains a landmine. The continuing ambiguity over what the clause means leaves the door open for future holdouts to argue that they, too, are entitled to an injunction similar to Elliott's successful efforts against Peru and Argentina. The claim for ratable payments is the argument that future holdouts can no longer advance. But they can still pursue an injunction blocking payments to other creditors on other grounds. Perhaps the landmine that remains embedded in the contemporary *pari passu* clause is not as dangerous as before, but only time will tell.

Mexico (2014)

Mexico was one of the first nations to fix its *pari passu* clauses in 2014 using the ICMA recommended language. But in revising their standard form to implement the ICMA language, the drafters inadvertently created a new landmine, thereby showing us a new way in which landmines can arise. To see how, consider Mexico's original clause. Starting in 1990, and for the next twenty-five years, Mexico used the *pari passu* clause with a heightened vulnerability to the ratable payments interpretation. Give or take a few word changes over the years, it provided:

> *The debt securities will rank pari passu* ***in priority of payment*** *with all other* ***External Indebtedness*** *of the Republic.*[20]

Focus now on the term, "External Indebtedness." It delineates the scope of Mexico's *pari passu* promise. The covenant is that the debt securities in question are, and will be, *pari passu* vis-à-vis those debts falling within the definition of "External Indebtedness." In the 1990s, that term covered *all* of Mexico's foreign currency debts.

Mexico is the largest trading partner with the United States, and since almost all of those transactions are in dollars, it has an extremely large foreign currency debt. But of this large outstanding debt, international bondholders only care how well Mexico handles other international bond transactions. Consequently, Mexico decided in the 2000s to limit the scope of its *pari passu*

[20] *E.g.*, United Mexican States, $1,000,000,000, 9.875%. Global Bonds Due Jan. 15, 2007 (Prospectus Supplement, Jan. 9, 1997).

promise to Mexican international bonds. "External Indebtedness" became "*Public* External Indebtedness." And "Public External Indebtedness" was defined as Mexico's foreign currency debts that were *listed or eligible to be listed on an international exchange*. That, of course, resulted in a much smaller set of obligations than "all" of Mexico's foreign currency denominated debt.

Things remained this way until 2014 when Mexico, leading the rest of the sovereign world, began revising its *pari passu* promise to disavow the ratable payments interpretation. Since the purpose of the revision was to correct an erroneous interpretation of *pari passu*, it had no effect on the scope of the clause. There was, therefore, no reason to expect any change to the scope of Mexico's *pari passu* promise. But Mexico went further and revised its *pari passu* clauses to provide:

> *The debt securities rank and will rank . . . equally ~~in right of payment~~ with all other public external indebtedness of Mexico. It is understood that this provision shall not be construed so as to require Mexico to make payments under the debt securities ratably with payments being made under any other* ***public external indebtedness.*** (emphasis added)

Our interest is in the term "public external indebtedness." The phrase is written in lower case and there is no other indication, such as through the use of quotation marks, that it refers to a specially defined term. Lacking any special designation, the term could be understood to refer to a colloquial meaning: all the debts of Mexico that are "public" and "external," whatever those two broad terms might mean.

Recall that the modifier "Public" on "External Indebtedness" had been inserted a decade earlier with the goal of narrowing the scope of Mexico's *pari passu* promise. The continued use of the modifier "public" for external indebtedness in the 2014 version suggests that Mexico wanted to continue narrowing the scope of the *pari passu* promise. However, the drafter failed to use capitalization or quotation marks indicating that the phrase incorporates the defined term "Public External Indebtedness." This creates a risk that the term might be given its plain language meaning and not the prior defined meaning. Ambiguity exists as to whether the lowercase "public external indebtedness" only includes public external debts that are listed or eligible to be listed on an international exchange as under the prior capitalized defined term. Almost surely, such an expansion of the *pari passu* promise was not what Mexico was intending.

The failure to signal either by capitalization or quotation marks (as had been done in previous Mexican bonds) that "public external indebtedness" referred to a defined term in the contract illustrates a different type of error from the errors discussed earlier. Errors appear to occur randomly from the actions of lawyers drafting sovereign bond contracts. But when a newly revised clause is introduced into the market, market participants may then experiment with different variations of language to embody the new clause or term. Once drafters determine to revise one aspect of the contract, the temptation is greater to further alter the contract language.[21] Thus, the purposeful changes to language following the adoption of a new or revised clause might well lead to a higher rate of errors. As in the case of Mexico's 2014 revision, these "innovation errors" typically favor activist creditors not present at the contract drafting stage who might use the inapt drafting to later undermine a proposed restructuring agreement.

Sri Lanka (2022)

In 2009, Sri Lanka was short on foreign currency reserves and unable to borrow adequate amounts from the international bond markets and it turned to a localized strategy. It issued foreign currency debt instruments to its local financial institutions and members of its diaspora. Although denominated in foreign currency, the bonds were governed by local Sri Lankan law and had few of the usual contractual protections of the typical international sovereign bond. One might then ask why any investor in dollar bonds would be willing to take the risk inherent in an instrument governed by local Sri Lankan law. The answer was that these investors, who were willing to bail out their country during this difficult time, expected to be treated well independently of their formal contract rights. If not, the country would not be able to turn to them for emergency financing in the future.

The strategy worked: ever since 2009, Sri Lanka has continued to tap its domestic and diaspora resource periodically by issuing these special "Sri Lanka Development Bonds." The fly in the buttermilk is that Sri Lanka failed to modify its standard form international bond contracts to enable the special treatment that the local investors in the special Development Bonds were

[21] For a discussion of this dynamic, see Stephen J. Choi, Robert E. Scott, & Mitu Gulati, *Investigating the Contract Production Process*, 16 Cap Mkts L. J. 414 (2021).

expecting. Specifically, the *pari passu* clauses in Sri Lanka's international bonds were not modified to limit their scope to debts governed by *foreign law*. Instead, the definition of "External Indebtedness" remained unchanged, applying to all Sri Lanka's foreign currency obligations eligible to be listed on a foreign exchange. And this meant that there would be a potential *pari passu* violation if Sri Lanka were to default and then give preferential treatment to the holders of its special Sri Lanka Development Bonds.

We've seen a version of this story before: Recall from Chapter One the landmine story involving Greece and its entry into the Euro area in 2000. The lawyers there failed to correct the definition of "External Indebtedness" to adjust for the fact that Greece's "external debt" was henceforth going to be in a domestic currency (the Euro) and the differentiating factor between "external" and "local" was not going to be the currency per se, but the governing law. In that case, the failure to adjust the scope provision gave Greece an advantage. It could pledge assets to new creditors without having to satisfy the negative pledge protection that the holders of bonds issued between 2000 and 2004 likely thought they had. In Sri Lanka's case, the landmine was much the same. The underlying conditions governing how the sovereign was issuing debt changed. Sri Lanka was now issuing local law governed debt to a subset of domestic investors that it wanted to exclude from the *pari passu* protections given to traditional foreign investors. And, indeed, traditional foreign investors would likely not have wanted the *pari passu* promise in their bonds to interfere with this means of raising capital since this emergency financing was helping all the creditors. But someone blundered.

In early 2022, Sri Lanka went into default for the first time in its history. Soon thereafter, a senior government official announced that the Sri Lankan Development Bonds (largely held by local banks) would be repaid in full. At the same time, it was clear that foreign creditors would face a haircut. Sure enough, a holdout creditor, Hamilton Bank, had purchased distressed Sri Lankan bonds and brought suit asking for an injunction barring Sri Lanka from paying the Development Bonds in full. Their claim: the *pari passu* promise had been violated.[22] And here their lawyers did not need to argue that they were entitled to ratable payments. They argued that Sri Lanka's announcement that it would treat some bonds more favorably than others amounted to a per se violation of the *pari passu* promise and justified the

[22] *See* Cleary Gottlieb, *Creditor Files SDNY Lawsuit Against Sri Lanka in Connection With Its Sovereign Debt Default, Asserting Breach of Contract and Pari Passu Claims* (Jan. 30, 2022).

court granting injunctive relief. *Pari passu* was back, and Hamilton Bank had easily circumvented the 2014 market-wide revision that was supposed to stymie holdout creditors.

For reasons unknown to us, Hamilton Bank withdrew the *pari passu* part of its attack on Sri Lanka.[23] Nevertheless, the story illustrates yet another way in which landmines can be created. In this case, a change in the economic conditions facing the sovereign made the clauses it was previously using obsolete. As suggested in Chapter Two, obsolescence is yet another way in which landmines appear in standardized contracts. An obsolete term in a commercial contract is not innocuous. As we have seen, commercial parties are often unable to update their contracts themselves even with the help of market institutions. And in the case of sovereign debt, the relevant institutions are weak. As the Sri Lankan story illustrates, the major concern with obsolescence is that a vestigial term could transition from being harmless but unhelpful to being dangerous. Such transitions can occur when the term *applies linguistically*, but not substantively, to the current version of the parties' contracting problem. A party behaving strategically, such as Hamilton Bank, may then attempt to exploit the linguistic fit to generate a judicial interpretation in its favor.

Lessons from *Pari Passu*

Tracing the *pari passu* clause from its introduction into the original standard form documentation for the sovereign bond market in the early 1990s to the present day illustrates each of the various landmine categories that we previously identified. This historical holdover from the syndicated loan market (or perhaps from cross-border corporate loans) seems very durable, despite or perhaps because it lacks a well-understood meaning or economic function. For the same reason, *pari passu* has been particularly susceptible to subsequent mutations. Human error apparently led to the introduction of the "in right of payment" language that significantly increased the risk of subsequent litigation. But other landmines continued to be embedded in *pari passu*. Mutations promising equality "except as otherwise provided by mandatory law," can best be understood as a product of the control that

[23] We suspect that Hamilton Bank realized that it was in a strong litigation position on conventional grounds without having to resuscitate the controversial *pari passu* clause.

sovereign-side lawyers exercise over the drafting process. It doesn't much matter whether this new landmine was introduced strategically (in order to blunt the efforts of holdouts to exploit *pari passu*) or just appeared randomly (and persists because sovereign lawyers have no incentive to remove it) since the effects of the landmine are the same either way.

The outcome of the infamous Argentine litigation, and the resulting windfall to activist creditors, created a near panic among market participants. Nevertheless, the market failed to act for three years after the appellate courts affirmed the verdict.[24] Meanwhile, individual issuers were effectively precluded from revising their own clauses. In a highly liquid market, any idiosyncratic or bespoke changes to the standard market terms raise the costs to buyers in the market who now must learn how much the deviant bond departs from "market." Learning is costly, and those costs would be reflected in the discount the individual issuer would have to pay to successfully issue its idiosyncratic bonds.

Perhaps the extraordinary costs of the successful Argentine holdout litigation were the trigger that stimulated the efforts of several large market players to agree on a way to repair the very dangerous clause. Yet, even after blunders are removed and misinterpretations are corrected, the clause remains in every international sovereign bond and it is still vulnerable to further mutations. In short, the lesson of *pari passu* is that once landmines are embedded in the standard contract, they are susceptible to further changes in the external environment that render them more or less dangerous, and to changes introduced randomly or intentionally to correct earlier irregularities. Some of these mutations appear to die out naturally, yet others are eliminated by extraordinary coordinated action, and yet others—such as the ubiquitous *pari passu* itself—continue year after year as deeply embedded features of the standard form contract.[25]

We should not conclude that the random errors or strategic insertions made by the lawyers initially responsible for changes in the *pari passu* standard form necessarily evince agency problems (although the same

[24] *See* Choi, Gulati, & Scott, *supra* note 2.

[25] To say nothing of the handful of issuers, such as Russia, who have failed to revise their obsolete *pari passu* clause, even after the coordinated change in the rest of the market. Perhaps this was not a matter of concern for the Russians given that Russia was such a strong credit for years. But then Russia went into default following the invasion of Ukraine and the resulting external sanctions in 2022. Litigation has not begun since there are no assets for creditors to attempt to seize (all assets are frozen, as of this writing). But when there is litigation, Russia's failure to fix its *pari passu* clause may come back to haunt it. *See* Robin Wigglesworth, *Pari Passu Saga 2.0*, FT ALPHAVILLE (Mar. 9, 2022).

cannot be said of the lawyers who fail to notice the landmines in subsequent iterations of the contract). It would be perfectly rational for a thoughtful drafter to add words such as "in right of payment" as part of a bargained for agreement with the sovereign, and equally rational for a sovereign-side lawyer to use the "mandatory law" proviso to insulate a client from actions that undermine legitimate efforts to restructure troubled loans.[26] But the rational or understandable actions of the originating drafters does impact the larger market where, as we have seen, terms once introduced tend to remain a part of the standard form, and parties thereafter must expend unnecessary costs to traverse the mine field of the standard form contract.

* * *

Part I of this book tells a story of discovery: systematic anomalies appear in different standardized terms found in multibillion dollar contracts, and they seem to mutate further as these terms are replicated in different contracts with different parties. These anomalies become landmines that are later weaponized in litigation. The question for us: Can we explain their differences and provide evidence of their prevalence and persistence? To answer that question, we turn in Part II to build a theory of the existence of landmines that can then be tested. To begin that task, Chapter Five describes the insights gained through interviews with over fifty experienced lawyers with expertise in drafting, restructuring, and litigating sovereign debt.

[26] Agency costs could well be the explanation if underwriter's counsel had failed to object to the insertion of the "mandatory law" proviso.

PART II
GURUS AND NOVICES
Building a Theory

Chapter Five
Gurus and Novices

Introduction

The stories in Part I raise questions about the ability of commercial parties in large markets to produce contracts that reflect their preferred designs. We have found instances of landmines in different commercial markets, and evidence that landmines persist in subsequent iterations of the standard contract even after the risk of strategic litigation is known. But are these landmines an inevitable by-product of the standardization of contracts? Do some types of landmines persist and yet others disappear? In this Part we search for a theory that might help us answer these questions and then work to test that theory with data. Our focus is on the standard form contract that is ubiquitous in a large, liquid market such as sovereign debt. Thereafter, in Part III we examine other markets to see how well the theory and supporting evidence explains those contracting environments.

* * *

The landmine stories that we were accumulating persuaded us that the deviations from the standard we had uncovered were not just errors. There was something more systematic at play; a dynamic more complex than the oft-told explanation of a 4:00 am drafting mistake made by an overworked and overcaffeinated junior associate. We heard that 4:00 am story many times in the course of this research. While it has a kernel of truth, we suspect that it is mostly a big-law folk tale. As an explanation for landmines, the tale does not work. Survival is the one thing animating junior associates at big law firms: if you bill the needed hours and do nothing to attract negative attention, you survive. Changing the text of a document when you would be safer doing nothing more than changing names and dates from an earlier precedent is not a survival strategy. If landmines were appearing systematically, there had to be a different story.

Contract Hazards. Stephen J. Choi, Mitu Gulati, and Robert E. Scott, Oxford University Press.
 DOI: 10.1093/9780197821770.003.0005

Background Market Structure

To this point we had puzzles, but no plausible theories. The way the sovereign bond contract is typically drafted implies that the only substantial changes to the standard form will be those proposed by the sovereign's own lawyers. The dominant drafting role played by the sovereign's lawyers does suggest that if these lawyers are experienced and mindful of their clients' interests, we might expect to find deliberate additions designed to enhance the sovereign's post-default position. But we would rarely expect to find careless errors by these same lawyers that would favor the interests of activist creditors. And yet, a number of the landmines that we initially found were inconsistent with these assumptions about standard drafting practices. Experienced lawyers can be expected to protect their clients' interests when they represent the sovereign but would not be expected to make careless mistakes that undermined those interests. Inexperienced lawyers might make these mistakes but would not be expected to attempt to draft new provisions that effectively expand the sovereign's post-default rights. We had a puzzle: What explained the peculiar combination of landmines that we were seeing?

The lawyers who draft the contract terms are the starting point toward understanding the market dynamics that affect contract terms. The provision of legal services in the sovereign bond market is dominated by a small number of large and elite corporate-focused law firms, mostly based in New York or London. Lawyers at these firms are experienced in sovereign bond deals and charge their clients accordingly. These lawyers have incentives to respond to the preferences of their clients. To be sure, the market for legal services is far from perfectly competitive, and long-term relationships likely create stickiness between specific attorneys and their clients. Nonetheless, lawyers who do not strive to implement the preferences of their clients are unlikely to remain long employed. In short, the lawyers in sovereign debt deals are motivated to be faithful agents for their clients. But the rub is determining who the clients are.

In the sovereign market, the immediate clients are, on one side, a sovereign country's debt managers and, on the other side, the underwriters for a particular debt offering. To answer the question whether lawyers will attend to landmines at the time of a debt offering, we need to examine the incentives of the clients. Debt managers are typically government officials, often in a country's treasury or similar department. These officials have career lifespans that are typically shorter than the term of ten-year and certainly thirty-year sovereign bonds. Moreover, in almost all cases, the government officials are compensated with a fixed salary and enjoy no upside connected with the long-term performance of any issued bonds.[1] To be sure, debt managers are invested in their country's economic prospects: yet they are still more likely to undervalue the long-term interests of the sovereign and its citizens relative to the short-term objective of raising capital quickly. A double agency relationship exists here: the lawyers act as agents for the debt managers who in turn act as agents for a political actor at the finance ministry who in theory reports to the country's citizens. The distortions caused by this multiple agency relationship motivate drafting lawyers to respond more to the short-term incentives of the debt managers (or the finance minister, in some cases) than to the long-term interests of the country's citizens who will bear the financial costs if a landmine disrupts a restructuring.

The other attorney-client relationship is between the underwriters for a debt offering and the lawyers for the underwriter. Here the agency problems are more severe. The investment banks that play the role of underwriter in debt offerings are compensated by successfully placing an offering in the market as quickly as possible. The bankers running the deal will focus on the sovereign for a particular deal and then, after the deal is completed, turn to the next offering. These bankers are indifferent to the long-term implications of landmines that may (or may not) create problems years later in a future restructuring. Like a country's debt managers, the underwriters in an offering are agents themselves.[2] Their ultimate principals are the still distant investors who will purchase the sovereign bonds. This double agency relationship from the underwriter attorneys to the underwriters to the ultimate investors strongly motivates the attorneys for the underwriters to satisfy the short-term interests of the underwriters rather than the long-term interests of the investors.

The Gurus

We set out to interview a sample of these sovereign debt lawyers. To move past the anticipated explanation of the hapless junior associate, we assembled

[1] For an in-depth examination of the debt manager perspective, see Anna Gelpern, Mitu Gulati, & Jeromin Zettelmeyer, *If Boilerplate Could Talk: The Work of Standard Form Terms in Sovereign Bonds*, 44 L. & Soc. Inquiry 617 (2019).

[2] For discussion of bank-side incentives as well, see Gelpern et al., *supra* note 1.

a set of landmines in contemporary standard form documents together with preliminary data showing how frequently these landmines appeared across deals by various sovereign issuers.[3] There were many landmines, some fraction appeared in literally every document, and each had subsequently exploded in one or more deals.[4] In all, we identified seventeen landmines present in at least a subset of the contracts. Each landmine had previously been invoked by a party seeking a more favorable outcome during negotiations over a debt restructuring. For every landmine, we prepared a detailed description of the country, the context, and the landmine's potential relevance in any debt crisis. We wanted our interview subjects sufficiently engaged with this material to offer insights on the source and extent of the landmine problem.

To develop a set of sovereign debt experts to interview, we started with lists of the lawyers involved in the four major endeavors to reform the architecture of sovereign debt over the past two decades.[5] Those lawyers, many of whom had retired, then gave us suggestions as to others who had inherited their roles as the leading experts of the sovereign debt market. Together, we developed a pool of roughly thirty sovereign debt experts whose intimate knowledge of the intricacies of the standard form debt contract qualified them as "gurus." That group then expanded to over fifty as our initial interviewees gave us suggestions of others who might have insights.[6] We emailed each subject a background memorandum explaining the seventeen landmines. We asked for their views on a series of questions: Had we identified a real phenomenon and, if so, did the examples qualify as landmines? How could irregularities like this arise? And why did some of them seem to persist and even spread, whereas others vanished?

[3] We started with a set of a hundred randomly selected bond sales documents for the period 2020–2022, supplemented by a handful of fiscal agency agreements and indentures. The actual contracts—fiscal agency agreements and trust indentures—are not available in meaningful numbers, but we have access to a large set of the sales documents that report the key terms of the bonds.

[4] When we say "exploded," we mean that one side or the other used the landmine in order to gain an advantage in restructuring negotiations. In a subset of those matters, the landmine was raised in litigation, and in a yet smaller set of cases, there was full scale litigation.

[5] This was the set of lawyers with sufficient depth of knowledge about the sovereign market to be asked by governments and international financial institutions to be on reform committees. The reform endeavors in question were those involving drafting and re-drafting "collective action clauses" (or CACs) and revising the *pari passu* clause. For discussions of these various reform efforts, see Chapter Four (on *pari passu*) and materials cited in notes 12 and 13, *infra* (on CACs).

[6] Every person we contacted responded to our requests. Conversations with the interview respondents generally lasted between a half hour to an hour on Zoom except for a handful of respondents with whom we communicated by email and text or spoke to in person. We began talking to sovereign debt experts informally in mid-2020. The interviews for this chapter were conducted starting in 2021 and continued through early 2025.

Since Lebanon had just gone into default at the time we began our interviews, we asked them to first evaluate the landmines in Lebanon's bonds.

Lebanon and Its Manifest Error Clause

Lebanon's debt crisis had been a slow moving train wreck for a number of years leading up to our interviews. For over three years, Lebanon had been unable to put in place the reforms necessary for an IMF program and to make progress on negotiating debt relief from its private creditors. And when it did get relief, it faced a heightened risk of holdouts.[7]

The risk of holdouts derives from Lebanon's decision not to use aggregated collective action clauses. These clauses were created to ameliorate the problem of holdout creditors and were widely adopted by sovereign debtors starting roughly a decade ago. This innovation allowed the debtor to conduct a single aggregated vote binding on dissenters across all of its bonds. Holdouts would be deterred, it was thought, because of the very large position the dissenting creditor needed in order to hold out.

Lebanon, however, retained its old non-aggregated clauses. Lebanon's international bonds thus require the approval of 75% of the holders, in principal amount, for *each* bond series before key terms can be modified. Holdouts could build a blocking position against approval if they accumulated over 25% of the bonds of a *single* bond series. Those single series CACs combined with the fact that Lebanon's foreign currency bonds were trading at under ten cents on the dollar were blood in the water for specialists in distressed debt.

But maybe not. Buried at the bottom of the typical Modifications section in a sovereign bond contract is the Manifest Error clause. This clause does

[7] The starting point was Lebanon going into default in March 2020. That caused many in the sovereign world to look at Lebanon's contracts more closely. Lebanon had been one of the first sovereigns to use collective action clauses (CACs) in New York law governed bonds. This early move to CACs in a New York law governed sovereign bond was a bold step; an innovation against the weight of the then-standard form that used unanimity action clauses that required all bondholders to approve a change to the terms of the bond. But in 2020, there was a need for a restructuring of Lebanon's bonds, and so, with Mark Weidemaier, we looked into the operation of the Lebanese CACs and realized that, from the sovereign perspective, some crucial features of the restructuring clauses didn't work as we expected. For more on the multiple dodgy features of the Lebanese bonds, see Mitu Gulati, *Figuring Out the Terms in the Lebanese Bonds (and Why do Agents in Sovereign Bonds Suck?)*, creditslips.org (Mar. 8, 2020); Mark Weidemaier & Mitu Gulati, *Lebanon's Vexing Modification Clause*, creditslips.org (Apr. 15, 2020); Mitu Gulati, *Lebanon's Unusual Pari Passu Clause and the Question of How to Construct Credible Priority*, creditslips.org (Apr. 7, 2020).

not attract attention because it covers technical corrections; minor matters that the debtor and its fiscal agent can modify without approval from the creditors. To protect against misbehavior, however, there are typically two conditions to any unilateral changes to the contract. First, the changes must not adversely affect the interests of any creditor. Second, the fiscal agent or trustee has to approve the change.

The standard Manifest Error clause is illustrated by Mexico's 2017 bond issue. It reads, in relevant part:

> *Mexico* ***and the trustee*** *may, without the vote or consent of any holder . . . amend the indenture . . . for the purpose of. . . . amending the . . . indenture in any manner that Mexico* ***and the trustee*** *may determine does not materially adversely affect the interests of* ***any*** *holders of the debt securities of that series.* (emphasis added)

Lebanon's Manifest Error clause, drawn from its 2010 Fiscal Agency Agreement, is different. The equivalent phrases in the Lebanon manifest error clause read:

> *Without the consent of any Holder of Notes, the Republic . . . may enter into one or more Supplements for any of the following purposes*
>
> *(a) to add to the covenants of the Republic* ***for the benefit of the Holders of the Notes,*** *. . .*
>
> *(f) to make any other change that does not adversely affect the rights of* ***any Holder***. (emphasis added)

The Lebanese clause modifies the standard manifest error term in two key ways. First, Lebanon's clause states that the Republic, *on its own* (without the agreement of the trustee) may add new provisions to the contract. Second, added provisions must be for the benefit of "the Holders." In other words, Lebanon, on its own can add new provisions to the contract so long as those provisions are for the benefit of the holders, arguably, *as a collective.*

One might ask: Who gets to decide whether a new provision is "for the benefit of the Holders"? Since Lebanon has the unilateral authority to insert new clauses, presumably it can decide in the first instance what changes benefit the holders. Were someone to argue that the matter is unclear, Lebanon's offering circulars from 2010 (and thereafter) shed light. They state:

> ***The Republic****, without the consent of the [creditors] may make any modification to any . . . of the provisions of the Fiscal Agency Agreement* ***which in its opinion*** *is for any of the following purposes:*
> - *to add to the covenants of the Republic for the benefit of the Holders.*[8]

What could Lebanon do with this power? Perhaps it could put in place a super aggregated voting mechanism (similar to Greece 2012) that would allow for a binding restructuring if over 50% of the creditors across all the bond series were to agree. Activist creditors would object that aggregation for voting purposes cannot possibly be "for the benefit of *the* Holders" because, by definition, the provision could be used to cram down the restructuring on *some* holdout Holders. But Lebanon has an argument based on clause (f) above that the change only has to benefit "the Holders" collectively as a class.[9]

Assuming the insertion of an aggregation provision, and the approval by a majority of creditors of a deal that pays creditors a premium over market price, would that be enough to overcome a legal challenge? We only note that a similar aggregation provision for Greece, inserted via legislation, survived multiple legal challenges. Thus, it appears that Lebanon's apparently innocuous Manifest Error clause contains a pro-sovereign landmine that might permit Lebanon to overcome the heightened risk of holdouts that it faces. Was this modification of the standard clause an example of what we have previously called a "subversive accretion," a modification inserted by an issuer's lawyer at some earlier time to provide just such protection down the road? Or was the modification a random error—an inexperienced lawyer tinkering with wording that should have been left alone? That is what we wanted the experts to tell us.

Respondents gave four principal explanations for Lebanon's modified Manifest Error clause as well as for other contractual irregularities that we

[8] A caveat here is that the offering circular is the sales document and not the contract. That said, it will be Exhibit A if a court decides that the clause in the Fiscal Agency Agreement is ambiguous, and it needs to resolve that ambiguity.

[9] Lebanon's argument supporting an aggregation modification would be that the clause in subsection (f) authorizes Lebanon "to make any other change that does not adversely affect the rights of *any* Holder" (emphasis added). Thus, Lebanon could say: "We know that the drafters, when they wanted to require the consent of *each* holder, knew how to say just that. But in clause (a) the drafters deliberately refrained from saying that the new covenant had to benefit every holder, thus implying that the change only has to benefit holders as a class. And the holders of a debt instrument—as a group—benefit from suppressing holdout-creditor opportunism."

had described as landmines. A final explanation is one that we posed to the respondents as a possibility.

Gurus Versus Novices

The largest number of respondents acknowledged that the mutations we had discovered were, in fact, landmines. Indeed, they were quick to disassociate themselves from these anomalies that they characterized as "embarrassing goofs," "the product of 4:00 a.m. drafting after too much caffeine," that reflected "badly on the profession." In the view of several of these respondents, the changes to Lebanon's Manifest Error clause was an example of a similar blunder. One explained:

> Most of these landmines, probably including the Lebanon case, are the product of a lawyer not understanding the sovereign context. The sovereign context is different. Just because it is a cross-border bond issue does not mean that you blindly use the same language that you used for the last three hundred corporate deals.... I am ashamed to say that this kind of language sometimes escapes the scrutiny of even the senior lawyers....
>
> These deals are done quickly, and there is not a lot of time given to scrutinizing the language. Errors are made. Worse, they sometimes get repeated.

The consistent refrain was that there were two categories of lawyers working in sovereign debt—experts and novices. The experts (the gurus) understand the sovereign context and the implications of the landmines because they work on restructurings as well as issuing new bonds. Indeed, a majority of the respondents described additional landmines that they had found during their careers.[10] In some cases, they had tried to correct errors without success because the lawyer on the other side was not able or willing to accept that the clause in question was flawed and could potentially harm their client's interests. A veteran sovereign-side specialist explained:

> I've seen Events of Default where the clause fails to say what the implications of the Events of Default are, or where the provision fails to state that the

[10] If we add the additional landmines the gurus identified, we would have a total of more than forty.

> event must be continuing as opposed to just having occurred once. These are big errors.... But they show up periodically. If one does not understand the big picture and how these things play out... then how does one know?
>
> There was one case... where I tried to point out the error to the young lawyer on the other side. But he was too petrified to change anything on his standard form. He had no authority to do anything. I decided that I had fulfilled my ethical obligations by telling him about the risks to his client.

There is a contradiction in the foregoing. The story is both of errors being introduced by novices and of novices being unwilling to change anything in prior forms. If novices are too reluctant to change any of the standard language, how do they introduce these landmines in the first place?

One answer to this contradiction is that there are two types of novices, one type knows they don't know anything, and so they cling to the standard form, refusing to change anything. This, as we have noted, is the paradigm of the junior associate working at 4 a.m. The other type does not know that they don't know anything—they may be relatively senior lawyers who are familiar with corporate debt instruments but are inexperienced with sovereign debt offerings—and they create errors by tinkering with language that goes unnoticed thereafter. For example, this may explain the modifications to Lebanon's Manifest Error clause. Errors made by senior lawyers unaware of what they do not know are more consistent with standard drafting practice: a junior lawyer has little incentive to change standard language that has been embedded in prior precedents. But that raises the question of just how errors arise when the drafting is being handled by the dangerous novice—the senior lawyer who is inexperienced in sovereign bond transactions.

Several respondents explained that sometimes there is no choice but to modify the standard form. For example, standard language has to be modified when the lead bankers change, and the new bankers might be used to a different standard form that had been drafted for a different type of issuer. An industry-wide move to change the standard form is another example of compelled modification—as when the market moved toward collective action clauses in 2003–2004,[11] or when the market coordinated

[11] For discussions of these moves, see Anna Gelpern & Mitu Gulati, *Public Syymbol in Private Contract*, 84 Wash. U. L. Q. 1627 (2006); Randal Quarles, *Herding Cats: Collective Action Clauses in Sovereign Debt: The Genesis of the Project to Change Market Practice 2001–2003*, 73 L. & Contemp. Prob. 29 (2010); W. Mark C. Weidemaier & Mitu Gulati, *A People's History of Collective Action Clauses*, 54 Va. L. Rev. 1 (2014).

around a revision to the standard *pari passu* clause in 2013–2014.[12] In these instances, a new clause is being incorporated into the standard document, and other portions of the document that are inconsistent with the new clause must be updated. A lawyer who neither fully understands the new clause nor has the time to determine how it might not cohere with the rest of the standard form runs the risk of making a mistake. One respondent, invoking the dog's breakfast metaphor for the second time in our interviews, explained:

> If you want to see a dog's breakfast of a document, just pick up the prospectus for [sovereign X] where a London firm was doing an issuance under New York law, trying to incorporate a combination of New York and English law-style provisions. It is a mess. And that mess kept getting repeated deal after deal, probably because no one understood the problems that had been created, or because it was [perhaps] too embarrassing to fess up later, [or because no one noticed after the first few deals went through successfully and an associate was assigned to copy and paste the prior deal].

The story of random errors that inexperienced lawyers never notice thereafter is an answer that we heard from more than a few respondents. Another respondent explained:

> Errors happen. . . . These documents are produced quickly. . . [and there can be] idiosyncrasies of the particular sovereign's requirements. Sometimes, with a clause that doesn't really make sense in the first place but has become "market" . . . like *pari passu*, you might add a few words just to have it make sense. But as we have seen with the Argentine case . . . that change might make it more of a landmine. . . .
>
> [K]eep in mind that this stuff is not literally boilerplate in the way in which you suggested. There are . . . variations in words across deals. The goal is to give your client what is "market"—that is different from boilerplate which suggests identical provisions.

[12] Mark Sobel, *Strengthening Collective Action Clauses: Catalysing Change—The Back Story*, 11 Cap. Mkts L. J. 3 (2016); Sergio Galvis, *Solving the Pari Passu Puzzle: The Market Still Knows Best*, 12 Cap. Mkts L. J. 204 (2017).

The Gravitational Pull of the Form

Prior research has investigated the reasons why the *pari passu* clause was retained for over a decade and a half despite widespread recognition in the market that this was a landmine.[13] The "gravitational pull of the standard form" was the primary explanation for the long period in which the *pari passu* clause was retained without revision.[14] Once a clause makes it into the standard form contract and onto the "check list" of core provisions that collectively determine "market," it is an artifact, virtually set in stone regardless of whether the clause makes sense or not.

As the respondents explained, the category of "check list" provisions had their origins in the source documents for the standard template that was created in the 1990s via the Brady bonds in the wake of the Latin American debt crisis.[15] One veteran of the Brady era explained:

> There were hardly any sovereign bonds at the time, except for a few from AAA rated nations. The Brady bonds helped create a . . . new bond market for emerging market nations. And the template that was used for these bonds was the corporate template. So, clauses such as the negative pledge and the *pari passu* clause . . . got into the standard template even though they didn't really work in the sovereign context where there was no bankruptcy and liquidation of assets. Once there . . . and part of the basic form. . . . no one wants to change what is market for fear [of market penalty] . . . . The worst of these, as you well know, was the unanimity requirement to change payment terms—a term borrowed from the corporate context where there was the backstop of bankruptcy.

This comment highlights the effects of the two-sided agency problem. Neither the government officials on the one side nor the underwriters on the other side care enough about what will happen in a future debt restructuring to urge the drafting lawyers to revise the core terms of the standard form.

[13] *See* Mitu Gulati & Robert E. Scott, The Three and a Half Minute Transaction: Boilerplate and the Limits of Contract Design (University of Chicago Press, 2013).

[14] Gulati & Scott, *id.*

[15] "Brady" bonds were a creature of the Latin American crisis of the 1980s, named after then US Treasury Secretary Nicholas Brady. For a description, see Neil Shenai & Marijn Bolhuis, *How the Brady Plan Delivered on Debt Relief*, IMF Working Paper WP/23/258 (2023).

At the start of this project, it was tempting for us to blame the lawyers for not making clear to their clients that they were incurring significant future risks that were trivially easy for expert lawyers to repair at the drafting stage. But respondents protested that their role did not include revising core feature of the standard form. Clients on neither side, they asserted, would tolerate the further delay that major changes to the standard form would require.

Tinkering at the Periphery

Not all our respondents agreed with the term "contractual landmines" to the extent it suggested that all of these were drafting blunders; consciously placed bombs meant to explode. Yes, they might present risks in the future, but they were often the product of considered choices in the negotiation process that were rarely intended to cause an explosion. Could it be that the Lebanon mutation developed in this way? In direct reference to the Lebanon case, a senior lawyer who had been responsible for numerous multibillion dollar deals with problematic *pari passu* clauses said:

> These drafting problems can arise in all sorts of ways. Take the SEC review process. You can get stuck with a junior lawyer at the SEC who knows nothing about sovereign deals, but feels like he needs to ask for some minor corrections and clarifications in the documents so as to justify his job. These clarifications are often harmful since they lend themselves to a completely different meaning for the clause than what was intended. But who wants to argue with an SEC staffer? If one gets them annoyed, that produces delay and then the client is pissed. You just do what they want and move on. But then the language gets reproduced in the next deal and on and on.

In a similar vein, another explanation was:

> For most of the landmines . . . I can tell you that there was a good reason why the provision was modified in the way that it was. Take the language granting the sovereign jurisdiction over matters of authorization and execution . . . for [the Republic of X]. During the negotiations for that document, the local Attorney General's office was uncertain as to whether it was legally allowed to have the legality of certain matters relating to the authorization of the lending be made under New York law. On the other

> hand, the underwriter's counsel took the position that investors would want New York law to govern. So, we had a compromise—New York law would govern everything except authorization and execution. Yes, that's ambiguous. But it was a compromise to get to the point where the issuance could happen. I can tell a similar story for some of the uses of ["to the extent permitted by applicable law"] that you point to or the use of the embassy as the agent for service of process.
>
> There is a risk when one does this sort of thing that there will be litigation later. But it is a small risk... Both sides are trying to get the deal done. These are context specific compromises that one would hope get removed when they are not needed. I worry, from reading your paper, that they sometimes migrate into deals where they are not needed.

Respondents explained that any rule-like provision—such as a broad waiver of sovereign immunity—was seen by investors as a standard clause they were entitled to receive (it was "market"). By a peripheral change, such as limiting the immunity waiver *"to the extent permitted by applicable law,"* the issuer was still able to state that it was granting the full waiver of immunity, and the question of what "applicable law" meant was, in effect, deferred for a later date when and if a dispute occurred. Thus, investors received a waiver of immunity—the market standard—and the sovereign was able to postpone difficult questions of application.

Timing the Market

A quote from a conversation that we had with two respondents together exemplifies the relevance of the time constraints that were a part of almost every respondent's story.

> You need to understand that these markets work quite efficiently. There are flaws, to be sure, in the standard contracts. But the markets work well and have done so for decades. These deals need to be done ... when there is a market window.... No one is willing to [delay to indulge the lawyers].
>
> The reality is that these bonds rarely default and when there is a default they are frequently renegotiated in an amicable fashion. No one is negotiating these deals with an expectation of default. Not even when Argentina is the issuer. Argentina and the *pari passu* litigation was an

> anomaly. And those clauses got revised, along with collective action clauses, through an industry-wide effort. Unless there is such an effort—and we only do that on rare occasions (maybe once a decade)—changes are hard to make. The issuers do not want to do them and the underwriters really do not. There is no appetite.

This, then, is a story justifying the drafters' failure to review the contract terms carefully: the fine details of contract drafting are too costly to worry about when a deal needs to quickly go to market. Because issuers are trying to time market windows and issue within a favorable window that might soon disappear, the cleanest and quickest way to get agreement on the deal is to use the documents that worked in the prior deal. A different version of the same argument was:

> Yes, there are ambiguities and problems if you read these documents with a magnifying glass as you do. But that's not the real world. In the real world, litigation is difficult and expensive against sovereigns. It is hard to effectively sue them and harder to attach assets unless you are . . . Elliott and other activists who have infinite patience. In the real world, sovereigns primarily repay because of reputation not because of fear of litigation. Plus, don't you think that smart judges in almost every case will figure out the right outcome? Judges in [England and New York] are much more nuanced [than you give them credit for].

But this "timing the market" argument doesn't explain how landmines get into the contracts in the first place. If it is rational to stick to the standard form and avoid making only minimal changes, then how to explain the anomalies—many of which are the product of additional words added to the contracts? Several possibilities surfaced in the discussion of novices and inexperience, but there seemed to be too many landmines to be explained simply by a change in investment banks or market-wide revisions of core clauses.

Context Matters

A few of the respondents who had worked both on restructurings and initial issuances noted how the difference in deal context might determine whether the deal documents could be corrected. In particular, changes are more feasible during restructuring negotiations when coordination with others can occur. One respondent described in particular his frustration at not being able to correct what he saw as an annoying landmine relating to beneficial owners and registered holders in a bond. The basic problem is that a number of the deal documents put the key litigation rights (the right to bring suit, waiver of sovereign immunity, etc.) in the hands of the "registered holder," an intermediary such as the Depository Trust Company, who has no interest in suing for defaulted payments. The result of this mismatch in many modern sovereign bonds is that costs are incurred when a subset of beneficial owners are first required to get authorization from the registered holder before taking a desired action. The respondent thought this arrangement was a holdover from the time when bonds were rarely traded and beneficial owners were the registered holders. When bonds began to be actively traded, the current mechanism evolved to permit quick changes in beneficial ownership without changing the identity of the official (registered) owner. Hence, the current structure. The respondent explained:

> This [mismatch between registered holder and beneficial owner] comes up on occasion . . . and not always in default . . . where you need to make a basic change in the bond structure. But to make the change, you need the registered holders to give permission and securing permission takes weeks and there are often delays. This is a real cost for the clients. But because one can always get the permissions eventually, no one wants to fix this problem.
>
> It would make sense to correct this in all documents. Argentina and Ecuador did fix the problem. But that was in a restructuring context. You can change things there because the real investors are at the table and there is no underwriter pushing for the deal to get done within minutes. If you dig deeper—maybe look at the origins of CACs, fixes to *pari passu*, hurricane clauses, GDP indexers and so on—they all came into being in restructurings, not in initial issuances.

In addition to the difference in opportunities to coordinate changes as between initial issuances and a restructuring, several respondents pointed to differences among the contract clauses themselves. Certain clauses, such as the tax provisions that matter to the sovereign issuer, are scrutinized in every deal. But clauses that are part of the historic artifact are particularly fertile ground for the growth of landmines: those that have always been on the standard checklist, such as *pari passu*, negative pledge and "manifest error" get little attention from deal to deal. These aren't the clauses that deal lawyers scrutinize, other than to make sure they are in the contract and "appear to be market." Governing law and jurisdiction clauses may get more attention, but the nuances of conflicts of laws and jurisdiction are not the province of deal lawyers.

Relatedly, other respondents pointed to the possibility that different law firm structures make a difference. A senior partner at a prominent English law firm was convinced that the English firms were better than their American counterparts in responding to problems in the documents for at least two reasons. First, English law firms have a tradition of having dedicated research departments. And second, the gurus in London have a tradition of meeting to coordinate changes to their documents that their New York sovereign debt counterparts do not have.

Strategic Drafting

Putting aside the historical clauses derived from the original source documents, more than half of the remaining landmines, like Lebanon's Manifest Error clause, favor the sovereign side. And, as in that example, a number of these "subversive accretions" involve the addition of several seemingly innocuous words or phrases that could provide the sovereign a significant advantage.

The question is how do these seemingly deliberate changes originate and why do they mostly advantage the sovereign rather than the investors as a group? One answer interrogates the standard practice of drafting these documents: this practice reveals a number of agency problems that lead to a misalignment of interests between the lawyers and their principals. As described in Chapter Two, the lawyers negotiating the contract are the sovereign's lawyers and the underwriter's counsel. There are no investors per se represented in the process. Indeed, the "designated underwriter's counsel" have been working for the underwriters deal after deal, even though the underwriters themselves may change.[16] And often these designated counsel are picked and paid for by the issuers.[17] Further, even if the underwriters were actively engaged during the drafting process, their incentives are short

[16] For a discussion, see Michael Bradley, Irving de Lira Salvatierra, & Mitu Gulati, *Lawyers: Gatekeepers of the Sovereign Debt Markets*, 38 Int'l Rev. L. & Econ. 150 (2014).

[17] This does not have to be the case. Some respondents told us of cases where underwriters had their favorite law firms. The issuer would still be paying.

term—to get the deal done and avoid incurring costs and time dickering over words in the contract. By contrast, the sovereign's lawyers (or at least the sovereign's law firm) are more invested in the process for the longer term. They have to pick up the pieces if the sovereign defaults.

We asked respondents whether sovereign-side lawyers might deliberately introduce new words or phrases to a standard form term such as Manifest Error. In our early interviews, some respondents resisted this framing. To be sure, negotiated changes could be introduced that are not then cleaned up in subsequent iterations of the contract, but strategic drafting, per se, was not an explanation we heard. No sovereign wanted (or rewarded) lawyers to be opportunistic during the drafting process. And once a reputation for strategic behavior developed, the underwriters would respond by scrutinizing the contract more carefully, and the goal of getting the deals done quickly would be undermined. One respondent explained (in response to our question about strategic or opportunistic drafting):

> The most I've seen is where the sovereign lawyer won't fight hard to correct language that benefits his client. I don't think anyone would actually try to insert language that would advantage the sovereign. . . . There is no reward for the transactional lawyer who does that—there is a completely different group of restructuring lawyers or litigators who deal with the default. They are not going to be asking the client to reward the clever deal lawyer who inserted a phrase or two at the front end that benefitted the sovereign's case.

In later interviews, however, we gained a more nuanced picture of how anti-investor subversive provisions might emerge. In response to the preceding quote, one respondent explained how a novice lawyer would not notice the inclusion of a subversive provision:

> I agree that no sovereign lawyer is going to affirmatively try to put in what you call landmines. But the way some of these landmines get in can be more complex. I've worked on deals where the other side isn't familiar with sovereign deals. Sometimes, they are the ones who put forward the initial form and it has features that disadvantage them. And they don't know it. I can't tell them either, because it could benefit my client. I was on one deal where there must have been a half dozen places where the other side was proposing features that disadvantaged them. Basic stuff—like failing to

> understand how one needed to define External Indebtedness in light of that sovereign's borrowing from China. These lawyers just didn't seem to know they needed to take it into account and update the standard form they had pulled from somewhere.

Another respondent did confess to inserting one of these pro-sovereign provisions:

> We had a deal where we were using an entirely new standard form. It was in a restructuring and the old forms were being tossed—new lawyers, new bankers. I was drafting the list of negative pledge clause exceptions. The prior list of exceptions that I took from another deal already had a long list of a dozen or so exceptions that allowed the sovereign to pledge assets. I added one more: the sovereign could pledge for new borrowing without violating the NP if it was in the national interest or something like that. It was broad—everything is in the national interest. No one said anything.
>
> It is a myth that lawyers notice every small deviation from the standard form. There is no real standard form, so how can anyone notice every deviation. Maybe from the prior deal's form, if you have to show changes. But for a new deal document all sorts of stuff can be put in. If the other side is not paying close attention, and no one is carefully reading the two dozen exceptions to the negative pledge clause, stuff gets in. Probably won't ever come into play, but this feature then becomes part of the form and the I[nvestment] bank lawyers themselves will refuse to change it because it is part of the form.

A final variant explained a sovereign's interest in counsel adding subversive terms to the standard form.

> The Russian bonds are full of these. After the invasion of Crimea, they became worried about future US and European sanctions . . . and they were right to be worried. And in those post-Crimea issues, the only investment bank willing to work with them was their own inhouse bank. Literally, no one is minding the store for the investors. Those bonds are full of clauses that disadvantage investors—and I bet no one raised a peep when the bonds were issued.

The Story so Far

The interviews yield five insights about the process of drafting sovereign debt contracts: (i) some lawyers writing these contracts are experts in sovereign bond contracting (most often the sovereign-side lawyers) and others are novices, and this division may explain how many landmines develop and persist; (ii) time constraints can impose costs on attempts to change (or even carefully review) the standard form; (iii) the original source document has developed a canonical status as artifact that constrains efforts to revise the core "market" terms; (iv) modest revisions to standard language are purposefully negotiated often to resolve sovereign's concerns about strict adherence to contractual duties, but thereafter drafters have inadequate incentive to eliminate these "subversive accretions"; and (v) the production context can matter, including regular opportunities for lawyers to coordinate: more landmines are defused during restructurings because traditional underwriter pressures are absent and all the lawyers are more likely to be experts.

The challenge is to organize these observations in a coherent way. The respondents left us with an important insight into lawyers and their role in the drafting of sovereign debt contracts as well as a puzzle. The insight that we develop more fully in Chapter Seven is that not all lawyers are the same. Some lawyers are gurus and have extensive skill in the language of sovereign bond contracts and the implications of this language for future restructurings. Other lawyers, as one respondent above put it, "aren't familiar with sovereign deals": These lawyers are novices in performing the task of drafting landmine-free documentation. The puzzle is why there seems to be an asymmetry that tends to favor the sovereign in the work of those with contract expertise and those without. After all, attorneys for both the underwriters and attorneys for the sovereign face potential agency cost concerns. Why would gurus for the sovereign care more than gurus for the underwriters about potential landmines? We address this puzzle in Chapter Seven.

But first we turn to Chapter Six to interrogate an assumption embedded in the analysis thus far, the conviction that market participants have a shared understanding of what constitutes the "standard" contract against which the degree of deviation from "market" can be observed. But what do we mean when we say that a term in the contract is "market"? And, what options are available to contract drafters to remove nonstandard deviations from the standard form contract?

Chapter Six
Contract as Artifact

Introduction

The *pari passu* story in Part I showed how resistant that particular landmine is to straightforward efforts to eliminate the problems it has caused. Bonds worth trillions of dollars were issued after the landmine risk was well understood, and yet not in a single instance did a drafter adopt the simple and effective solution of deleting the clause from the standard form. In the interviews we reported in Chapter Five, the sovereign debt gurus repeatedly invoked "the gravitational pull of the standard form." The *pari passu* clause, we were told, could not be deleted because *pari passu* was "market."

What does "market" mean? It means at a minimum that the standard form contract used in these environments is quite different from the conception of contract familiar to most litigators, law professors, and the general public. The standard form contract that is reified as "market" emerges as an artifact; it has a canonical status that effectively precludes major changes to the documentation. The language of a *pari passu* clause can be modified to reverse the result of a single court judgment, but the clause itself must remain in the standard form even though the absence of any understood meaning creates litigation risk. This conception of a standard form contract as a kind of fossil whose surface appearance can be cleaned and polished but not fundamentally changed has implications for the persistence of the various landmines described in Part I.

To make progress toward understanding not only the existence but also the persistence of landmines, we need to better understand exactly what it means that a given standard form contract has become "market." Must each boilerplate term in the standard form have identical language or phrasing? If not, what exactly constitutes a boilerplate term that is acceptable to the market? We examine these questions here. We begin by reviewing the academic literature on boilerplate terms and then turn to the quite different way in which a boilerplate term is understood among the participants in the market. Harmonizing the theoretical and the real worlds provides

Contract Hazards. Stephen J. Choi, Mitu Gulati, and Robert E. Scott, Oxford University Press.
 DOI: 10.1093/9780197821770.003.0006

an opportunity to determine the meaning of "market" in commercial contracting and thereby to determine what linguistic anomalies can properly be characterized as landmines.

Boilerplate Theory

Academic researchers have long been interested in boilerplate terms in standard form contracts. But the focus has been on contract regularities, rather than the types of irregularities that are our concern.

Most of the research on boilerplate contracts has concentrated on consumer contracts and on whether the typical consumer boilerplate allows for meaningful consent to the terms in question. Many commentators see this phenomenon to be particularly problematic in transactions where there is a large commercial enterprise that is offering terms on a "take it or leave it" basis to dispersed, uncoordinated, and unsophisticated consumers. Given that assent to a bargain is supposed to be the foundation of welfare improving contracting, many argue that these transactions do not fit within the contract paradigm.[1] Our focus, however, is on the use of standard form contracting among sophisticated commercial entities. In this setting, it is tempting to treat standard form instruments the same as other contracts where the terms are deemed to be individually negotiated. And this is what courts often do. Faced with a corporate bond indenture or a private equity merger deal, what the court sees is a high dollar value contract among sophisticated commercial parties. The terms are given a formalist interpretation: the assumption is that every word in the instrument was carefully considered to embody the actual agreement between the participants.[2] Courts, then, treat a commercial boilerplate term as implementing the goal of efficient contract design: it is a complete and carefully bargained provision that maximizes the expected joint surplus from the transaction.

[1] There is a vast literature on this topic. *See, e.g.*, NATHAN OMAN, THE DIGNITY OF COMMERCE: MARKETS AND THE MORAL FOUNDATIONS OF CONTRACT, CH.7 (University of Chicago Press 2017); MARGARET JANE RADIN, BOILERPLATE: THE FINE PRINT, VANISHING RIGHTS AND THE RULE OF LAW (Princeton University Press 2013). A fuller set of references is in Robert E. Scott, Stephen J. Choi, & Mitu Gulati, *Commercial Boilerplate: A Review and Research Agenda*, 20 ANN. REV. L. & SOC. SCI. 201 (2024).

[2] Elisabeth de Fontenay, *Complete Contracts in Finance*, 2020 WISC. L. REV. 533; Jared Elias & Elisabeth de Fontenay, *Law and Courts in an Age of Debt*, 171 U. PENN. L. REV. 2025 (2023).

Over the years, a growing chorus of scholars have begun to question the efficiency of commercial boilerplate.[3] Coming at the issue from both theoretical and empirical perspectives, researchers on commercial boilerplate contracts have pointed out flaws in the optimal design assumption. Empirical work has uncovered many examples of terms in these agreements that the parties recognized as suboptimal and yet they have persisted.[4] Theoretical work has explored the trade-offs between optimal design and the benefits of standard language.[5]

The research that developed out of these insights built on the work of Marcel Kahan and Michael Klausner. In a series of articles in the 1990s, Kahan and Klausner set forth the foundations of the "law and economics of boilerplate."[6] Kahan and Klausner focused on a puzzle: Why do suboptimal terms seem to persist in financial contracts among sophisticated commercial parties? They suggested that the answer lay in the trade-off between the efficiency benefits of tailored contract terms and the positive externalities of using standard forms in thick or liquid markets where financial products needed to be tradeable. When the positive value of the latter outweighs the benefits of the former, the market could be in an equilibrium where all parties were using suboptimal terms. Boilerplate contract terms could be "sticky."[7]

Following the work of Kahan and Klausner, a substantial literature revealed the persistence of suboptimal terms across a range of contracts including sovereign debt contracts, investment treaties, M&A agreements, insurance contracts, and even trust documents.[8] Scholars also explored

[3] *E.g.*, Charles Goetz & Robert E. Scott, *The Limits of Expanded Choice: An Analysis of the Interactions Between Express and Implied Contract Terms*, 73 CAL. L. REV. 261 (1985); Marcel Kahan & Michael Klausner, *Path Dependence in Corporate Contracting: Increasing Returns, Herd Behavior and Cognitive Biases*, 74 WASH. U. L. REV. 347 (1996); Stephen J. Choi & Mitu Gulati, *Innovation in Boilerplate Contracts*, 53 EMORY L. J. 93 (2004).

[4] *E.g.*, William A. Klein, David Anderson, & Kathleen McGuinness, *The Call Provisions of Corporate Bonds: A Standard Form in Need of Change*, 18 J. CORP. L. 653 (1993); Marcel Kahan, *Anti-Dilution Provisions in Convertible Securities*, 2 STAN. J. L. & BUS. FIN. 147 (1995).

[5] Goetz & Scott, *supra* note 3; Kahan & Klausner, *supra* note 3.

[6] Kahan & Klausner, *supra* note 3; Marcel Kahan & Michael Klausner, *Standardization and Innovation in Corporate Contracting (or "The Economics of Boilerplate")*, 83 VA. L. REV. 713 (1997).

[7] *See* John Pottow & Omri Ben-Shahar, *On the Stickiness of Default Rules*, 33 FLA. ST. U. L. REV. 651 (2006).

[8] *E.g.*, Stephen J. Choi, Mitu Gulati, & Robert E. Scott, *The Black Hole Problem in Commercial Boilerplate*. 67 DUKE LAW J. 1 (2017); Christopher French, *Insurance Contracts: The Grandfathers of Black Holes*, 67 DUKE L. J. 102 (2017); David Weisbord & Reid Horton, *Boilerplate and Default in Wills Law: An Empirical Analysis*, 103 IOWA L. REV. 663 (2018); John F. Coyle, *Choice-of-Law Clauses in Bond Indentures*, 13 CAP. MKTS L. J. 152 (2018); John F. Coyle & W. Mark C. Weidemaier, *Interpreting Contracts Without Context*, 67 AM. U. L. REV. 1673 (2018); Robert Anderson & Jeffrey Manns, *Boiling Down Boilerplate in M&A Agreements*, 67 DUKE L. J. 219 (2019); Stephen J. Choi, Mitu Gulati, Matthew Jennejohn, & Robert E. Scott, *Contract Production in M&A Markets*, 171 U. PA. L. REV. 1881 (2023).

the factors that stimulate the revision of sticky terms. Here context matters a great deal: markets operate differently and the degree of stickiness and suboptimality varies as a function of factors such as capacity for coordination within that industry.[9]

One aspect of the research on standard forms bears particularly on our project. The central insight from these original set of papers was the increasing returns to scale that resulted from standardization. The value of a contract form increased as a function of how similar it was to other contracts. This insight was particularly important in the context of financial transactions. The fact that the core legal terms in a large number of debt instruments were identical meant that loans could be traded without buyers having to examine hundreds of pages of legal documentation. All one needed to know were key financial terms such as yield, rating, and maturity. Moreover, provisions that had been used for long periods of time became well understood, and these terms were readily priced. Any problems with the precise language in these terms would be resolved with repeated use and what survived should be optimal.

The logical extension of this story is that contracts in markets that value tradability and liquidity should evolve to near identity. To be sure, there will be some suboptimality because of the reluctance to depart from standard provisions that have worked well for long periods of time, but all parties in the market will have an identical level of suboptimality. And to the extent there is variation, it will be in newly introduced terms. Here, we would expect to see some experimentation until the market comes to rest on an agreed upon standard version. That version will then be used by everyone and it will be sticky.[10]

The second generation of research on boilerplate found empirical disjunctions with this theory of contract identity. Contrary to the predictions of the conventional theory—that boilerplate provisions will become better understood, more accurately priced, and more uniform over time—scholars reported market-wide data showing that provisions in the standard form were not understood at all, were not priced, seemed to spread, and were sticky.[11] Some standard provisions appeared to lose meaning through

[9] *E.g.*, Stephen J. Choi, Mitu Gulati, & Robert E. Scott, *Comparing Contract Production: Private Equity M&A, Corporate and Sovereign Bonds*, 74 Case West. L. Rev. 48 (2023).

[10] For an empirical examination of this dynamic, see Stephen J. Choi, Mitu Gulati, & Eric A. Posner, *The Dynamics of Contract Evolution*, 88 NYU. L. Rev. 1 (2013).

[11] Among the recent additions to this literature are Adam Badawi, Vincent Buccola, & Greg Nini, *Price Discipline for Non-Price Terms*, University of Chicago Law School Working Paper (Aug. 2024); Robert Bartlett, *Standardization and Innovation in Venture Capital Contracting*, Stanford

constant repetition but remained embedded as part of the standard form. This rote usage proved to be dangerous when opportunistic actors asserted new meanings for words that were not well understood. Importantly, the reasons for suboptimal provisions being repeated were not just the positive externalities from having identical and perfectly understood provisions as posited by Kahan, Klausner, and others. There was more going on.

In more formal terms, having a set of boilerplate provisions that are perfectly identical, accurately priced, and fully understood by all parties is not the only possible equilibria. Other equilibria are also possible in a market where the great value of a standard form is that no one has to pay any attention to it. But if no one is paying attention to a particular boilerplate term, another equilibrium can exist where the meaning of the term is lost over time because everyone assumes someone else knows its meaning—in other words, a term can become a contractual "black hole." Even after parties in the market realize that the clause is useless historical debris, it cannot be removed easily because it has become part of the standard package of terms. Across a range of markets, including M&A, sovereign bonds, insurance contracts, trust agreements and more, scholars began to identify such "black holes" in the standard boilerplate.[12]

A complication in all of this work is that the focus is on the importance to market participants of having highly standardized forms. If the packages of terms in the market are identical, traders can price them without having to attend to variations in the boilerplate for different issuers. To be sure, there might be the occasional black hole, but those are seen as aberrations. The problem was that empirical work discovered that many of these so-called boilerplate terms were not that similar if one looked carefully enough.

Mark Weidemaier was among the first to recognize that market participants had a much broader conception of boilerplate than the academic theory assumed.[13] Contract terms that one might assume were the most uniform, such as the governing law and jurisdiction provisions, had dozens of linguistic variations even though the market perceived them as being "identical." This fact complicates the search for landmines. Some of

University Law School Working Paper (Feb. 2024) (available on ssrn.com); Roberto Tallarita, *Dual Class Contracting*, 49 J. Corp. L. 971 (2024); David Hoffman & Vincent Buccola, University of Pennsylvania Law School Working Paper, *Precedent Terms* (2025).

[12] *Supra* note 8 (citing studies).

[13] W. Mark C. Weidemaier, *Disputing Boilerplate*, 82 Temple L. Rev. 1 (2009).

the variations in the language of the boilerplate terms are benign, while other variations raise the landmine threat. To be sure, one could dismiss all the variations as mere surplusage. Yet, as any first-year law student would say, "words matter" in contracts.[14]

It does not take much effort to find that differences in wording, if pushed far enough, can change the meaning of a clause that the parties understood as the standard package of terms. The question, then, is how this state of affairs occurs within the world of contracts among sophisticated commercial parties. How do these potentially disastrous differences in wording appear, sometimes persist, and occasionally spread? The answer to the question of why this state of affairs results again and again in the world of highly sophisticated and high dollar value transactions can only be found by studying the processes of contract production. Contract production, as contrasted with contract design, has long been ignored in contract law and theory. But if we want to understand why contracts are the way they are—and that is surely a central project in contract theory and law—we need to understand how and why production processes are the way they are and what results from those realities.

To be sure, other scholars have urged that attention must be paid to contract production if features such as the ones we have noted are to be understood. Over a decade ago, Barak Richman pointed out that the process of contract production in settings such as sovereign bonds more resembled Henry Ford's automobile production lines than the idealized version taught in law school.[15] Claire Hill noted in several papers that errors in high end corporate contracts were not aberrations but rather a systematic part of the way law firms and lawyers did business.[16] Trevor Clark connected law firm

[14] Alex Ritchie writes about Oil and Gas contracts:

> While these [especially boilerplate] provisions [at the back of the contract] seem harmless enough, for those transactional lawyers unfortunate enough to see 50- or 100-page contracts that are the subject of litigation, experience shows that crafty litigators with ample time and will to research and argue the meaning of each word in the contract will claim that notices are defective, implied waivers have been granted, and anti-assignment clauses are invalid. Worse yet they may materialize a previously unknown claimant that sues on a theory of third party beneficiary rights.
>
> *How Contract Boilerplate Can Bite?* 50 ROCKY MOUNTAIN MINERAL L. FOUNDATION J. 240 (2013)

[15] Barak Richman, *Contracts Meet Henry Ford*, 40 HOFSTRA L. REV. 77 (2011).

[16] Claire Hill, *Why Contracts are Drafted in "Legalese"?* 77 CHICAGO-KENT L. REV. 59 (2001); Claire Hill, *What Mistakes Do Lawyers Make in Complex Business Contracts, and What Can and Should Be Done About Them?* in REVISITING THE CONTRACTS SCHOLARSHIP OF STUART MACAULAY 223–241 (Jean Braucher, Jean Kidwell, & William C. Whitford, eds., Bloomsbury 2013).

and market structural features and practices to contract outcomes.[17] Indeed, Kahan and Klausner, although they did not look at the features we describe, argued in their initial papers that examining the contract production process was crucial to understanding why contracts look and function the way they do.[18] We also took that tack in our prior work on standardization, noting both the positive externalities as well as the barriers to innovation resulting from standard forms.[19]

Yet, previous discussions of the relevance of contract production were primarily focused on particular subsets of contracts (e.g., highly standardized and readily tradeable financial contracts) or on the particular dynamics of elite law firms. In a sense, these efforts were informing contract law and theory at the far margins. But the stories we described in Part I (and the subsequent discovery of many more exemplars) persuaded us that the need to take contract production seriously applies to all of contract law, not just the idiosyncratic corners where we find fast-paced, high-volume trading. So, we began with the hypothesis that every commercial contract is the product of some amount of borrowing from preexisting standard forms. And this implies that every contract may be subject to landmine risk. The complication is that while boilerplate terms may be everywhere, the legions of standard terms embedded throughout the universe of commercial contracts are not the identically worded formulations that many had imagined them to be.

The story of Suriname's definition of "External Indebtedness" illustrates the dimensions of the problem we now began to tackle.

Boilerplate in Practice

In 2022, Suriname was in default on its sovereign debt and trying to negotiate with a variety of creditors including Chinese state-owned companies, foreign bondholders, local debtholders, and members of the Paris Club.[20] As is the case with many nations that have recently gone into default (Ghana, Zambia,

[17] Trevor Clark, *Transactions Costs and Big Law*, Kings College Working Paper (May 2024); *see also* Elisabeth de Fontenay, *Law Firm Selection and the Value of Transactional Lawyering*, 41 J. Corp. L. 393 (2015).

[18] *Supra* note 6 (citing studies).

[19] Goetz & Scott, *supra* note 3; Choi & Gulati, *supra* note 3.

[20] For a fuller treatment of this story, see Mark Weidemaier & Mitu Gulati, *The Perils of (Bond Contract) Faith*, FT Alphaville (Feb. 17, 2023).

Sri Lanka, among others), there was a heightened level of tension and suspicion among the creditors. Part of this additional tension was because of the emergence of China as a new creditor. Over the past decade, China had grown from an inconsequential participant in the sovereign lending market to a dominant player via its myriad state-controlled companies.[21]

A number of countries in the global south were in debt distress and needed to restructure their debts after the massive expenditures required to deal with COVID-19, and China was thought by some to be treating the rest of the lenders unfairly. Specifically, the non-China creditors feared that China might use its greater leverage over the borrower countries to obtain a larger recovery. In the case of Suriname, our old friend *pari passu* and its use of the term "External Indebtedness" was causing particular concern among foreign bondholders whose lawyers had begun parsing the fine print of the bonds.

Suriname's 2026 dollar bond promises that:

> *The Notes . . . will rank* pari passu, *without any preference among themselves and equally with all other unsubordinated External Indebtedness of the Republic.*

Usually, the term "External Indebtedness" is defined as debt denominated in a foreign currency. The logic is that if the debtor runs out of foreign currency it may want to favor some creditors over others. Foreign creditors don't much care what happens to local currency debt since the sovereign, having control of the printing presses, can just print as much of that currency as they need. Suriname's 2026 bond defines External Indebtedness in two parts, with a definition for each of the two words:

> *"Indebtedness" is "actual or contingent payment obligations for borrowed money . . ."*
>
> *"External" is "any Indebtedness* ***issued and placed*** *outside of the territory of the Republic."* (emphasis added)

At first cut, the "issued and placed" language might seem innocuous. But in the context of a country borrowing money repeatedly from Chinese state-owned operations, there was a possible problem. At least it seemed so for

[21] Anna Gelpern et al., *How China Lends: A Rare Look into 100 Debt Contracts with China*, 38 Econ. Pol'y 345 (2023).

some of the foreign bondholders of the country worried about China exploiting them.

A worried external bondholder might have begun to ask, what is debt "issued and placed" outside the Republic? The definition is unproblematic for a bond issue done in New York or London and sold through a syndicate of banks located there. But what about Suriname's debt to the Chinese Export Import Bank ("Ex Im"), which also lent in dollars? If the loan was finalized in a signing ceremony in Paramaribo, might China Ex Im argue that this loan was "issued and placed" within the Republic. And, if so, it falls outside the ambit of the *pari passu* clause.[22]

The specific wording of the Suriname External Indebtedness clause (the "issued and placed" language) looked to be unique. But the lawyers who discovered this variation in language saw resemblances in the standard External Indebtedness definition in Russia's bonds. The language had apparently emerged in the context of the breakup of the Soviet Union and the creation of the Russian Federation and then migrated as a standard formulation into the bonds of a number of post-soviet republics. And then into Suriname.[23]

We tell this story because it provides a window into how market experts understand the process by which linguistic variations arise and spread and yet remain "market." In this case, unusual circumstances occurred (most likely the break-up of the Soviet Union and creation of the Russian Federation) that might have required a modification of the wording of the standard clause. But the modification had to be done so that the bankers could still market the bond as having standard terms. Then, once accepted as "market," and within the body of acceptable precedents for issuers of that same type (e.g., post-Soviet republics), the language migrated. And once in the standard form, it was repeated. And so on and so forth.

[22] In addition, consider the Negative Pledge clause in Suriname's 2006 bond that constrains the sovereign's collateralized borrowing. What if Suriname were to pledge its gold reserves as collateral for the Ex Im loan? Normally, such an act would violate the contract's Negative Pledge clause, which forbids the creation of new secured debt unless the debtor grants a similar security interest to existing creditors. Except that Suriname's Negative Pledge clause limited the creation of security interests only when granted to secure "*Public* External Indebtedness."

[23] We tried to determine the origins of the unusual language in the Suriname clause, but this was one that befuddled even our sovereign debt experts. The best answer was that the language might have migrated from Russia's clauses that had to have nonstandard External Indebtedness provisions when the Soviet Union broke up. We then consulted some of the lawyers who had worked on post-Soviet Union sovereign bonds. Together we surveyed the various post-Soviet Union sovereign bonds for the different countries and failed to find much evidence. But as the experts cautioned, we only had access to a limited set of those debt instruments.

In response to our question about how boilerplate could be both a "market" standard and yet have language that migrates from bond to bond, one sovereign debt expert responded:

> Standard form contracts are not static creatures that are repeated by rote and never change. They evolve. You can think of a standard form contract as the body of an aging prize fighter. His body is going to be covered with scars. . . .
>
> Each scar tells a story. The process is Darwinian. As events occur, modifications have to be made for survival. And many of these modifications occur quietly, in some pocket of the industry. Some survive; others die out. Lawyers do not write any of this down. Nothing is recorded. So, years later, the only way to figure out why the modification was made is to try and pinpoint the origins and who the initial users were and figure out why.

Another senior lawyer offered his gloss:

> These deviations [from the standard form] are always intended to be within certain bounds. Modifications can only happen if the investment bankers can sell the notes as containing the standard set of provisions. You cannot change, unless the change is within certain bounds: at the deal stage that means that there is no price change for the modified language. Boilerplate can change, but it must remain market—so the change must be slight. This all goes sideways at the back end when there is a litigator and then a judge who reads the strict language without any understanding of the basic market understanding of the provision. Then, if there is a court decision that goes down some crazy path, the whole thing is off kilter. To use your language, that's when the landmine blows up.

Three insights follow from the evidence of migrating language in commercial boilerplate. First, boilerplate does not mean identical wording. In a market where different actors have varying needs, minor modifications will occur as a function of different contexts and particularized needs even though everyone involved sees themselves as still using the standard set of provisions for the particular deal type. Among those variations in language, some will be benign but others will be vulnerable to a strategic attack. Second, we should see clauses accumulate increasing levels of variation the longer they are around. Third, things blow up when contract terms that transactional parties understand as having a shared meaning land in the hands of the lawyers who specialize in conflict—the litigators and restructuring specialists who weaponize certain variations to extract maximal advantage for their side.

In sum, the notion of a standard form or boilerplate contract term in the real world is broader than academics and controlling legal doctrine have been assuming. And that broader notion of what could fit within the rubric of being accepted as "market" is the breeding ground that allows landmines to germinate, arise, persist, and spread.

From Variation to Landmine?

We now faced a conundrum: boilerplate language is not identical wording; there are tolerable variations in the words used to express the market's understanding of the meaning of particular provisions. Yet, on the other hand, the language must be a sufficient equivalent of that understanding in order to be considered "market."[24] How then can we know when a variation exceeds the market's boundary and becomes a landmine? One answer is to use the concept of functional equivalence. Different words can be used to express the same concept. It is not enough to argue that those differences must be syntactic synonyms. Rather the market judgment is that the variation cannot undermine the core promise that the term embodies. In the patois of the market, unexpected variations are landmines if they (eventually) affect the price of the contractual instrument. Our strategy has been to limit the designation of "landmine" to clauses that have actually been weaponized in a crisis environment. The presence of a landmine can affect the bargaining leverage of either creditors or the debtor near or in financial distress. Landmines are typically not priced prior to financial distress. But if the market becomes aware of them in that distress context, they do get priced then, a point we return to later in Chapter Eight.[25] Based on the importance of landmines in restructuring negotiations for sovereigns in distress, we are able to draw

[24] For a study of how participants in the sovereign bond markets understand the concept of what it means for terms to be "standard" or "market," see Anna Gelpern, Mitu Gulati, & Jeromin Zettelmeyer, *If Boilerplate Could Talk: The Work of Standard Form Terms in Sovereign Bonds*, 44 L. & Soc. Inquiry 617 (2019).

[25] For an example of ex post pricing, see Stephen J. Choi, Mitu Gulati, Ugo Panizza, Robert E. Scott, & W. Mark C. Weidemaier, *Obscure Contract Terms: An Inadvertent Pricing Experiment*, 19 Cap. Mkts L. J. 230 (2024).

the distinction between our landmines and acceptable variations based simply on subsequent facts. To paraphrase Justice Potter Stewart: "We know a landmine because we have seen it." But this implies that there are more landmines than the ones we have chronicled for this project. There are likely many other "putative" landmines lurking in bond contracts, waiting for a litigating lawyer to find and exploit them.

Notwithstanding the linguistic variations that are the reality of boilerplate in standardized contracts, landmines do exist. And they have different characteristics: some are exploitable by debtors, others by activist creditors, some persist, and others are eliminated through coordinated actions. These differences raise questions. If careful lawyers who have drafting responsibilities are capable of introducing changes that favor their clients' interests, why then don't these drafters eliminate harmful mutations (at least those that impair their clients' interests) as theory predicts they would? What explains a world in which the process of drafting contract terms seems so indifferent to the lawyer's professional responsibility to anticipate (and plan for) future litigation? And how do deal lawyers judge the difference between a harmless variation in the language of a standard provision and the dangerous irregularity that might eventually be deployed as a landmine? To begin to answer these questions, we focus in the next section on how the conception of contract as artifact changes the ways in which boilerplate is commonly understood.

Reconceiving Boilerplate as Artifact

We have identified two puzzles with the standard boilerplate story. First, standard terms are not identical but instead often have minor variations in language. While there is a market expectation for the presence of a particular type of clause within a particular architectural structure connecting the clauses, there is no expectation that the specific clause will contain the exact same language. Second, we find stickiness in some aspects of the terms in the boilerplate but not in others. Sometimes historical terms lose meaning even while remaining sticky. But we also find lawyers willing to change items around the margins. For example, in the Cerberus negotiations described in the Introduction, lawyers added a walk away clause but instead of deleting the otherwise standard specific performance clause, modified it with a "notwithstanding" caveat (end result being litigation).

The artifact conceptualization helps to explain both of these puzzles in a way that the standard boilerplate story does not. When contracting parties in the large liquid markets refer to a given contract as "market," they mean something more than that the contract is composed of many boilerplate clauses. It is that difference that is captured by the metaphor of contract as artifact. Artifacts are different from the standard boilerplate story: their core terms are interconnected both historically and symbolically.

As we suggested in the Introduction, an apt metaphor to capture this different perspective is to imagine the artifact contract as a complex instrument with many parts. Different parts of the contract will serve varying functions that combine to serve a common goal of encapsulating the rights and obligations of the contracting parties. In a prototypical sovereign bond contract, for example, there will be, among other components, a section governing payment terms, a section detailing the method of payment, a section covering what happens if the debtor defaults on payments, and a section specifying when parties can make modifications to the rest of the agreement (including what cannot be modified unless most creditors agree). These sections work together to create a specific balance of rights and obligations between creditors and debtors.

The deal lawyer who is using this contractual instrument to transact a particular deal does not have the skill, time, or motivation to design a new or different instrument. Moreover, any attempt to create a new contractual architecture will likely be met with, at best, skepticism in the market, and at worst, alarm and suspicion at the attempt to deviate from the market standard. Instead, as we have suggested, the deal lawyer views modifying a contract in the same way as a mechanic (or even more crudely an assembly line worker) views working on a car: She is competent to repair or install particular parts at the margins, but she will not attempt to change the underlying purpose of any particular component section nor the overall design of the contract in how the various components fit together. Indeed, attempting wholesale change to just a portion of the contractual instrument—say refashioning the modification clause in a loan agreement—will have a far-reaching impact across other components of the contractual instrument that depend on the functioning of that clause. Instead, drafting lawyers will typically leave the contractual architecture more or less functionally the same as when the contract was first assembled.

How much of a contract is artifact as opposed to how much flexibility lawyers in a particular deal have to make changes will vary based on several factors including the history of the uses of the clause and the importance of sticking close to the "market" standard. This is particularly important for deals that must be completed quickly and where the resulting contract is available for resale in a secondary market that values standardization. The complexity and degree to which different components of a contract are interconnected will also affect the cost of changing any one component. Within a specific contract, how central a component is to the bargained for balance of rights and obligations will also affect what portion of the contract is artifact. The more central the component, the more likely parties will hesitate to make changes out of a fear of making an error that will negatively affect their clients' interests.

The contract as artifact perspective is crucial to understanding the world of landmines. Lawyers are hesitant to change terms that are within the core artifact portion of the contract even if circumstances have rendered the meaning of the term contrary to the initial intent of the drafters or, at the extreme, undecipherable. We need, therefore, to learn much more about the operation of the market in which contracts as artifacts function, including the market for the lawyers who work on these instruments. To understand the factors that produce the different patterns of landmines, we turn in Chapter Seven to the theory of incomplete contracts as a frame for illuminating the insights that have come from the lived experience of the lawyers, an experience unfiltered by any conceptual frame.

Chapter Seven
Landmines and Incomplete Contract Theory

Introduction

The paradox that prompted this book is the trade-off between an efficiently designed contract and the efficiencies of contract production. In the sovereign debt market, our focus thus far, the demands of a liquid secondary market suggest that production efficiencies will dominate concerns about efficient contract design. In short, there will always be landmines in sovereign debt contracts. To understand why that is so, and to develop some conceptual coherence from the responses to our interviews, we turn to contract theory.

Contract theory has yet to engage with the ubiquity of commercial boilerplate and the landmines that are its incident. To the extent conventional contract theory recognizes irregularities such as the landmines we have described, they fall in the category of "incomplete contracts." What makes landmines an unusual phenomenon is that the effect of a landmine is to turn a relatively complete market contract into a more incomplete contract. The contract with the landmine is incomplete because now the contract doesn't specify the outcome (who wins, who loses) for every possible future state that might arise. Especially in the case of what we have called "subversive accretions," the landmine changes a clear statement of obligation into a discretionary obligation that turns on subsequent facts.[1] To be sure, in some cases the modified contract terms specify a clear, literal meaning. But interpreting the clause in the context of background market understanding renders the outcome of the ex post event indeterminate. So, in a sense, this also is a form of contractual incompleteness since the contract language no longer dictates the outcome the parties intended.[2]

[1] The "except as provided by mandatory law" proviso is an example of this type of subversive accretion.

[2] The metaphor of an incomplete contract most obviously applies to a gap in the contract—a contingency that has not been addressed by the parties in their agreement. We do not tackle explicit

Contract Hazards. Stephen J. Choi, Mitu Gulati, and Robert E. Scott, Oxford University Press.
 DOI: 10.1093/9780197821770.003.0007

Transactions costs and asymmetric information are standard explanations for incomplete contracts: either contingencies are too numerous or remote to be worth taking into consideration in the drafting process or they depend on facts known only to one of the parties.[3] But landmines of the type we've identified do not quite fit either of these categories. With the landmines, it is not that a contingency hasn't been taken into account or a party has critical private information. Rather, it appears that the contingency was dealt with in a way that makes little sense in light of what typical parties seeking to obtain the standard package of terms are trying to achieve. And, if the prospect of default looms large and the party advantaged by the aberrant term recognizes the strategic possibilities, the landmine provides an advantage that can be used to devastating and unexpected effect.

Reasons for Incompleteness

Beyond the transaction cost of accounting for future contingencies or the prevalence of private information, scholars have suggested other reasons for incompleteness. Three reasons are relevant to the puzzle of landmines.

Optimal Contract Design

What we call Optimal Contract Design explains parties' motivation to optimize total contracting costs by shifting contracting costs from the front end

gaps in this book because that would require greatly increasing the length of our treatment. But gaps do exist and they are close cousins of landmines in that many of them cannot be rationalized by standard design explanations. On some of these gaps, see Patrick Bolton, Mitu Gulati, & Ugo Panizza, *Sovereign Debt Puzzles*, 15 Ann. Rev. Fin. Econ. 239 (2023).

[3] Robert E. Scott & Jody Kraus, Contract Law and Theory, p 43 (Carolina Press, 6th ed. 2023). Another cost of writing complete contracts is the resource costs of negotiating and reducing to a written form the agreed upon allocations of risk. Those resource costs, in turn, include not only the time and effort to negotiate and draft the clauses in question but also the possibility that in doing so the parties might make a mistake in formulating their written contract. A clause that they regard as clear may, upon subsequent examination, appear ambiguous or vague. This "formulation error" may then lead to litigation over the appropriate meaning that should be given to the clause in question. Charles J. Goetz & Robert E. Scott, *The Limits of Expanded Choice: An Analysis of the Interactions Between Express and Implied Contract Terms*, 73 Cal. L. Rev. 261 (1985). Other explanations of incompleteness might include a reluctance to impede the deal making process by raising objections that could signal a lack of trust or the presence of strong informal means of enforcement that make legal enforcement rights unnecessary.

of a contract (the negotiating and drafting stage) to the back end (the performance and enforcement stage) by substituting a vague standard in place of costly efforts to specify every possible action that might constitute an act of default.[4] The addition of new language that creates the landmine effectively changes a contract term from a bright line rule to a vague standard thereby rendering the contract incomplete. Despite the enhanced risk of litigation over the meaning of the now-vague language, the change is justified if the addition of new language saves even more front-end negotiating costs. Drafters may find it cost-effective to forgo disagreements negotiating over specific exceptions to a contractual obligation and instead substitute a vague term that delegates that function to a later court. For example, in an effort to satisfy a sovereign's concerns that a broad waiver of immunity might violate some domestic constitutional requirements, parties may forego bargaining over a detailed list of qualifications to the waiver. Instead, the parties can negotiate for a vague standard such as "we waive sovereign immunity to *the extent permitted by applicable laws*," a provision that postpones to a later litigation the determination of possible conflicting domestic constitutional requirements. One interview respondent advanced this theory explicitly, claiming that "you take risks to please a particular sovereign and know that the risks are low in context because sovereigns can't change the law for a single issue."

Optimal contract design may explain why vague language is introduced, but it does not explain why it is retained in subsequent bonds, since careful lawyers, like the respondent, would always remove risky terms if they had no context-specific reason to keep them. Moreover, this explanation for incompleteness cannot explain simple errors and glitches that are not inserted purposefully to respond to a client's concerns.

Satisficing

Satisficing explains incompleteness as a function of the opportunity cost of time, where expending additional negotiating costs to write better contract terms causes parties to miss even more profitable opportunities.[5]

[4] *See* Robert E. Scott & George G. Triantis, *Anticipating Litigation in Contract Design*, 115 YALE L. J. 814 (2006).

[5] Patrick Bolton & Antoine Faure-Grimaud, *Satisficing Contracts*, 77 REV. ECON. STUD. 937 (2010). Bolton and Faure-Grimaud model time constraints as a source of incomplete contracting. Parties

The claim here is that there is no time to engage in front-end negotiations because the market moves so quickly that taking time to negotiate is not cost-effective. Satisficing theory thus fits the factual assertion offered by some interview respondents that there is often only a "small window" for timing the placement of sovereign bond issues (probably for corporate bonds, too). Timing constraints may explain errors that arise from haste and also explain why those errors are often not eliminated once they have been introduced. Another way of expressing the satisficing motivation is that front-end costs are too high relative to the much lower back-end risks to justify getting the legal contract terms right.

Several respondents argued that the legal contract terms are largely irrelevant because "a sovereign loan is simply a gift that is repaid when the sovereign needs more money." Another respondent opined, "who knows what a term such as the issuer's right to correct a 'manifest error' means, but does it matter?" In short, because sovereigns are reputationally constrained, there is no payoff in clarifying ambiguous language if making those changes impairs the opportunity to issue the bonds at the best available price.

Satisficing theory predicts that no lawyer would make deliberate changes in the standard form if they could avoid it, but as we have seen there appear to be a number of these pro-sovereign changes. Satisficing theory, therefore, cannot explain purposeful changes that create landmines where none existed previously.

Agency Costs

Contracts will be incomplete when the misalignment of interests between drafting lawyers and their clients and between the nominal clients—underwriters and debt managers—and the "real" clients—bondholders and the citizens of the sovereign state—leads to hyperbolic discounting of future risks in order to capture present returns.[6] Sovereign debt contracting

in their model satisfice in equilibrium by assigning control rights to one of the agents as a means of deferring time-consuming deliberations. The model suggests that the fact that agents tend to resolve most conflicts up front implies that contracts are excessively complete. This theory, then, might support the argument that lawyers negotiate too much and that the imposition of time constraints is efficiency enhancing.

[6] Hyperbolic discounting is also known as "present bias": overweighting present considerations vis-à-vis future ones. For discussion of this feature in the sovereign debt contracting context, *see*

is particularly subject to agency costs. In the case of sovereign bonds, the individual interests of the key market participants are inconsistent with the interests of their respective principals—the investors in the market and the citizens of the sovereign. The private interests of the drafting lawyers are the mirror image of their de facto clients, the debt managers (the agents of the sovereigns) and the investment banks (the agents of the investors).[7] And both sets of agents are subject to hyperbolic discounting of future risks that are unknown to the sovereigns and investors. The key agents are motivated to minimize the ex ante costs of a bond issue (transaction costs plus negative price effects) even though expected ex post costs (restructuring cost, the cost of holdouts, etc.) are thereby increased by an even greater amount.[8]

A number of the respondents offered a version of this agency cost story: Landmines result from various instances of careless drafting, including the introduction of language from corporate bonds (by lawyers who don't adjust for the fact that sovereigns have control of domestic law) and other random errors. One respondent explained: "careless language is not removed [from the standard form] because only a few skilled lawyers know to make changes." Another said: "No one who is not an expert—generally those who don't work on restructurings—cares and the underwriters don't care because litigation is a very low probability."

These errors, and the admitted failure to read the core boilerplate terms in the standard form contract carefully, are a product of time constraints that are only partially attributable to the client's interests in doing the deal promptly. The client believes that the lawyer's skill suffices to ensure that the words in the contract match the contractual intent as the client understands it. But the novice lawyer understands that her level of skill requires an additional investment of time in order to guard against risks embedded in the artifact contract of which the client is ignorant. That difference in

Gulati & Scott, *supra* Ch. 4, note 2; *see also* Choi, Gulati, & Scott, *The Back Hole Problem*, *supra* Ch. 6, note 8; Stephen J. Choi, Mitu Gulati, & Robert E. Scott, *Contractual Arbitrage*, in Oxford Handbook of Institutions of International Governance and Market Regulation, chapter 7 (Eric Brousseau, Jean Michel Glachant, & Jerome Sgard eds. Oxford University Press, 2019).

[7] *See* Mitu Gulati & Robert E. Scott, The Three and a Half Minute Transaction: Boilerplate and the Limits of Contract Design (University of Chicago Press, 2013) (reporting on interviews; and emphasizing the agency cost issue).

[8] Excessive discounting by agents leads to bond issuances that are less efficient than they could be (for details from interviews, see Gulati & Scott, *id.*). An efficient sovereign bond contract optimizes total contracting costs by trading off the ex ante or front-end costs of the contract and the ex post or back-end costs of default.

understanding is the source of the misaligned incentives between client and drafter.

Agency costs imply that drafting lawyers will rarely change terms purposefully: lazy and risk averse lawyers would prefer not to make any changes at all, and thus agency costs cannot explain changes that were designed to give ex post discretion to the sovereign. Contracts infected by agency costs will, however, have a higher risk of careless errors and thoughtless importation of terms from other documents as drafters ignore the core boilerplate terms while racing to "fill in the blanks in the contract."[9] In short, this theory can explain both the creation and the retention of the historical holdover and random error landmines but it cannot explain how "subversive accretion" landmines develop, at least not if the magnitude of agency costs are the same on the part of both sovereign and creditor lawyers.

We see that each of these reasons for incompleteness in sovereign debt contracts appear to fit some of the landmines that we have discovered. The problem is that none of these reasons can, by itself, explain the universe of landmines. Optimal contract design cannot explain how simple blunders and errors emerge, nor can it explain the persistence of pro-sovereign terms where the original purpose of the clause no longer applies. Neither satisficing nor agency costs can explain purposeful or deliberate changes that were designed to give the sovereign a strategic advantage.[10] The problem is not that we have no theory of incompleteness. It is that we have too many theories and none fit the universe of our landmines.

The question is whether a coherent story can be told that purports to explain the different characteristics of the landmines in our dataset and harmonizes the theories of incompleteness we have derived from the interviews with market experts.

[9] One lawyer described the process of drafting sovereign debt contracts in the following terms:

> You have to understand the system. No one pays that much attention to the minute details like this. One cannot afford to, if one wants to stay competitive. The firm has a computer program. You know . . . one that a junior associate can go to and plug the relevant parameters into—you know, type of issuance, type of issuer, which side we are representing, etc.,—and the computer generates a standard contract. The firm spent [a large amount] on putting together this system. Associates can now produce a contract for one of these deals *in three and a half minutes*. This is the future of contracting in these markets.
>
> Gulati & Scott, *supra* note 7 at 9 (quoting an interview with a senior law firm partner, June 18, 2007). (emphasis added)

[10] *See also* Anna Gelpern, *The Importance of Being Standard*, European Central Bank Annual Legal Department Conference Proceedings (Jan. 2017).

The Divided Market Hypothesis

To make progress, let's begin with the most salient factor identified by our respondents: the market for sovereign debt lawyers appears to be divided into two separate populations with different levels of experience and different motivations. In the first cohort are the "gurus" who are experienced in both issuing *and* restructuring sovereign debt, and who represent their sovereign and banker clients faithfully and negotiate modifications to standard terms that their clients request. The "guru" group is small relative to the second cohort, the "novice" lawyers who are unfamiliar with the intricacies of the standard form contract, and whose practice experience in the sovereign area is limited to issuing the bonds. These less experienced lawyers, while not meaning to change substance, may introduce random errors through inexperience and haste. The separation between the two cohorts undergirds a prediction that some landmines result from the efforts of gurus, who anticipate the risks of a downstream default and provide client service, while other landmines—for example, careless importation of language from inapt precedents—result when inexperienced lawyers, unmindful of the downstream risks of litigation, are responsible for drafting the initial contract documents.[11]

But there is a puzzle: assuming gurus work for both sovereigns and underwriters, the presence of both gurus and novices in the market does not fully explain the prevalence of pro-sovereign subversive accretions. Moreover, hyperbolic discounting by the agents of both the sovereign and the creditors would seem to predict that gurus on either side would not have much of an incentive to care about the longer term and the risk of potential restructurings.

The solution to the puzzle is that the magnitude of the agency costs is not the same on both sides: Despite the presence of gurus on both the sovereign and investor side of a sovereign bond deal, gurus utilize their expertise effectively only on behalf of the sovereign. On the creditor side, the underwriter's focus is purely on the short term. The investment banks that play the role of underwriter in sovereign deals are never involved in any restructuring that

[11] The separation between gurus and novices is primarily a function of the nature of their practice experience. The interview respondents who we characterize as gurus practice at both ends of the sovereign debt market—restructuring distressed debt as well as issuing new bonds. They have litigation experience as well as transactional expertise while novices tend to only practice on the transactional end.

may take place many years in the future. In addition, the ultimate clients—those investors who purchase the sovereign bonds from the underwriters—often are professional money managers who also focus on immediate short-term returns and care only that the contract looks "market." The focus on the short term for the creditor side is thus at a maximum.

Things are different on the sovereign side. Government officials may have a career life span shorter than ten-year and thirty-year sovereign bonds, but their interests extend to the sovereign's financial distress in the intermediate term. Moreover, most government officials have a stake in the long-term economic health of their country. Unlike the underwriters, therefore, government officials will often balance closing the deal with the prospect of financial distress that may occur sooner rather than later. Indeed, one respondent vividly explained a contemporary sovereign's interest in counsel adding subversive terms to the standard form: "The Russian bonds are full of these. After the invasion of Crimea, they became worried about future US and European sanctions . . . and they were right to be worried."

This asymmetry in the magnitude of agency costs gives gurus on the sovereign side greater leeway to use their expertise to favor the sovereign and helps explain the effects of the divide between gurus and novices. To the extent the sovereign cares relatively more about having discretion in responding to financial difficulty, a guru on the sovereign side will exert more attention to the contract terms than a guru on the underwriter side. In addition, over time more gurus will represent sovereigns than creditors: the sovereign will pay more for lawyers with a reputation for skill in drafting contracts and handling restructurings. As a result, lawyers who work for the sovereign will be motivated to hone their knowledge of the intricacies of sovereign debt contracts. Not coincidentally, our respondents believe that the most prominent sovereign debt attorneys, including Lee Buchheit, have worked primarily on the sovereign side.

The divided market hypothesis, informed by the asymmetry in agency costs as between debtors and creditors, thus appears to explain the origin of the different types of landmines that we have discovered in the sovereign bond market. To test that explanation, we turn to another puzzle: What explains the evidence that some of these landmines persist and mutate, becoming part of the boilerplate in the standard form, while others appear to die out rather quickly? The answer turns on an empirical inquiry. To begin that inquiry, we start by linking each of the three landmine categories that we discovered in the sovereign debt market to the reason for incompleteness that may explain how that landmine was introduced into the standard form.

First, are the large number of purposeful changes to well-understood standard terms are made to give a sovereign leverage if it should ever attempt to restructure the debt.[12] These subversive accretions are not necessarily opportunistic efforts to seek advantage. Vagueness may be introduced when there is a negotiating impasse between the investors' interest in holding the sovereign to strict repayment terms and the sovereign's interest in carving out reasonable exceptions to those duties. Because these landmines are introduced by sovereign-side lawyers who control the drafting process, they should be prevalent and persistent in contemporary bond contracts.

Second, are errors that disfavor the sovereign and that likely arise randomly from novice attorneys drafting contracts and making mistakes. We expect that the gurus in the market will work to clean up these errors: errors will be introduced inadvertently, get cleaned up when noticed, and then arise again.[13] Numerous changes to language following the adoption of a new clause or term will predictably lead to an even higher rate of errors as these new terms are introduced to the standard form. These innovation errors should be prevalent initially and then diminish more rapidly as the market ultimately settles on the new standard. Both random and innovation errors typically favor activist creditors not present at the contract drafting stage who attempt to use careless drafting to undermine a proposed restructuring agreement. Since activist creditors only appear when the debtor nears default, it is difficult to characterize any of these irregularities as "purposeful."[14]

Third, are "historical holdovers," terms and concepts introduced when the current standard form debt contract was evolving from corporate transactions.[15] These holdovers from the original source documents that

[12] In addition, gurus working on behalf of the sovereign may purposefully elect not to correct mistakes made by novice lawyers that favor the sovereign, leading to pro-sovereign errors accumulating over time.

[13] Few, if any, attorneys were gurus at the beginning of the modern sovereign debt market in the early 1990s, but the cohort of gurus increased over time as attorneys gained expertise in restructuring sovereign deals. In equilibrium, the fraction of bonds with these errors will depend on the balance between the number of novices introducing new errors and the number of gurus correcting such errors. This equilibrium may shift over time as the ratio of novices and gurus changes.

[14] If the value to activist investors were priced in at the outset of deals, there would be an incentive for the underwriters to retain these activist-favoring glitches (indeed, they would no longer be glitches). But we have seen little evidence, in either data on prices or interviews, of this kind of pricing effect. *See e.g.*, GULATI & SCOTT, *supra* note 7 (examining the matter in the context of the *pari passu* clause).

[15] The *pari passu* clause is a prime example of the problems caused by the historical holdovers that are embedded in the contract. Another example is the negative pledge clause.

formed the sovereign bond template enjoy a canonical status derived from their presence at the origin of the modern debt contract. Once embedded in the artifact's core, these landmines are unlikely to disappear even over long periods of time. They will be more persistent over time.

A variant of the historical holders are terms that once may have maximized the joint surplus of contracting parties but have become obsolete as legal or economic conditions change and require updating in the standard form contract. Here, coordination difficulties that are prevalent in large multilateral markets such as sovereign debt may prevent the updating of the artifact's core that is necessary to eliminate these obsolete terms.

In sum, the assumption of a divided market for sovereign debt lawyers generates these four predictions on the nature and dispersion of landmines that we should expect to observe in that market: (1) Subversive accretion landmines will be prevalent and more persistent in contemporary bond contracts than human errors: (2) Of the human errors, the random errors will tend to diminish over time, while the errors that arise as a byproduct of innovation should be prevalent initially and then diminish more rapidly; (3) Historical holdovers from source documents will be more prevalent and persistent over time than both subversive accretions and human errors; (4) Obsolete terms will persist because of difficulties in coordinating changes to the artifact's core will deter updating.

We turn in Chapter Eight to report on our test of these predictions using a dataset of randomly selected sovereign bond issuances.

Chapter Eight
Prevalence and Persistence

Introduction

Earlier chapters document the existence of multiple landmines. Even so, finding a handful of landmines that appeared but then disappeared over a period of several decades would not be too surprising. Adherents to an efficient contracting model would expect the market over time to eliminate any problematic provisions that may emerge. The question we ask in this chapter, therefore, is prevalence over time. How often do landmines appear and then, importantly, persist?

One goal in this project has been to explore the existence question across a range of transactions. We are, after all, starting from the conventional wisdom that landmines do not exist. But once landmines are credibly found in a particular transactional market, new questions arise as to the nature of these landmines. Are there discernable patterns in the landmines? Are there, for example, particular provisions of the contracts where landmines appear more frequently? Do landmines favor one type of contracting party over another: in the case of sovereign bonds, do sovereigns benefit from landmines more than creditors? Do structural features of the drafting process, such as who drafts first, matter? This chapter provides preliminary answers to these questions.

Before proceeding, a few caveats on the data we summarize in this chapter. Our focus in this chapter is on the persistence of landmines in sovereign bond contracts. But we do not provide a complete analysis of every landmine in sovereign bonds. We cannot do that since we are unable to observe the entire set of landmines that may have been present at one time in a sovereign bond contract. This is due partly to the difficulty in defining what constitutes a landmine. We could take the "I know it when I see it" approach and subjectively select as a landmine any provisions that we believe could be weaponized in litigation. A more objective approach, and the one we adopt, defines landmines based on their functional properties. Has an idiosyncratic contractual provision blown up over the past two decades when one party

Contract Hazards. Stephen J. Choi, Mitu Gulati, and Robert E. Scott, Oxford University Press.
 DOI: 10.1093/9780197821770.003.0008

attempted to secure an advantage during a debt restructuring? From this objective approach, we identified seventeen landmines.[1] All of them are present in documents that are currently being used in the sovereign market.

Our approach is underinclusive: it misses those provisions that potentially could have—under different circumstances—resulted in a landmine that exploded during a debt restructuring. Not all sovereign debt, for example, is restructured. Even for those contractual provisions that did surface during a restructuring, we only know about the events that our research has identified. That said, given that sovereign bonds have been the subject of a significant portion of our research, we are optimistic that we have learned of most of the meaningful instances of landmines that affected a restructuring. From our interviews, we know that there are other landmines but for whatever reason the aberrant terms have not yet been weaponized. What we report, therefore, is an undercount of the prevalence of landmines in sovereign bonds.

The theory in Chapter Seven predicts that we should see differences in the evolutionary pattern for the three categories of landmines. Here, we examine the data to see whether we see such differences. To assess the prevalence and persistence of landmines in sovereign bond contracts, we constructed two sets of random samples of bonds.[2] Our first sample is a set of one hundred contemporary bond issuances from 2020 to 2022.[3] This sample assesses the prevalence of landmines in modern sovereign bond contracts. Unless one assumes that all the landmines just appeared in 2020, the existence of landmines in the 2020–2022 period indicates that earlier landmines have persisted, uncorrected, into the 2020–2022 period. Starting with a sample from 2020–2022 period thus provides a measure of how many of the landmines that have appeared over the past two decades (e.g., the seventeen landmines we discussed earlier) are present in contemporary bonds. The goal is to provide a sense of prevalence.

We go one step further. The second sample is a random selection of historical bonds from 1990 to 1995.[4] Using the 1990–1995 sample, we are able to

[1] We describe each of the seventeen landmines we found in the Appendix. The material for this chapter is drawn from: Robert E. Scott, Stephen J. Choi, & Mitu Gulati, *Contractual Landmines*, 41 Yale J. Reg. 307 (2024). We provide a more detailed analysis of the seventeen landmines in our *Contractual Landmines* article. For those who are interested in going down the rabbit hole, we have a larger set of close to fifty possible landmines (including the initial seventeen). At fifty, we stopped collecting.

[2] Additional details are in Scott et al., *id.*

[3] We obtained the bonds from the Filings Expert/Perfect Information database. We selected forty bonds each from 2020 and 2021 and twenty bonds from 2022, collected up to June 1, 2022.

[4] Due to a relative lack of bond issuances in this period, we randomly selected only seventy-five sovereign bond issuances using bonds obtained from Perfect Information.

see whether any of the landmines we find in the 2020–2022 period were also present in the 1990s, consistent with a decades-long period of persistence. The 1990–1995 period, when emerging market sovereigns began issuing international bonds, is generally seen as the birth of the modern sovereign debt market.[5]

The two samples of randomly selected bonds include contracts governed by different law and bonds guaranteed by a sovereign that are issued by nonsovereigns. Each bond is denominated in a currency other than the sovereign's own currency and, importantly, structured for sale to the international market. In theory, the need to sell to the international market motivates the sovereign to account for the preferences of the investors in this market. To the extent investors are sophisticated commercial parties with interests represented by investment banks seeking to place the bonds, conventional wisdom holds that the bond contracts, even if boilerplate, should reflect those terms that maximize the expected joint surplus of the sovereign and the investors. Under the conventional view, therefore, we would not expect to find any landmines in the bonds we have collected. We find, however, that landmines are pervasive in our sample. In the sample of one hundred bonds from 2020 to 2022, 100% had at least one of seventeen landmines. There were nine landmines on average in each bond in the 2020–2022 sample, and the minimum number of landmines in any bond was five.

PREVALENCE

To assess the Divided Market Hypothesis developed in Chapter Seven as well as the associated theories of why landmines are prevalent and persistent in sovereign bond contracts, we grouped the landmines into the categories we first identified in Chapter Two.

Historical Holdovers

Our first category, historical holdovers, captures those landmines that have existed from at least the start of modern sovereign bond issuances in the early

[5] There were a handful of sovereigns who issued bonds in the 1960–1990 period, but the market was thin and populated mostly by highly rated issuers.

1990s. These landmines are most likely to persist because they are embedded in the core terms of the artifact contract. They were part of the initial template for these bonds, and market participants expect to have them in their contracts, even if they don't fully understand their purpose. To quote the sovereign bond experts we interviewed, they are "market." In our sample of sovereign bonds, we found three landmines in the historical holdover category. For our analysis, we focus on one of the historical holdover landmines: the *pari passu* clause described earlier in Chapter Four.[6] The *pari passu* clause may have had a purpose once, but this purpose is now not clear. Simply removing the *pari passu* clause would address the concern of sovereigns that holdout creditors may use the ambiguity of the *pari passu* clause to demand pro rata payments on the holdouts' bonds. But instead of removing the *pari passu* clause, sovereigns typically patched the clause to make clear that whatever the clause meant, it did not require pro rata payments. Despite this patch, retention of the ambiguous *pari passu* terminology potentially provides activist creditors opportunities to advance strategic claims.

The historical holdovers, to the extent they are a long-standing part of the artifact's core, will be difficult to remove from the sovereign bond contract. We predicted that there would be a relatively high prevalence of historical holdover landmines in 2020–2022. Consistent with this prediction, the *pari passu* landmine was present in 100% of the bonds in our 2020–2022 sample.[7]

To test the progression of historical holdovers, we turn to our 1990–1995 sample of sovereign bond contracts, the period when the modern sovereign bond issuances began.[8]

Table 8.1 compares the fraction of bonds with the *pari passu* clause for the 1990–1995 and 2020–2022 periods. It shows that the incidence of the *pari passu* clause was not only high in 2020–2022 but also at the start of the modern sovereign bond issuances in the 1990–1995 period.[9] Table 8.1 is based on pooled cross-sectional data from the 1990–1995 and 2020–2022 periods. To assess the persistence of the historical holdover landmines for a *specific* sovereign, we looked at the sovereigns that included the historical holdover

[6] The other two historical holdover landmines involve the Negative Pledge and Buy Back clauses. See the Appendix for a description of the landmines in the historical holdovers category.

[7] We found similar results for the other historical holdover landmines, each of which is present in over 80% of the bonds in the 2020–2022 period.

[8] Due to a relative lack of bond issuances in this period, we randomly selected only seventy-five sovereign bond issuances using bonds obtained from Perfect Information.

[9] We found similar results for the other historical holdover landmines, each of which is present in over 70% of the bonds in the 1990–1995 period.

Table 8.1 Historical holdover comparison

Clause	Fraction of bonds: 1990–1995	Fraction of bonds: 2020–2022	*p*-value
Pari Passu	0.987	1.000	0.247

Note: *p*-value is from a chi-squared test of the difference between the 1990–1995 and 2020–2022 periods for the clause.

landmines in 1990–1995 and assessed whether these same sovereigns still used the same landmines in 2020–2022. Here, we find high levels of persistence for specific sovereigns: 100% of the fourteen sovereigns using a *pari passu* clause in 1990–1995 continued using it in 2020–2022.[10] In sum, every single sovereign continued to use a *pari passu* clause.

Subversive Accretions

Our second category, subversive accretions, captures those landmines that became embedded when gurus representing the sovereign issuer used their expertise and access to insert terms that favor the sovereign over investors. Eight of the landmines in our dataset fall in this category. For our analysis, we focus on the Manifest Error subversive accretion landmine.[11] As we discussed in Chapter Five, the manifest error clause normally does not attract attention as it deals with minor errors in the contract. The clause typically allows the debtor and the fiscal agent to modify the contract to correct a minor error without approval from the creditors. Variations in the manifest error clause go beyond mere technical corrections and provide, in some versions of the clause, that the debtor at its sole discretion (without agreement of the

[10] We found similar, albeit weaker, results for the other historical holdover landmines: 63.6% of the eleven sovereigns using a Buy Back clause in 1990–1995 used a Buy Back clause in 2020–2022; 77.8% of the seven sovereigns using a Negative Pledge clause in 1990–1995 used a Negative Pledge clause in 2020–2022. We leave for future research the analysis of what explains differences in persistence for the historical holdovers. It is possible, for example, that the market is focused more on some historical holdovers (e.g., *pari passu*) as part of the standard form at the beginning of the modern sovereign bond market in the early 1990s than others (e.g., Buy Back clauses), leading the market to penalize the absence of one more than the other.

[11] The other subversive accretions involve landmines that affect the following clauses: Fiscal Laws, *pari passu* Mandatory Law, Sovereign Immunity by Law, Sovereign Immunity Exclusions, Prescription, Governing Law Authorization and Execution, and Jurisdiction. See the Appendix for a detailed description of the subversive accretion landmines.

fiscal agent) can make its own determination of what is a manifest error and modify the contract accordingly. This variation of the manifest error clause seemingly allocates unlimited authority to the debtor to modify the contract to correct what the debtor self-identifies as a manifest error.

We predict widespread prevalence of subversive accretions, particularly as a function of time from the early 1990s to today. Subversive accretion landmines are found frequently in the sovereign bond contracts from 2020 to 2022. In our 2020–2022 sample, 67% of the bonds contained a Manifest Error landmine.[12] As we hypothesized in Chapter Seven, the relative expertise, first drafter advantage, and asymmetric incentives between sovereign-side lawyers and their underwriter counterparts appear to explain the presence of subversive accretion landmines. It follows that subversive accretions should not be as prevalent at the start of the modern sovereign bond issuances in the early 1990s. This would be true if subversive accretions were inserted onto bond contracts as sovereign-side lawyers developed expertise in handling distressed debts and used this expertise and their first drafter advantage to favor the sovereign.

A simplified version of this story clarifies this claim. We begin our data analysis in the early to mid-1990s, after the sovereign financing market switched from syndicated loans to bonds. Here, in this new market—the product of the many defaults on sovereign syndicated loans in the 1980s—everyone who worked on these instruments was essentially a novice. The initial template for the standard bond form contract was likely borrowed from a combination of the standard templates then in use for corporate bonds and syndicated loans for sovereigns. Over time, as market volume exploded and countries inevitably began to experience crises, a handful of lawyers who were engaged in the resulting restructurings developed expertise in the documents. If these "gurus" then participated in drafting new issuances, they may have been able to effect marginal changes in the standard form contract to the advantage of their clients. And since, as we have noted, the lawyers with interests most closely aligned with the ultimate client were sovereign-side lawyers, we'd expect to see the marginal adjustments in language that benefits the sovereigns.

[12] The other subversive accretion landmines were not as prevalent in 2020–2022. The other subversive accretions range from 22% of the bonds (Pari Passu Mandatory Law) to 57% of the bonds (Prescription) in 2020–2022.

Table 8.2 Subversive accretion comparison

Clause	Fraction of bonds: 1990–1995	Fraction of bonds: 2020–2022	*p*-value
Manifest Error	0.200	0.670	0.000

Note: p-value is from a chi-squared test of the difference between the 1990–1995 and 2020–2022 periods for the clause.

Table 8.2 compares the fraction of bonds with the Manifest Error landmine for the 1990–1995 and 2020–2022 periods. Consistent with the Divided Market Hypothesis, the Manifest Error landmine has grown in prevalence over time.[13]

The phrase "subversive accretion" implies a degree of intentionality. Recall from the interviews that respondents resisted the notion of naked opportunism as an explanation. But subversive accretions may also arise from somewhat less direct, yet intentional, methods. If we assume that errors occur randomly over time in boilerplate terms, these errors are as likely to favor creditors as they are to favor sovereigns. But if gurus are better at identifying these errors and tend to correct only anti-sovereign errors, then one would expect more pro-sovereign landmines to accumulate over time in the standard boilerplate contract.

While we leave a more detailed time series analysis for future research, we can focus here on the adoption of the Manifest Error clause for Ukraine. Here, we collected bond contracts at roughly five-year intervals in order to assess changes in Ukraine's Manifest Error clause over time. In Table 8.3, we show the results of this analysis.

We can see that Ukraine used the same basic Manifest Error clause in its bonds from 2002 to 2014. Each clause leaves it to the "Trustee and the issuer" to make modifications that are of a "formal, minor or technical nature or is to correct a manifest error." The clause also provides that modifications may

[13] Including the Manifest Error landmine, seven of the eight subversive accretion landmines increased in prevalence from the 1990–1995 period to the 2020–2022 period. The increase for five of the eight subversive accretions is significantly different from zero. Only the Fiscal Laws landmine decreased somewhat in prevalence from 29.3% in 1990–1995 to 23% in 2020–2022 but the difference is not statistically significant. One of our gurus offered an explanation for the difference in prevalence of the Fiscal Laws landmine. This particular landmine was always likely to behave differently from the others because it is a tax-related provision, and tax provisions receive greater scrutiny than other provisions such as a governing law or jurisdiction clause. This is because investors at the outset want to know the taxes they will be assessed and because the tax provisions in the contract receive an additional level of scrutiny in every deal from a tax specialist.

Table 8.3 Ukraine's "Manifest Error" time series

Offering date	Manifest Error clause
November 27, 2002	The *Trustee and the Issuer* may, without the consent of the Noteholders, agree (i) to any modification of these Conditions or the Dollar Trust Deed (other than in respect of a Reserved Matter) which is, in the *opinion of the Trustee*, proper to make if, in the *opinion of the Trustee*, such modification will not be materially prejudicial to the interests of Noteholders and (ii) to any modification of the Dollar Notes or the Dollar Trust Deed which is of a formal, minor or technical nature or is to correct a manifest error.
October 12, 2005	[Substantially the same as in 2002].
September 22, 2010	[Substantially the same as in 2002].
February 17, 2014	[Substantially the same as in 2002].
October 13, 2018	The Agency Agreement may be amended without the consent of the holder of any Note for the purposes of, as determined *by the Issuer*, curing any ambiguity or of curing, correcting or supplementing any defective or inconsistent provisions contained therein or herein, to take into account further issues of notes pursuant to Condition 15 (Further Issues) or in any manner that the Issuer may deem necessary or desirable and that will not adversely affect, *in the opinion of the Issuer*, in any material respect, the interests of the Noteholders.
December 16, 2020	[Substantially the same as in 2018].
July 23, 2021	[Substantially the same as in 2018].

be made if in the "opinion of the Trustee" such modifications are "not . . . materially prejudicial to the interests of Noteholders." The trustee works on behalf of the Noteholders and thus, in theory, should only invoke the Manifest Error clause when the action is not materially prejudicial to the interests of Noteholders. The last offering in this series was in 2014, and Ukraine used VTB Capital, a Russian state-controlled investment bank, as the underwriter.

Subsequently, Ukraine shifted alliances in the direction of the European Union, and in response Russia invaded Ukraine in 2014 and occupied Crimea. That was a jolt to Ukraine's future economic prospects, and Russian financial support was no longer available. By 2018 (the next data point we have), Ukraine had dropped VTB Capital as the underwriter. Coinciding with these changes, Ukraine's 2018 Manifest Error clause no longer refers to the Trustee. Instead, the clause now contains a landmine: the *issuer alone* may make modifications to cure ambiguities, defective provisions, and so on. Moreover, modifications may be made if the modifications "*will not adversely affect, in the opinion of the Issuer, in any material respect, the interests of the Noteholders.*" The landmine-infected Manifest Error clause now provides the sovereign with full authority to determine what does and does not adversely affect the interests of the Noteholders in any material respect. Unlike the trustee, the sovereign does not act on behalf of the Noteholders and thus one can wonder whether the "opinion" of the sovereign will accurately reflect any adverse impact on the interests of the Noteholders.

The question then is whether this is a subversive accretion or a drafting error. The fact that language is changed in a specific way suggests this is a subversive accretion but context provided by one of our respondents complicates the analysis. She pointed out that in 2018, Ukraine had both switched underwriters and moved from using a Trustee structure to an Agency form probably because the new underwriters had used an Agency structure in their prior deals. Because they were switching from a Trustee to an Agent, all references to the Trustee had to be removed. But simply removing the Trustee reference without requiring consultation with the investors left control of any changes entirely in the hands of the sovereign. In any event, this landmine is a likely subversive accretion whether initially purposeful or the result of an error that a subsequent sovereign-side lawyer saw no reason to correct.[14]

Errors

Our third category captures those landmines that arose due to errors or blunders. We identify six landmines as errors in our dataset.[15] We focus initially on scope-related error landmines. The Negative Pledge, Cross Default, and *pari passu* clauses of a typical sovereign debt contract are triggered based on an event affecting some other obligation (i.e., the granting of collateral, the occurrence of an event of default, or the payment of money) and

[14] In addition, the timing of this change coincided with a military and economic shock to the country and the move away from an investment bank, VTB. It is also possible that Ukraine, after the Crimean invasion by Russia, became increasingly concerned about the potential for default and wanted language to protect itself from any restructuring that could follow from the default.

[15] The error landmines include the following clauses: *pari passu* Scope, Negative Pledge Scope, Cross Default Scope, Governing Laws Always, Reverse Acceleration, and CAC Strategy Disclosure. See the Appendix for the details describing each of these landmines.

Table 8.4 Error comparison

Clause	Fraction of bonds: 1990–1995	Fraction of bonds: 2020–2022	*p*-value
Cross Default scope	0.260	0.110	0.010
Negative Pledge scope	0.307	0.030	0.000
Pari Passu scope	0.480	0.420	0.429

Note: p-value is from a chi-squared test of the difference between the 1990–1995 and 2020–2022 periods for each clause.

result in a contractual consequence for the debt governed under the contract in question. In a scope-related landmine, the clause fails to define the scope of the other obligations to which the provision applies, potentially leaving the sovereign vulnerable to a claim that the clause applies even to types of obligations of the sovereign (such as the obligation to pay the salary of a state employee) that are unrelated to the sovereign's activities in raising capital from the international market. Such mistakes, at least to the extent they pose a potential risk to the sovereign, should be weeded out by the sovereign's attorneys. Thus, we can predict a diminishing incidence of mistakes over time and a relatively low incidence of scope-related mistakes as a result in 2020–2022.

Three of the six error landmines are scope-related landmines involving the Cross Default, Negative Pledge, and *pari passu* clauses. Table 8.4 compares the incidence for the Negative Pledge Scope, Cross Default Scope, and *pari passu* Scope landmines in the 1990–1995 and 2020–2022 periods.

Unlike subversive accretions, the incidence of these errors diminished over time. The decreasing incidence of Cross Default Scope and Negative Pledge Scope landmines was large in magnitude (drops of 15.0 and 27.7 percentage points, respectively) and statistically significant. This decrease in these error landmines is consistent with the assumption that gurus, working on the sovereign side, weeded out the errors that negatively affected the sovereign.[16] Even if errors are part of the standard form contract, the low incidence of these errors is consistent with the market's ability (at least for the sovereign's side) to correct such mistakes eventually.

[16] The relatively low incidence of such errors is consistent with an equilibrium where such errors arise randomly and the gurus (in particular, the sovereign's attorneys) eventually remove these landmines.

One puzzle in this weeding out process is why the *pari passu* Scope error did not appreciably decrease from 1990–1995 to 2020–2022. One answer might be that that the weeding or persistence of errors depends on how errors originate in the first place. Some errors occur randomly. Here, the passage of time should result in the correction of many of these errors. But errors may also arise through a different process. A change in legal or economic conditions may create a fertile ground for new errors to arise in the process of revising an existing provision or introducing a new term. The more recent the changes, the more prevalent will be errors due to these innovations. Our definition of an innovation error focuses on errors directly related to the innovation itself. But when lawyers begin to change a particular clause for one purpose, other unrelated errors may occur as well. Put another way, once lawyers "open the hood" to repair a clause for one purpose, the chance for unrelated errors being introduced increases—particularly if the lawyers are not experts at understanding the entire document.

To assess the "open the hood" hypothesis, we can look at a time series of bond issuances by Mexico at roughly five-year intervals from 1995 to 2020. While not comprehensive, this time series provides insight into how Mexico modified the *pari passu* clause over time. These modifications correspond to the presence of new errors occurring in the Mexico contract. Recall that these errors arise when the *pari passu* clause fails to limit its scope to external indebtedness that is payable in a foreign currency.

We see from Table 8.5 that Mexico had a *pari passu* clause in each of the offerings we examined from 1995 to 2020. Mexico used the same issuer's counsel and underwriter's counsel in all the offerings. Despite the continuity of law firms, Mexico varied its *pari passu* clause over the years. From 1995 to 2010, it provided a definition limiting the scope of the clause to foreign currency denominated debt. In 1995, the foreign currency scope limitation was specified directly in the *pari passu* clause. From 2000 to 2010, Mexico's clause incorporated the foreign currency scope limitation for "public external indebtedness" contained in the definition found in the Negative Pledge clause for the same contract.

But in response to the Argentine litigation described in Chapter Four, Mexico modified its *pari passu* clause in 2015, specifying that the clause did not require ratable payments. Along with this purposeful change, Mexico embedded a landmine: it omitted the previous reference to a definition that limited the scope of the *pari passu* clause to foreign currency debt. The decision to modify the *pari passu* clause for one purpose (addressing ratable

Table 8.5 Mexico *Pari Passu* time series

Offering date	Pari Passu clause text
November 28, 1995	The Debt Securities will rank pari passu . . . with all other unsecured and unsubordinated obligations of Mexico . . . relating to external indebtedness. "[E]*xternal indebtedness" means any indebtedness for money borrowed which is payable by its terms or at the option of its holder in any currency other than the currency of Mexico* . . . and "indebtedness" means all unsecured and unsubordinated obligations of Mexico in respect of moneys borrowed by Mexico and guaranties of Mexico in respect of moneys borrowed by others.
January 10, 2000	The debt securities will be the direct, general and unconditional external indebtedness of Mexico. They will rank equal in right of payment among themselves and with all Mexico's existing and future unsecured and unsubordinated *public external indebtedness, as defined under "Negative Pledge" below.*
January 4, 2005	[Substantially the same as in 2000].
September 2, 2010	[Substantially the same as in 2000].
February 16, 2015	The debt securities rank and will rank without any preference among themselves and equally with all other *unsubordinated public external indebtedness of Mexico.* It is understood that this provision shall not be construed so as to require Mexico to make payments under the debt securities ratably with payments being made under any other public external indebtedness.
January 31, 2020	[Substantially the same as in 2015].

payments) seems to have simultaneously generated an unrelated error, the removal of the foreign currency debt scope limitation, resulting in a new landmine.

Innovation may thus explain the occurrence of new error-induced landmines and their high incidence in 2020–2022 owing to a relatively recent underlying innovation. But what about the correction process for these innovation-type errors? Another error landmine we found in our sample of sovereign bonds involves the Reverse Acceleration clause. In a typical sovereign bond, the occurrence of an Event of Default generally gives a certain fraction of the holders of the bond (typically 25% in principal amount), the right to accelerate payment if the default event is not cured within a specified time. On occasion, though, there may be circumstances where a minority asks for acceleration but the majority is in the process of working out a deal with the debtor. To protect this circumstance, bonds typically contain a reverse acceleration provision where the majority can reverse the acceleration that a minority have requested. Some bonds, however, appear to subject the Reverse Acceleration clause to a condition precedent that arguably undermines the clause—for example, requiring the sovereign to "cure" the event of default that defeats the purpose of the Reverse Acceleration clause in giving the majority time to work out a deal with the debtor.

The Reverse Acceleration landmine arose with the introduction of collective action clauses (CAC) into the standard form sovereign contract in the early 2000s.[17] In the 2020–2022 period, there is a high incidence of the Reverse Acceleration landmine—86% of our bonds contained the landmine. As an example of the path of an innovation error for a particular sovereign, we examined the Reverse Acceleration clause for Italy at approximately five-year intervals from 2000 to 2020. Table 8.6 shows how Italy moved from a unanimity action clause (UAC) in 2000 to a CAC by 2005. Italy used a CAC from 2005 to 2019. Then, in 2020, Italy adopted a modified CAC with specific provisions that allow for the aggregation of votes across different Italian bonds.[18] Table 8.6 also shows the changes in the Reverse Acceleration clause that correspond to the modification clause in each Italian offering.

When Italy used a UAC in 2000, the Reverse Acceleration clause allows the sovereign to reverse any acceleration if the sovereign has "cured all defaults." Because each bondholder in a UAC regime may individually seek to accelerate payment upon a default in payment, the requirement of "cure" simply provides that the default event applies unless there no longer is a default (i.e., it has been cured). Because a UAC *already* gives each creditor the power to act as a holdout, requiring a "cure" to each creditor does not change the allocation of power to potential holdouts.

But when Italy shifted to a CAC in 2005, the CAC reduced the power of potential holdouts. The Reverse Acceleration clause accordingly took on greater importance. Reverse acceleration in the context of a CAC allows a majority of creditors to pause a default in order to facilitate a deal for the sovereign to resume making restructured payments. Requiring the sovereign to cure the event of default by paying the full amount of a debt to all the creditors defeats the purpose of the clause. A single holdout could resist any

[17] The Appendix provides an explanation of these landmines.

[18] Across these offerings, Italy used the same issuer's counsel (its in-house lawyers) and the same underwriter's counsel (Skadden Arps).

Table 8.6 Italy Collective Action Clause innovation error time series

Offering date	Modification	Reverse Acceleration
September 6, 2000	UAC	Principal may be declared due and payable if a holder gives a written demand to us and the fiscal agent, unless we have *cured all defaults* prior to receipt of the demand.
January 13, 2005	CAC	The holders of at least 66.67% of the aggregate principal amount outstanding of the debt securities may rescind a declaration of acceleration *if the event or events of default giving rise to the declaration have been cured or waived.*
January 19, 2010	CAC	[Substantially the same as in 2015].
October 10, 2019	CAC	The holders of more than 50 per cent of the aggregate principal amount outstanding of the Notes may rescind or annul a notice of acceleration.
November 18, 2020	CAC Aggregation	[Substantially the same as in 2019].
April 28, 2021	CAC Aggregation	[Substantially the same as in 2019].

attempts to reverse the acceleration if a "cure" of the default is required before the reversal of the acceleration can occur. This new landmine was likely an innovation error.

Italy eventually recognized their error with the Reverse Acceleration clause. In 2019 and thereafter, Italy's clause no longer requires that the issuer "cures" the default or that there must be a "waiver" of the default before a majority of the outstanding debt may reverse acceleration.[19] The move to correct this innovation error occurred after several years, perhaps after Italy's lawyers learned of the error from other sovereign deals.

Postscript: When Do Landmines Get Priced?

Theory tells us that contractual landmines are unicorns. They should not exist, and empirical testing using price data would show them to be mirages. If a landmine confers an ex post advantage to one party or the other,

[19] There was no change in Italy's issuer's or underwriter's counsel.

sophisticated contracting parties will incorporate that into the price at the time the contract is made.

Since landmines of the type we have described impose potential costs upon default, the value to the parties at the time of contracting will be negative. Landmines do not increase value but serve only to transfer value between parties at the time of default. This transfer is not cost free; litigation and negotiation costs are incurred as well as costs associated with delaying a restructuring. Accordingly, contracts that retain value-reducing landmines should incur a price penalty, particularly in a competitive and thick market, such as the market for sovereign debt. This pricing penalty should result in competitive market forces eliminating landmines over time. A believer in the efficiency of the competitive market would, therefore, take the view that contractual landmines are a mirage. Yet, landmines do exist in sovereign bond contracts. Why aren't the landmines priced ex ante? One answer is that the classic pricing story does not apply to a market such as that for sovereign bonds.

This classic pricing story does not apply to a market where investors systematically ignore linguistic anomalies in contractual terms. If the investors only care about having the standard "market" clauses but otherwise ignore the precise language in these clauses, they will not price the failure to remove landmines, even if removal would increase the expected contractual surplus. Investors' neglect of landmines in the contract is rational. The cost to investors to learn about the landmines and effect their removal would significantly exceed any pricing penalty. Only expert lawyers can cost-effectively find and remove dangerous language that creates landmine risk. Novice lawyers attempting such a fix not only bear higher costs but also run the risk of adding new landmines. Moreover, the immediate clients, the debt manager (or the investment bank), will not pay for removal efforts since their time horizon likely will not encompass any later need to restructure the debt. And if lawyers, responding to the incentives of their immediate clients do not act to remove landmines, the landmines will remain notwithstanding the highly competitive market. This straightforward agency cost story thus appears to explain in theory the prevalence and persistence of landmines in the sovereign debt market.

In a world in which everyone sees themselves as using a "market" set of terms, even motivated sovereigns with expert lawyers may not remove all landmines from their contracts unilaterally. Individual deviations from the artifact contract to remove a landmine might send a negative signal. Investors are prompted to ask why this proposed contract deviates from "market." At a minimum, a proposed deviation from the market standard will delay the deal as parties pause to assess the changes in language; more lawyers are consulted, placement is delayed, and ultimately borrowing costs are increased all in service of an uncertain risk of future litigation. From the perspective of the sovereign's finance ministry, an increase in borrowing costs to revise several words in a boilerplate clause that others in the market are using without revision is more costly than the failure to correct a landmine in a commonly used version of the clause. In a sense, everyone in the market accepts the use of a flawed standard form; one that they know is likely to be vulnerable thereafter to transactions costs when litigating lawyers fight about the meaning of the flawed terms.

A Test of Pricing

Because the claim that landmines are *not* priced ex ante is significant to the story of why landmines persist, we provide a pricing test. In an ideal pricing test, one could compare the price of two otherwise identical sovereign bonds issued at the same time that differ in only one respect: one bond has a landmine and the other does not. No one has the data to implement this test, and it runs afoul of the fact that landmines are obscure. To run a test, then, we need a landmine that is in some bonds and not others, and we need an event that makes the market aware of the landmine.

Somewhat inadvertently, we were able to take advantage of a pricing experiment. The technical details are published in an article with our coauthors, Ugo Panizza and Mark Weidemaier.[20] Below, we describe the basics of what we did and what we found.

Our inadvertent experiment was the product of one of us (in collaboration with Mark) writing several short pieces in FT Alphaville (and producing a few podcasts) about landmines we believed were in bonds for Ghana and Sri Lanka, two countries in financial distress at the time. Had the market been pricing the presence of these landmines, our articles should have had

[20] *See* Stephen J. Choi, Mitu Gulati, Ugo Panizza, Robert E. Scott, & W. Mark C. Weidemaier, *Obscure Contract Terms: An Inadvertent Pricing Experiment*, 19 Cap. Mkts L. J. 230 (2024); Robin Wigglesworth, *Do Investors Actually Read Bond Docs: An Accidental FT Alphaville Experiment*, FT Alphaville (Apr. 24, 2024).

no effect on market prices of the bonds with the landmines (in comparison to the bonds without landmines for those same issuers).

We then compared prices across time for the two bonds with similar maturities for the same sovereign that differed in one (but perhaps not the only) important respect: one bond has a landmine (the treatment bond) and the other did not (the control bond). We focused on the price difference between the treatment and control bonds both before and after our podcasts and articles. This difference could be due to the landmine or to unrelated factors. Crucially, we used the set of shock events to the market (articles/podcasts) that we posited acted as a public announcement to the market about the existence of a landmine in the treatment bond. We used a measure of the *relative* price change for the treatment and control bonds to gauge the market's price response to the landmine.

We assumed that news of the existence of a landmine would not affect the market price of the treatment bond if the market was already continuously pricing in the value of the landmine. But if the market was not yet pricing the presence of the landmine, then news of the existence of a landmine would move the market price of the treatment bond relative to the control bond. This movement will be particularly acute for sovereigns near default. Then, if we found that the market was not pricing in a landmine as a sovereign neared default, it is likely that the market also did not price the landmine at the time of the bond's issuance. The relative price response of the treatment bond with the landmine compared to the control bond without a landmine on the date when news of the landmine was made public provided a test of (a) how the market viewed the ex post value of the landmine once a sovereign is in distress and (b) the lack of fully informed ex ante pricing of the landmine prior to the public announcement.

Our two sets of experiments told the same story. Disclosure of the landmine produced a significant relative price movement between the treatment and control bonds in the direction one would predict if the landmine existed but was not priced ex ante.[21] The lack of pricing prior to the public announcements and as a sovereign nears default was consistent with a lack of pricing at the time of the issuance of the bonds. We started with a simple question: Are landmines priced at the time of issuance purely by virtue of their presence in the contracts? The answer from this experiment was,

[21] Choi et al., *id.*

"No." Only later, once the sovereign neared default, and the existence of the landmines was made public, did the market price the landmines.

* * *

The results from our analysis of the prevalence and persistence of landmines shed light on the predictions developed in Chapter Seven. A sample of current sovereign bond contracts reveals numerous instances of harmful landmines—vague and apparently purposeful changes to standard language that increases a creditor's nonpayment risk, coupled with errors in expression and drafting and a continuing use of terms that were historically imported from corporate transactions. These landmines differ from each other in important respects: purposeful changes to the standard form reflect careful lawyering on behalf of sovereign clients, while errors that only benefit subsequent activists reflect haste in adapting precedents to new transactions. The market for sovereign bond lawyers, divided between experts and novices, provides at least a partial explanation for why each of these quite different landmine types can be found in a single contract. Together with the asymmetry in the power to control the drafting process between sovereign's counsel and underwriter's counsel, these market forces negatively impact contract design.

Our findings suggest reasons to doubt the standard view that the terms in large market commercial contracts are finely tuned representations of the *parties'* ex ante intentions. Assumptions about the efficiency of market contracts and the extent to which they reflect the shared intentions of the contracting parties must account for the distortion that these lawyer-side agency costs have on the contract production process in these markets.

PART III

OTHER ARTIFACTS

Lawyers, Legal Culture, and Landmines

Chapter Nine
Landmines All the Way Down

Introduction

Part III pivots away from the large and liquid sovereign debt market. As we turn to other markets where commercial contracting is prevalent, we ask whether the landmine problem is unique to sovereign debt. On the one hand, the answer is clearly, No: we find landmines in every other setting we study. Moreover, the landmines we find in these other settings are familiar: we find historical holdovers, subversive accretions, and simple errors; the same categorizations that we examined in detail in the sovereign bond market. Upon reflection, we should have expected that to be so. The paradox of contract production—where the efficiencies unique to standardization inevitably lead to landmines—exists in commercial contracts of every type. But on the other hand, the lifecycle of the landmines changes from market to market. We had expected to see some variation across types of contracting; we thought we would see fewer landmines in settings where agency problems and the pressures of a secondary market were not as acute as in sovereign debt. And, we were not altogether wrong: those factors matter. But other factors that we would not have anticipated, such as the culture of the drafting lawyers, turn out to be important determinants of the shape of landmines as well.

The Contracting Continuum

Our exploration of landmines in other commercial markets begins with a single question: Can contracting parties in these other settings exploit production efficiencies without degrading the contract terms that motivate performance?

We can best grapple with this question by formally separating the contracting process into two stages. At the design stage, parties negotiate to reach agreement on the assignment of duties and the allocation of risks; the

Contract Hazards. Stephen J. Choi, Mitu Gulati, and Robert E. Scott, Oxford University Press.
 DOI: 10.1093/9780197821770.003.0009

substance of the exchange that will maximize their expected joint surplus. At the production stage, parties reduce that "agreement" to a "contract" by drafting the "formulations" of contract terms that collectively communicate that agreement to each other and to courts. Standardization plays an outsized role in this formulation process. Using a standard form expression of a substantive entitlement reduces the effort costs of formulating that expression individually. Moreover, standardization has another value: a standard term that has been used successfully in the past reflects the learning and experience of many parties in formulating similar agreements that courts have interpreted correctly per the parties' intentions. This standard formulation has been "tested" over time and, in theory, such standard terms are better than individually crafted ones at implementing a particular design. But the question is whether these benefits necessarily come with a cost: Do contracting parties inevitably settle for the standard formulation even if it doesn't fit their design goals?

To begin to answer that question, imagine a production continuum with contracting that takes place in a thick liquid market (such as sovereign debt) at one pole and with individualized, bespoke contracting in thin markets at the other. At the pole represented by the now familiar sovereign debt contract, we have seen how traders exploit the economies from standardizing the production of all the contracts in the market. Economies of scale result in contracts that address a wide range of contractual contingencies by accumulating universally adopted boilerplate terms. This facilitates pricing and trades in the underlying assets covered by the contracts and imposes a high cost on those that do not use the standard form. These costs further tilt the parties in this market to retain the boilerplate terms. The terms themselves are resistant to attempts to eliminate mutations or adapt to changed conditions: production efficiency is maximized in the world of sovereign debt at the cost of inefficiencies in design.

But what about the bespoke transaction at the other pole of the production continuum? Consider a one-time sale to a buyer of a seller's interest in specified oil and gas properties.[1] The lawyers agree upon and then formulate the terms necessary to resolve the critical issues of price, quantity, and performance, including the payment schedule for the purchase price,

[1] *See, e.g.*, the Purchase and Sale Agreement entered into on April 19, 2016, by and among BSM Energy LP, a Texas limited partnership, Crux Energy, LP, a Texas limited partnership, Zaniah Energy, LP, a Texas limited partnership, and Callon Petroleum Operating Company, a Delaware corporation and Callon Petroleum Company, a Delaware corporation (Available on Westlaw's What's Market database).

valuing royalty income, estimating future maintenance costs, allocating tax advantages, and so on. Since the transaction is one of a kind, the parties' production cost considerations are limited to the costs of formulating the terms relevant for that contract. These costs may cause the parties not to allocate risks for all contingencies, but risks that are allocated are tailored to the particular transaction. In theory, this contract should not be plagued by obsolete terms, mutated terms, or holdover terms that lack meaning: design efficiency is maximized for the specified terms but at a high per contract production cost.

But this description of a completely customized contract is more myth than reality. The truly bespoke commercial contract perhaps existed for a time in the mid-nineteenth century as contract law was evolving. Consider for example, *White v. Toncray*, the first case in the United States to adjudicate an open-quantity contract.[2] The handwritten contract consisted of three terms. The seller agreed to provide the buyer "between 1,200 and 5,000 barrels of salt," at the "rates of fifty cents a bushel," and delivery "at seller's place of business within six months" from the date of contracting. The contract was incomplete in that many future contingencies were unaddressed. This was the common feature in nineteenth-century bespoke commercial contracts. Courts were left with the task of filling the gaps with appropriate default rules.

The dispute in *White* focused on one of these gaps: Which party—the seller or buyer—could invoke the contract's flexible quantity term? The Virginia Supreme Court of Appeals held that the buyer, being in the best position to determine its needs, should be permitted to decide the quantity that the seller was required to provide.[3] For the next one hundred years, common law courts continued to fill similar gaps in incomplete bespoke contracts with legal default rules. But as courts continued filling the gaps in incomplete contracts, they invited parties with different preferences to contract out and design their own allocation of risks. And parties did so. How? By using customary language that had proven successful in other cases for signaling an opt out. This customary language, used to displace common law rules, formed the basis for a set of standardized terms used even in bespoke one-on-one contracting.

[2] *White v. Toncray*, 36 Va. at 353–354 (1838).

[3] *Id.* at 354-355 ("[I]n general, where a latitude is given in contracts of this description, the right to fix the quantum must depend upon the question,—what is the principal motive to the contract? [A]nd he whose concern constitutes that motive, must have the election in preference to the other party.")

Today parties cannot escape the gravitational pull of standardization even in the most personalized contracting environment. Bespoke contracting parties can save production costs by using standardized language that was used by parties in previous transactions to opt out of disfavored court supplied default rules. As a result, most if not all contemporary commercial contracts have language that is highly standardized and repeated in one form or another from contract to contract. Features of the contract as artifact can be found throughout the contractual space.

Quasi-Bespoke Commercial Contracts

Commercial contracts in thin markets are better understood, therefore, as "quasi-bespoke." They are one-off deals that are highly negotiated, reflecting substantial efforts in contract design for the terms most relevant for the specific transaction. But portions of the contract are historical artifacts: standard language borrowed from prior transactions that is used to opt out of common default rules that are ill-suited for these commercial contracts. This includes standardized choice of law and choice of forum clauses replacing common law jurisdictional rules, as well as remedy limitations that displace common law damages rules. These standardized terms are attractive to the drafting lawyer: a provision widely used by others inspires confidence and measurably reduces the cost of formulating an alternative. There will be negotiations over price and over many other terms in the quasi-bespoke contract but the balance of the contract will be borrowed without careful scrutiny from earlier but unrelated transactions.[4]

[4] For readers who want yet more about sovereign bonds, we have seen examples of landmines in bespoke contracts in sovereign guarantee bonds, such as the infamous World Bank guarantee for Ghana. The guarantee portions of this bond was specially designed for this transaction: sovereign guarantee contracts such as these are not standard products; they have to be specially tailored to the transactions in question. In the case of the World Bank guarantee, separate lawyers were hired to draft the guarantee portion of the bond. And they did that. But the lawyers drafting the main portion of the bond apparently failed to coordinate with those doing the guarantee and failed to modify their portion of the contract to adjust for the guarantee. The result is a landmine in a transaction that combines standard and bespoke language. *See* Mark Weidemaier & Mitu Gulati, *FUD and the Ghana 2030 Bond*, FT Alphaville (Nov. 29, 2022). There are other examples of sovereign debt transactions that were bespoke going awry because the drafters erred in the bespoke aspects of the bonds. Among these are the Argentine FRAN bonds and its GDP Warrants. For podcast discussions of each of these landmines, see Mark Weidemaier & Mitu Gulati, *What Is the FRAN?*, Clauses and Controversies (Apple Podcasts) (Nov. 13, 2023); Mark Weidemaier & Mitu Gulati, *Unpacking the Argentine GDP Warrants Case*, Clauses and Controversies (Apple Podcasts) (Aug. 7, 2023).

Efficient design theory holds that any mutations to the standard language in these quasi-bespoke contracts will be scrubbed clean by successive generations of transactional lawyers: they will update language for their own deals to accommodate changes in legal or economic conditions, and clean up errors and ambiguities in the standard form. We have already seen that Smith and Warner's axiom is violated in the thick sovereign bond market. But the axiom doesn't hold even in the thin market of the quasi-bespoke transaction. Consider the agreement referenced earlier of the one-time purchase and sale of oil and gas properties. That contract contained a common standardized exclusion clause that is designed, in theory, to replace the regnant default rule that assigns liability for breach of contract for *all* reasonably foreseeable damages to the seller.[5] The clause reads in part:

> *[Seller's] damages shall not include any loss of profits that are consequential, indirect or special, or other consequential damages suffered by the [Buyer], nor any punitive damages.*

The design objectives of the parties in negotiating for this clause are clear. The common law default rule fails to account for the buyer's ability to bear the risk of certain losses that may result from breach better than the seller. Typically, the seller, as the party in control of its own performance, is best able to insure against the risk of defects in the promised quality of the contracted for goods or services and thus will agree to bear those "loss of bargain" risks. But buyers, who have some control over the uses to which they put the seller's goods or services, are better able to reduce either the likelihood or the impact of other losses as long as they are reasonably foreseeable: buyers can insure against those losses more cheaply than can the seller. By opting out of the default rule and allocating foreseeable losses beyond the loss of bargain to the buyer, the parties can draft a contract that effectively reduces the joint cost of future risks and thereby increases the joint value of the contract for both parties. The clause, then, is an effort to implement this design objective: opting out of the default rule permits a more efficient allocation of future risks.

[5] This default rule derived from the venerated case of *Hadley v. Baxendale,* 29 EXCH. 341 (1854) that limited a seller's damage liability for breach of contract to those losses that were reasonably foreseeable at the time of contract. For a history of the *Hadley* v. *Baxendale* rule and its evolution, see Wayne R. Barnes, *Hadley v. Baxendale and Other Borrowings from the Civil Law,* 11 Tex. Wesleyan L. Rev. 627 (2005).

What is the problem with using this standardized version of a damage exclusion clause? The same words and phrases are repeated virtually verbatim in thousands of commercial contracts where buyers contract to limit their liability in this way. The problem is that each of these terms have been interpreted differently by different courts: as a consequence, the meaning of the clause is ambiguous and imprecise; replete with undefined words. And as more courts rule on standard exclusion clauses, the confusion over what the case law really says about the ambiguous and unclear language only increases. In the end, the standard clause fails to express the design objective clearly and succinctly and thus often risks a lawsuit to determine what the parties were attempting to accomplish.

To point out just a few problems: punitive damages cannot be recovered in contract so that language is an unnecessary encrustation, the words "special" or "indirect" have no understood meaning in contract damages doctrine, and the phrase "consequential damages" is itself an ambiguous generalization. Consequential to what event? Unforeseeable consequences would be excluded under the common law rule but foreseeable consequences of the breach could be recovered by a buyer. Does the clause mean to exclude both?[6]

There is a justification for a well-drafted exclusion clause, but not this one. Yet, parties often resort to borrowing unclear boilerplate language to express terms that are only relevant if the contract is breached (e.g., choice of law, jurisdiction, and limitations of liability). There is reason for doing this, and it implicates yet another agency problem. Although each of these terms might appear simple on its face, each connects to changing bodies of law such as *Conflicts of Laws* or *Remedies* about which most transactional lawyers have only a passing familiarity.[7] When clients are eager for a transaction to be

[6] For a discussion of these and other problems with many of the contractual formulations of an exclusion clause in the private M&A context in particular, see Glenn D. West & Sara G. Duran, *Reassessing the "Consequences" of Consequential Damages Waivers in Acquisition Agreements*, 63 Bus. Law. 777 (2008); Glenn D. West, *Consequential Damages Redux: An Updated Study of the Ubiquitous and Problematic "Excluded Losses" Provision in Private Company Acquisition Agreements*, 70 Bus. Law. 971 (2015).

[7] On landmines in choice of law and forum selection clauses, John Coyle's work is exemplary. In a recent blog post pointing out the numerous problems in Microsoft's standard form choice of law and jurisdiction clauses, he noted: "Reading the clause for [Microsoft's deals in] Myanmar is like watching a traffic accident unfold in real time." John F. Coyle, *Microsoft Contract Day 2025*, Transnational Litigation Blog (June 12, 2025). *See also* John F. Coyle, *Short History of the Choice of Law Clause*, 91 U. Colo. L. Rev. 1147 (2020); John F. Coyle, *The Puzzle of Floating Forum Selection Clauses*, 56 NYU. J. Int'l L. & Pol. 183 (2024); John F. Coyle, *The Mystery of the Missing Choice-of-Law Clause*, 56 U.C. Davis L. Rev. 707 (2022); John F. Coyle, *"Contractually Valid" Forum Selection Clauses*, 108 Iowa L. Rev. 127 (2022). On stickiness with dispute resolution clauses, see Julian Nyarko, *Stickiness and Incomplete Contracts*, 88 U. Chi. L. Rev. 1 (2021).

done quickly, few drafters understand the complex contract law rules governing damages or choice of law well enough to readily craft a defined term that is compatible with contemporary case law. In the end, many transactional lawyers elect instead to borrow ambiguous terminology from an earlier document despite the dodgy language. In this way, the bespoke contract embodies portions that are artifacts and is potentially subject to the same landmine problems we have identified earlier. Production *inefficiency* in the bespoke situation, just as production *efficiency* in the thick market, thus leads to the use of flawed standardized language.

Optimizing Between Design and Production

To frame the project going forward, we have described in some detail the poles of a continuum formed by thin market contracting at one end and thick market contracting at the other end. In either market, the reliance on a core artifact necessarily leads to terms that may not fit the preferences of the specific contracting parties and with language that contains potential landmines.

As a first cut, this analysis suggests that landmines will occur across the contractual continuum but that the prevalence and persistence of landmines will vary as contracts are examined in different markets that fall along this continuum. The largest liquid markets—including sovereign and corporate bonds—likely have the largest number of landmines due to the markets' pervasive reliance on historic holdover terms that produce contractual rigidity. The liquidity of these contracts in the secondary market depends on the faithful reproduction of standard terms that have been used in many prior transactions. It is this ability to trade the contract readily that our interviewers mean when they refer to the key standard terms as "market."

The quasi-bespoke contract form falls at the lower end of the continuum. These contracts will contain many individually negotiated terms but features of the contract as artifact remain. Standardized language is most prevalent in the terms that parties have used to opt out of disfavored default rules. And so, landmines will be found in these contracts as long as drafters continue to reject these defaults. However, these landmines should be less prevalent in number and in persistence than those found in large market transactions. We explore this claim in Chapter Ten.

The remaining questions, therefore, turn on understanding markets that fall in spaces between these two poles where parties might have an opportunity to optimize total contracting costs by trading off the costs of contract production and contract design. We will examine two such markets.

In Chapters Eleven and Twelve, we look into the world of Mergers and Acquisitions (M&A) agreements. We focus in particular on private deals, an environment with sophisticated parties with the resources and, on occasion, the motivation to craft bespoke contracts. The market also includes repeat players, including private equity funds and their law firms, who need to do deals quickly and who benefit from employing standardized terms across deals that provide greater certainty and reduced transaction costs. In such a market, parties should value both the option to employ bespoke terms and the ability to draw upon a pool of standardized terms. With such a preference, we might expect a market structure that allows for the prevalence of standardized terms as well as the freedom for individual actors to employ their own bespoke terms.

In Chapter Thirteen, we move to the world of private equity sponsors and syndicated leveraged loans, a market that falls somewhere between M&A and sovereign debt on our continuum. As we saw in Chapter Three, this market has recently been roiled by aggressive actions by debtors and activist creditors. By collaborating with private equity sponsors, activist creditors can exploit loopholes in the standard loan contract and secure priority positions in the debtor's collateral at the expense of other creditors. Here, a robust secondary market supports a high degree of standardization of terms that resist modification. Passive investors who are damaged by these actions frequently fail to block these liability management transactions.

The Collective Action Problem

The appearance of a landmine in any given commercial contract is not an occasion for general alarm. Even Smith and Warner's famous axiom, on which rests the claim of efficient debt contracting, recognizes that occasional landmines may arise, but only then to die out. It is the persistence issue, therefore, that lies at the root of the landmine problem. Given the nontrivial possibility that a court may err in interpreting terms that are embedded with landmines, commercial parties have incentives in all these markets to ensure that their standardized contract terms are continually revised. Updating the standard terms in these markets is essential to preserving a common *and contemporary* meaning. Despite these incentives, however, we now have evidence that parties in readily fail to convert standardized terms into new and efficient formulations.[8] Inertia results from costs that collectively deter individual participants in the market from revising the standard terms.[9] Since the production of network externalities is a primary value of standardized contracts, particularly in these large liquid markets, contract terms are slow to change, even after market participants identify costly errors and ambiguities.[10]

There is a solution to the impediments that prevent individual traders in commercial markets from repairing landmines. If the market participants acted together, they could coordinate to create a network of traders and their lawyers who collectively advance new standard market terms with clear meaning and purpose. But creating a functioning network that can coordinate the efforts of all participants is very challenging. Consider once again the continuum between the poles of thick markets and thin quasi-bespoke markets. At the thick market pole, we find first the sovereign debt market where the fourteen-year battle over the meaning of the *pari passu* clause suggests there are significant impediments to coordination. As detailed in Chapter Four, the clause remained unchanged in all sovereign debt contracts for over a decade even after a court in Brussels endorsed the claim of activist creditors to full payment on their debt.[11] Even after the more authoritative rulings by federal courts in New York[12] put the multitrillion dollar bond market at real risk, revisions to the language of the *pari passu* term did not begin until more than three years after the federal courts had ruled.[13]

The *pari passu* story demonstrates two things: First, the costs are high when private parties fail to revise boilerplate clauses embedded with landmines. Retaining an historical holdover rather than developing an apt

[8] *See* Chapter Eight, *supra* (citing research) and Stephen J. Choi, Mitu Gulati, & Robert E. Scott, *Variation in Boilerplate: Rational Design or Random Mutation?*, 20 Am. L & Econ. Rev. 1 (2017).

[9] Anna Gelpern, Mitu Gulati, & Jeromin Zettelmeyer, *If Boilerplate Could Talk*, 44 L. & Soc. Inquiry 617 (2019); Elizabeth de Fontenay, Josefin Meyer, & Mitu Gulati, *The Sovereign Debt Listing Puzzle*, 71 Ox. Econ. Papers 472 (2019).

[10] For discussion, see Marcel Kahan & Michael Klausner, *Standardization and Innovation in Corporate Contracting (or "The Economics of Boilerplate")*, 83 Va. L. Rev. 713 (1997); Marcel Kahan & Michael Klausner, *Path Dependence in Corporate Contracting: Increasing Returns, Herd Behavior and Cognitive Biases*, 74 Wash U. L. Q. 347 (1996).

[11] *See* Mitu Gulati & Robert E. Scott, The Three and a Half Minute Transaction: Boilerplate and the Limits of Contract Design 53–119 (University of Chicago Press, 2013).

[12] *NML Capital, Ltd. v. Republic of Argentina*, No. 08 Civ. 6978, 2011 WL 9522565, at *2–3 (S.D.N.Y. Dec. 7, 2011), *aff'd* 699 F.3d 246 (2d Cir. 2012), *aff'd* 727 F.3d 230 (2d Cir. 2013).

[13] Choi, Gulati, & Scott, *Variation in Boilerplate*, *supra* note 8; Stephen J. Choi, Mitu Gulati, & Robert E. Scott, *The Black Hole Problem in Commercial Boilerplate*, 67 Duke L. J. 1 (2017).

alternative creates opportunities for strategic litigation.[14] Second, despite the high costs, parties in these markets can be trapped in inefficient contracting equilibria for long periods of time. Changing a core term puts the status of the contract as artifact at risk. Too much change and the contract will be viewed as idiosyncratic, measurably increasing learning costs for investors. As a consequence, the market is likely to punish idiosyncratic terms by imposing a price penalty. In the absence of any institutional mechanism, a large market may simply lack the capacity to solve its coordination problem readily.[15]

Paradoxically, coordination failure can also exist at the thin market pole of the continuum, where parties are negotiating quasi-bespoke contracts. Although individual bespoke contractors have ready access to precedents, either in the form of contracts used by other drafters or commercially supplied model contract terms, they are generally reliant on those other sources to update the terms appropriately. If that fails, there are few if any market participants around whom an informal network can develop that might promote updating the obsolete terms used in these one-off contracts.

This raises a further question: Might coordination networks develop more readily in markets where contracting parties trade information on strategies for revising risky terms? In Chapters Eleven and Twelve, we investigate the hypothesis that lawyers drafting M&A purchase agreements are able to respond in a coordinated way to new developments in the law and do so in an "organic" fashion.[16] But before we examine whether M&A drafters can overcome the collective action problems that impede efficient contracting elsewhere, we turn first in Chapter Ten to document the existence of persistent landmines even in the environment characterized by quasi-bespoke contracting.

[14] *See* Lucy McNulty, *The Future for Pari Passu*, 32 INT'L FIN. L. REV. 6, 19–20 (2013) (explaining that the market agreed on the need for change but could not overcome the challenges of moving to new standard).

[15] *See* Alan Schwartz & Robert E. Scott, *Obsolescence: The Intractable Production Problem in Contract Law*, 121 COLUM. L. REV. 1659 (2020).

[16] For prior work that studies advisory networks as conduits for information transfer and coordination among deal lawyers, see Kristina Bishop, Matthew Jennejohn, & Cree Jones, *Top Ups and "Telephone,"* BYU Working Paper (2022); Matthew Jennejohn, Julian Nyarko, & Eric Talley, *Contractual Evolution*, 89 U. CHI. L. REV. 901 (2021); Matthew Jennejohn, *The Architecture of Contract Innovation*, 59 BOSTON COLLEGE L. REV. 1 (2018).

Chapter Ten
Landmines in Bespoke Contracts

Introduction

Chapter Nine framed the landmine problem in terms of a continuum of contracting types, ranging from thick market contracts characterized by sovereign and corporate bonds to purely bespoke contracts, the one-off highly customized deals that have been the idealization of contract for many contract theorists. Yet, a look into the history of contract law persuaded us that the purely bespoke contract, with all terms custom drafted, disappeared after the early period of commercial contracting in the nineteenth century. Today, even commercial contracts made in thin markets are replete with standardized clauses: drafting a contract for a new type of deal still involves the borrowing of standard terms; albeit from other, adjacent, deals. Terms such as governing law, jurisdiction, and liability limitations, are among those that are unlikely to be individually drafted even for an entirely new transaction. They will be copied from other deals and then modified, but if that replication process fails to update the obsolete language, landmines can and will arise.

A Prototype: The Commercial Agreement

In terms of our contracting continuum, commercial agreements sit at the thin end of the continuum opposite from sovereign debt. These agreements cover a range of topics including joint venture research collaborations, supply and distribution agreements, and one-time sales of specific assets.

The "commercial agreements" that we examine in this chapter are between sophisticated, business-oriented parties. The contracting parties are typically large entities that do not face the problems that affect dispersed creditors purchasing sovereign bonds but neither are they members of any informal network that shares information on best contracting practices. These firms have the resources to hire large law firms to negotiate and draft the contractual

Contract Hazards. Stephen J. Choi, Mitu Gulati, and Robert E. Scott, Oxford University Press.
 DOI: 10.1093/9780197821770.003.0010

language governing their agreements. As principals, the parties in a commercial agreement can convey their preferences to and monitor their attorneys for compliance with these preferences in drafting contracts.

But having the resources to negotiate and draft bespoke contractual language does not mean that the principals and their attorneys will choose to do so. Drafting a new contract from scratch is costly, including the costs of selecting appropriate language to formulate the parties agreement, as well as the uncertainty costs of how a future court will interpret this language if a dispute arises. While the parties may craft bespoke language for the price and other terms they care most about, formulation costs will push the parties to use boilerplate language for other, non-price terms such as the choice of law or limitation of liability provisions.

The wide variety of commercial agreements necessarily reduces the pool of similar contracts from which drafting attorneys may find useful precedents. A drafter dealing with an isolated commercial agreement is more likely to be ignorant of how other lawyers formulate bespoke terms for their contracts because of the dissimilarity of the transactions. This in turn raises the cost for any drafting lawyer who chooses to use original language to formulate the contract's non-price terms. Moreover, the drafting lawyer faces resistance should they attempt to charge the client for the costs of originality that could have been avoided by choosing serviceable language drawn from other sources.

Unfortunately, the range of choices among these other sources is constrained. There are few if any entities in the market who can coordinate efforts among the disparate attorneys drafting specific types of agreements. The drafting lawyers who search for model language thus often must choose between an ill-fitting precedent in their own archives or a commercially available, one-size-fits-all collection of contract terms. Far from being the contracting ideal, the bespoke context can lead to a *decentralized* form of robotically repeated boilerplate, specific to particular lawyers and their law firms, one that rarely changes and thus becomes embedded over time with outdated and possibly value-decreasing landmines.

The Confusion Over "Consequential" Damages

Our starting point for looking beyond the thick market context was a blog post by contracts guru Glenn West whom we met in Chapter Three. You will recall that Glenn is a retired partner from the Weil Gotschal law firm in Dallas, where he specialized in private equity and M&A deals. He is unusual among transactional lawyers in many ways, including that he reads contract clauses for fun and has an encyclopedic knowledge of the relevant (and irrelevant) case law. Glenn's extensive writing about contract terms was our introduction to landmines in the M&A world.

In his writing, Glenn had expressed dismay at the blind copying and repetition of phrases in consequential damages exclusion clauses.[1] His focus was on M&A agreements, but he suggested that these problems existed in other areas of contracting as well. What particularly interested us was his surmise that the problematic language had even migrated into the world of bespoke commercial agreements. Other prominent practitioners commented as well on the confusion surrounding boilerplate provisions purporting to exclude consequential damages. These problematic formulations had proved hard to excise from market practices despite the efforts of the experts in the field to do so.

As discussed in Chapter Nine, the standard default rule in American contract law is that the seller of goods or services is liable for all the reasonably foreseeable damages that follow from the seller's breach of contract.[2] Coupled with the trend in contract law to relax the definition of "foreseeable,"[3] the default rule as applied imposes the risk of certain losses for breach of contract on the supplier of goods or services that the parties often would prefer to allocate to the purchaser. The purchaser is generally better able to take precautions to avoid or reduce the risk of losses that are, at least in part, within its control. A defective widget may explode and cause a fire in a buyer's plant causing extensive damage to the facility. The buyer is typically able to more cheaply insure against such losses and also may be better able to limit the damage should such an explosion occur. For that reason, parties to commercial agreements often opt out of the default rule: consequential damage waivers are ubiquitous. These waivers, sometimes referred to by practitioners as "no consequential damages" (NCD) clauses, divide the risk of losses from breach of contract *between* the parties. The seller retains the risk of defects

[1] Among Glenn's blog posts on the topic are, Glenn West, *Lost Profits May or May Not be Consequential Damages*, Weil Private Equity Blog (July 11, 2023); Glenn West, *Excluded Loss Provisions and the Danger of Contractually Slaying Mythical Dragons*, Weil Private Equity Blog (Dec. 13, 2021).

[2] *See* UCC Section 2-714(1),(3) & 2-715(2).

[3] *See* Richard Epstein, *Beyond Foreseeability: Consequential Damages in the Law of Contract*, 18 J. Legal Stud. 105 (1989).

in the contracted for goods or services—losses that deprive the buyer of the loss of its bargain.[4] The buyer, in turn, accepts the risk of any collateral losses beyond loss of bargain by agreeing to an NCD clause. The failure of drafting lawyers to explicitly explain this distinction in their contracts has led to confusion over the extent and meaning of these "excluded losses."

The problem is that drafters do not use tailored language to clearly delineate this division of responsibility. Rather, they rely on standardized language centered on the generic word "consequential" that courts have interpreted in different ways. The absence of any judicial consensus on the scope of the term "consequential" should, in theory, motivate drafters to provide a clear, bespoke explanation of those losses that are allocated to the buyer. Instead, drafters have attempted to define "consequential" by adding undefined synonyms to the consequential damages exclusion. Terms such as "indirect," "special," "incidental," and "no lost profits" are among the modifiers that are often used. But instead of adding clarity, these modifiers introduce even more ambiguity to the clause thus risking unexpected interpretations.

The confusion over the language in NCD clauses has been remarked upon by many lawyers and academics.[5] In two articles in the *Business Lawyer*, Glenn West (writing first with Sara Duran and then on his own) described the numerous problems embedded in many of the NCD provisions that were being used in the M&A market at the time.[6] Glenn suggested that widespread use of these clauses might have begun in the supplier and construction context—where well-drafted exclusion clauses made sense.[7] Thereafter,

[4] Often, a seller will limit the form of the loss of bargain risk by promising to repair or replace any defects in its performance.

[5] For a sample, *see*, David Leinwand, *Considering the Consequential Damages Waiver*, Mergers & Acquisitions and Corporate Governance 6 (Oct. 2011); Sarah Kupferman & Christian Matarese, *Like Bigfoot, a Clear and Settled Definition of "Consequential Damages" Remains Elusive*, Dechert (Apr. 6, 2017); Edward P. Smith & Patrick J. Navaez, *Lost Profit Waivers: Beware of Unintended Consequences*, Chadbourne & Park (Apr. 28, 2014); Rick Climan & Joel Flaum, *Using "Buyer Power Ratio" to Negotiate Consequential Damages Exclusions in M&A Deals*, Hogan Lovells (July 16, 2019); Tim Dodsworth, Maggie Hemsworth, & Severine Saintier, *Hadley v. Baxendale*, Unpacking Contract Law (Apple Podcasts) (Apr. 1, 2024); Victor P. Goldberg, Rethinking the Law of Contract Damages 171–172 (Edward Elgar Publishing, 2019).

[6] *See* Glenn D. West & Sara G. Duran, *Reassessing the "Consequences" of Consequential Damage Waivers in Acquisition Agreements*, 63 Bus. Law. 777 (2008); Glenn D. West, *Consequential Damages Redux: An Updated Study of the Ubiquitous and Problematic "Excluded Losses" Provision in Private Company Acquisition Agreements*, 70 Bus. Law. 971 (2015). For a somewhat different view of the enforceability of NCD clauses, see Goldberg, *supra* note 5, at *id.*

[7] *See* West, *Consequential Damages Redux*, *id.*, at 9 (describing what might have been the key case from the construction context that then resulted in the spread of NCD provisions). For articles in the construction contracts area discussing the importance of these provisions *see, e.g., Consequential*

inattention to changes in the case law, thoughtless copying, and the unhelpful addition of extra words may have resulted in the spread and evolution of standardized provisions that are obsolete in light of the conflicting case law and poorly crafted for the particular context.[8]

Legal scholars have expressed similar frustration with the formulation of standardized NCD clauses: one scholar writes that "the most common way parties learn what consequential damages actually means is the same way 'road bugs learn about MACK trucks.'"[9] The author of the *Corbin on Contracts* treatise, complained: "Too often, our contracts resort to generic, cookie-cutter language that excludes consequential, special, and indirect damages without further explanation. This practice is fraught with peril . . . [and] exposes clients to unnecessary risk."[10]

We cannot tell whether any given standardized NCD clause represents the optimal bargain among the parties.[11] What we can tell, however, is the extent to which clauses with obsolete terminology contain landmines that measurably increase expected litigation costs. Before turning to the data, we provide two examples.

Two Examples

We describe two cases, both involving collaborations to develop new products, where the landmines in NCD clauses led to litigation. In each case, there were large dollar transactions, fancy lawyers, and wasteful litigation as a result of provisions burdened by puzzling boilerplate.

Damages in Construction—The Silent Killer, JDSupra.com (Aug. 12, 2020); R. Edward Boucher & Jacquelin Kaltz, *Beware of Consequential and Liquidated Damages*, Kotz Sangster (Aug. 30, 2016).

[8] *Id.*

[9] Roy Ryden Anderson, *Incidental and Consequential Damages*, 7 J. L. & Com. 327, 353 (1987).

[10] Timothy Murray, *Drafting Exclusion of Consequential Damages Clauses*, LexisNexis (Dec. 19, 2018). Indeed, it takes little effort to find dozens of warnings from senior lawyers that NCD provisions can be landmines for the unwary. A 2012 client alert by Gibson Dunn M&A partners warned: "[C]ounsel may intend that these provisions prevent liability arising from . . . unforeseeable future events; however, because these terms are poorly understood . . . the exclusion of these categories of damages may have unexpected consequences." Eduardo Gallardo, *Avoiding Unintended Consequences of Damage Waiver Provisions*, Harvard Corporate Governance Blog (July 26, 2012); Chris Babcock & Robert Little, *Avoiding Unintended Consequences of Damage Waiver Provisions in M&A Agreements*, Gibson Dunn (July 10, 2012).

[11] *See* Eric A. Posner, *Economic Analysis of Contract Law After Three Decades: Success or Failure*, 112 Yale L. J. 829, 830 (2003).

Biotronik

In May 2004, Biotronik, a manufacturer and distributor of medical devices, and Conor Medsystems, the developer and manufacturer of CoStar, a drug-eluting coronary stent, entered into a distribution agreement. Biotronik was to be the exclusive distributor of CoStar and to use "commercially reasonable efforts to promote, market, and distribute" the stents in the territory. Conor, for its part, agreed to supply Biotronik with "all reasonably required support to comply with any local regulatory law and requirements" and to assist with the registration of its trademarks. The agreement allowed Conor to terminate unilaterally in the event of a change of control "that has, or in the reasonable opinion could have, a material adverse effect on the distribution" of CoStar. At the time of the agreement, Conor was in the process of seeking regulatory approval in both Europe and the United States. European approval was obtained in 2006, and sales by Biotronik began while FDA approval in the United States was still in progress.

Conor was acquired in February 2007 by Johnson and Johnson, a firm that had its own stent that was in competition with the Conor stent. In May 2007, Conor withdrew its application for FDA approval on the grounds that the CoStar stent was not competitive with others in the market. Conor then recalled all the stents that it had sent to Biotronik, paid the contractually specified recall fee, and announced that the contract was terminated. When Biotronik sued for breach of contract claiming damages for the profits it had lost, Conor pointed to the following provision:

> NEITHER PARTY SHALL BE LIABLE TO THE OTHER FOR ANY INDIRECT, SPECIAL, CONSEQUENTIAL, INCIDENTAL OR PUNITIVE DAMAGE WITH RESPECT TO ANY CLAIM ARISING OUT OF THIS AGREEMENT (INCLUDING WITHOUT LIMITATION ITS PERFORMANCE OR BREACH OF THIS AGREEMENT) FOR ANY REASON.

Lost profits, Conor asserted, were a type of consequential damages. And since consequential damages could not be recovered, lost profits could not be recovered. Litigation ensued, all the way to New York's highest court, with the different levels of court disagreeing with each other and, ultimately, at the Court of Appeals, the judges split 4–3.[12]

[12] For the court decision, see *Biotronik A.G. v. Conor Medsystems Ireland, Ltd.*, 22 N.Y.3d 799 (2014).

What is interesting to us here is not whether the term "consequential damages" encompasses all claims for lost profits (it clearly does not)[13] but that the parties drafting this quasi bespoke contract didn't make their intentions clear. The boilerplate NCD clause was incorporated in the contract by the drafters without any effort at clarification. And clarification was needed: the liability limitation provision uses a set of phrases—"indirect, special . . . incidental"—that are undefined and vague. None of these phrases have been interpreted uniformly by common law courts in previous litigation. Moreover, the case law has been muddled for many decades about precisely what damages are encompassed by the term "consequential." In short, the boilerplate clause contained several landmines and, predictably, this blew up when there was a breach, and damages had to be estimated. In a multimillion dollar agreement, with experienced lawyers who were drafting a quasi-bespoke contract, a crucial term was left undefined and unexplained because the lawyers relied on the safety of a standardized formulation borrowed from other sources.

Biotronik was decided in 2014,[14] and the resulting confusion over lost profit damages and NCD clauses was much discussed in both press and legal circles.[15] Therefore, it is appropriate to ask: Would this dodgy language be clarified in future contracts, at least as to whether the term consequential damages encompasses "lost profits?" Decided almost a full decade later, the 2023 case of *Endless River Technologies v. Trans Union* provides one answer to that question.

Endless River

In 2014 (the year *Biotronik* was decided), Endless River and Trans Union entered into an agreement looking toward the joint development and commercialization of a method for providing insurers online, real-time comparison price quotes to consumers. Subsequently, Trans Union pulled out of the agreement and Endless River sued for breach claiming, inter alia, that it had lost profits as a result of Trans Union's actions. Trans Union

[13] See Robert E. Scott & Jody P. Kraus, Contract Law and Theory 1002–1016 (Carolina Academic Press, 6th ed. 2023).

[14] See *Biotronik*, *supra* note 12.

[15] *E.g.*, Elizabeth Edmondson & Jenna E. Ross, *Lost Profit Damages Three Years After "Biotronik,"* 258 N.Y. L. J. (Aug. 16, 2017); *Lost Profits: Direct or Indirect Damages*, King & Fisher (July 30, 2017); Jeremy Sher, *Biotronik v. Conor: Lost Clarity on Lost Profits*, N.Y. Daily Record (Aug. 20, 2014).

responded by pointing to the provision in the contract limiting damages for lost profits.[16]

The damages constraining provision reads:

> IN NO EVENT SHALL EITHER PARTY BE LIABLE FOR, AND BOTH [TRANSUNION] AND [ENDLESS RIVER] HEREBY WAIVE AS TO THE OTHER PARTY, ANY CONSEQUENTIAL, INCIDENTAL, INDIRECT, SPECIAL OR PUNITIVE DAMAGES INCURRED BY THE OTHER PARTY AND ARISING OUT OF THE PERFORMANCE OF THIS CONTRACT, INCLUDING BUT NOT LIMITED TO LOSS OF GOOD WILL AND LOST PROFITS OR REVENUE, WHETHER OR NOT SUCH LOSS OF DAMAGES IS BASED IN CONTRACT, WARRANTY, TORT, NEGLIGENCE, STRICT LIABILITY, INDEMNITY, OR OTHERWISE EVEN IF SUCH PARTY HAS BEEN ADVISED OF THE POSSIBILITY OF SUCH DAMAGES. THESE LIMITATIONS SHALL APPLY NOT WITHSTANDING ANY FAILURE OF ESSENTIAL PURPOSE OR ANY LIMITED REMEDY.

The provision is not a model of clarity, but both parties agreed that the lost profits Endless River was claiming would be excluded by the boilerplate language *only if* they were a type of "consequential, incidental, indirect [or] special" damages. Unfortunately, the answer to the question of precisely what damage claims were included by those words was itself unclear. Therefore, so was whether the "lost profits" claimed here were excluded. In sum, the boilerplate language contained a landmine and litigation predictably ensued. Had the contract used bespoke language to exclude, or alternatively to include, all claims for the loss of profits contemplated by Endless River none of the drama would have ensued.

Landmines in NCD Clauses

In this section, we set out a set of simple measures of the extent to which NCD provisions in quasi-bespoke commercial agreements have

[16] For the court decision, see Endless River Technologies LLC v. Trans Union LLC, 2023 WL 24101 (N.D. Ohio, Jan. 3, 2023). One of Glenn West's blog posts discusses *Endless River* in depth. *See Lost Profits May or May Not be Consequential Damages*, Weil Private Equity Blog (July 11, 2023).

landmines of the type that produced problems in the two cases discussed above.[17]

Drawing from the literature, we can isolate the different problematic phrases that are often used in these boilerplate provisions. Then, we code commercial agreements contained in Securities and Exchange Commission (SEC) filings from 2010 to 2023 to see how the key language in NCD provisions varies over time in commercial agreements. The typical boilerplate formulation begins first with a broad definition of "Losses" that may be recovered in the event of breach. Then, there is a clause (often titled "Limitation on Losses" or "No Consequential Damages") that purports to limits these losses by excluding the recovery of certain types of specifically described losses.[18]

The problem lies in the description of excluded losses: in addition to "lost profits," the typical boilerplate uses words (e.g., "special," "indirect," and "incidental") that have no accepted meaning in contract doctrine nor any meaning distinct from each other. These words are apparently intended to add to or, in the alternative, clarify the losses that would otherwise be excluded by the term "consequential." The troublesome language in these clauses is different in kind (but not risk) from the landmines that we identified in sovereign bonds. The undefined words are "encrustations": the overlayering of legal jargon to the point where the intelligibility of the language deteriorates. This type of boilerplate language weakens the communicative properties of standardized terms, reducing their reliability as signals of what the parties really intend. The potentially problematic phrases are described below.

Ambiguous Exclusions

Each of the purported exclusions noted below presents a risk to both parties in the transaction because the term will potentially be unclear to the courts:

- *Consequential damages*: The case law demonstrating that courts are unsure of what this term encompasses goes back at least a half

[17] The analysis in this chapter is drawn from: Tara Chowdhury, Faith Chudkowski, Amanda Dixon, Rishabh Sharma, Madison Sherrill, Hadar Tanne, Stephen J. Choi, & Mitu Gulati, *Consequential Damages: Alien Vomit or Intelligent Design?* 102 Wash. U. L. Rev. 601 (2024).

[18] In many agreements, there is a third piece of the puzzle, which is a dollar limitation on how much can be recovered. We do not go into that aspect here.

century.[19] In an optimal design world, we might expect parties drafting quasi-bespoke contracts to define this term with specificity. Many do not. Glenn West suggests that many drafting lawyers believe that the term refers to speculative and remote damages.[20] Not only is that not clearly the meaning of the term, but speculative and remote damages typically are not recoverable anyway.

- *Indirect damages*: Glenn West and Sara Duran note that "many deal professionals and their counsel [exclude indirect damages] because they believe, wrongly, that the term 'indirect damages' . . . is simply a synonym for 'consequential damages'" (consequential damages being a term that is itself unclear).[21] But the concept of "indirect" versus "direct" damages muddies the waters further because it adds the question of causality to the mix of what damages can be recovered.[22]
- *Special damages*: It is unclear what "special" means. These "special" damages are sometimes equated with consequential damages. But, again, who knows what either of those term means?[23] Special is perhaps the opposite of normal or ordinary. But abnormal damages are not recoverable anyway, unless the contract explicitly says they are.[24]
- *Incidental damages*: The common law courts have not defined incidental damages. But to the extent the goal of excluded loss provisions is to eliminate indirect damages, the term incidental damages can easily cover some direct damages as well. As an illustration, in the Uniform Commercial Code, incidental damages comprise any "commercially reasonable *expenses* incident to delay or other breach."[25] That includes a range of damages that could be direct, such as the costs incurred by a nonbreaching party to mitigate damages.[26]
- *Treble*: The exclusion of recovery for "treble damages" seems to be a reference to punitive damages as well. But, again, one can't recover these as a matter of contract damages. So, there is no reason to exclude them.[27]

[19] West, *Consequential Damages Redux*, *supra* note 6 at 987.
[20] *Id.*
[21] West & Duran, *supra* note 6 at 793.
[22] West, *Consequential Damages Redux*, *supra* note 6 at 993–994.
[23] West, *Excluded Loss Provisions*, *supra* note 1.
[24] *Id.*
[25] *See* Uniform Commercial Code, $ 2-715.
[26] *Id.*
[27] *Id.*

What Do the Data Tell Us?

We decided to test our hypothesis that parties to commercial agreements face high contract production costs and, as a consequence, resist repairing the hazards in their NCD clauses.[28] For our analysis, we compiled data on NCD provisions over a thirteen-year period, from 2010 to 2023. To construct our sample, we took a random draw of roughly forty-five commercial agreements each year from SEC filings between 2010 and 2023 as obtained from the Practical Law database on Westlaw. Our goal was to get a rough measure of the prevalence of NCD landmines over time. The commercial agreements in our sample cover a wide range of different types of agreements involving commercial parties.[29]

Unlike thick markets with frequent trades of nearly identical instruments by numerous market participants, the one-off commercial agreement market consists of isolated deals that occur relatively infrequently without the benefit of many precedents to use in drafting a new contract. When we examined the incidence of standardized NCD clauses, we found that 79% of commercial agreements in our sample contained a potentially hazardous NCD clause.

To analyze the persistence of standardized NCD clauses over time, we focused on a particular "shock" derived from the market's response to *Biotronik* and the extensive commentary by Glenn West and other senior practitioners. In a world in which drafters are paying attention to every clause, or even

[28] These are the agreements that are reported as part of required filings of "material contracts" with the Securities and Exchange Commission.

[29] Our sample includes: (1) Collaboration agreements such as strategic alliance agreements, joint ventures, and other collaboration type agreements to research, develop, manufacture, and commercialize new products among other joint objectives; (2) Distribution-Marketing agreements such as agreements for one party to purchase and resell products (including, for example, refined petroleum gasoline and diesel products) from another party; (3) Purchase-Sale agreements (including supply agreements) by one party to provide a particular good (such as sand or liquid natural gas) over a specified period to another party; (4) Services-Consulting agreements that include, among other things, agreements for former executives to continue as consultants after the acquisition of a company and agreements to obtain assistance from a particular individual with expertise; (5) Services—Management include agreements by one party to provide management services to another party; (6) Services—Transition include agreements by a selling shareholder of a target company to continue to provide the acquirer certain administrative, management, operating, and other services related to the target company post-acquisition; (7) Services—Other services include all other types of services agreements including agreements in conjunction with an existing joint venture to provide administrative services to jointly owned companies and agreements for two companies to provide services to each other, among others; (8) Other agreements include inventory intermediation agreements, franchise agreements, lease agreements, and engineering agreements, among others. The distribution of agreements by type of contract varied from 1.6% to 24.7% of the sample.

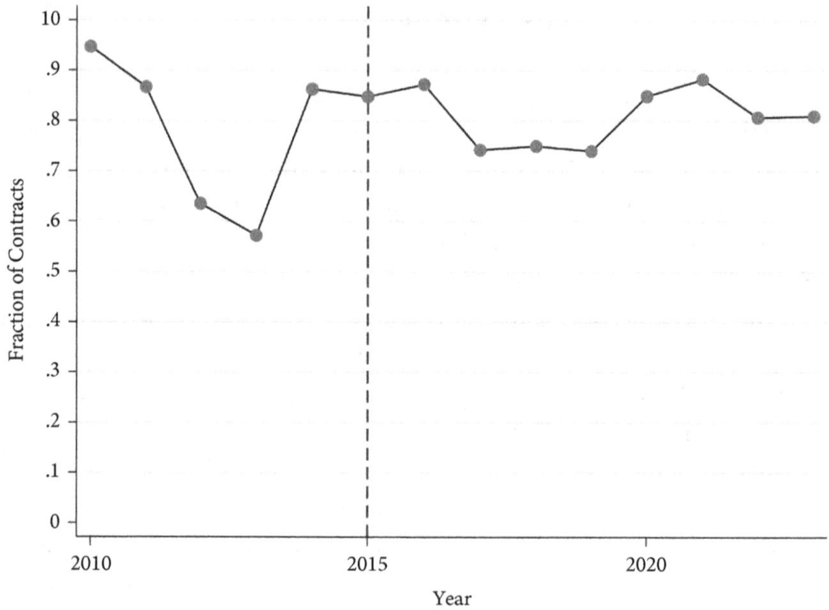

Figure 10.1 Presence of a No Consequential Damages clause

every important clause, these events should have alerted parties to define precisely the exclusions in their standard NCD clause particularly around and after 2015. Our hypothesis was that bespoke contracting poses high contracting costs for those parties who wish to modify an existing standard term, leading to slower, if any, changes to the standardized terms over time. We find that not only are encrusted NCD clauses prevalent in the sample of commercial agreements, but that these clauses persist across the entire period of our study, both prior to and after 2015.

Figure 10.1 shows the fraction of commercial agreement contracts with a standardized NCD by year with the dashed line indicating 2015. There is no discernable decrease in the use of NCD clauses after 2015. Indeed, the percentage of contracts with a suspect NCD *increases* for all commercial agreements in the post 2015 period (80.3%) from the earlier period (77.9%), although this difference is not statistically significant. Despite the calls for change in the market, there is no evidence that parties in the commercial agreement market reduced the usage of a standard form NCD clause after 2015.

That said, the fact that contracts continue to have an NCD clause does not tell us much about landmine prevalence. Perhaps the clauses being

Table 10.1 Average Number of Ambiguous Exclusion per No Consequential Damages Clause

	Contracts with an NCD	Average number of ambiguous exclusions
Commercial Agreement	498	3.0

Note: Number of exclusions are computed only for contracts with a NCD clause.

used both before and after 2015 did not fail to define any of the ambiguous terms. We next sliced the data more finely by examining the prevalence of the Ambiguous Exclusions in each of the clauses.

Table 10.1 gives the summary statistics of the number of undefined ambiguous exclusions in a NCD clause in our sample. The average NCD clause in our sample has on average, three undefined exclusions. In other words, there is a high prevalence of the language that caused problems in the two cases we described. Ambiguous exclusions, for our purposes, include at least one of the hazardous undefined terms like *consequential, indirect, special*, or *incidental* in a standardized NCD clause. Their presence is problematic to both parties because no one—courts and practitioners alike—knows quite what they mean. If the NCD clause is encrusted with ambiguous words, the clause is vulnerable to attack if the contract is subsequently litigated.

As Figure 10.2 reflects, prior to 2015, NCDs in commercial agreements regularly employ exclusions that are undefined and thus create a landmine risk. The events discouraging the use of ambiguous exclusions around 2015 led to only marginal change: NCD clauses had 3.1 ambiguous exclusions on average for 2015 and earlier and 3.0 ambiguous exclusions after 2015 (the difference is not statistically significant). This lack of any change in the number of ambiguous exclusions in NCDs is consistent with the high costs of replacing a standard clause with a more tailored version for one-and-done bespoke deals.

Implications

The basic problem with the standard NCD clause is the assumption that stringing together a series of terms that different courts have interpreted differently will somehow clarify an otherwise ambiguous clause. It does not,

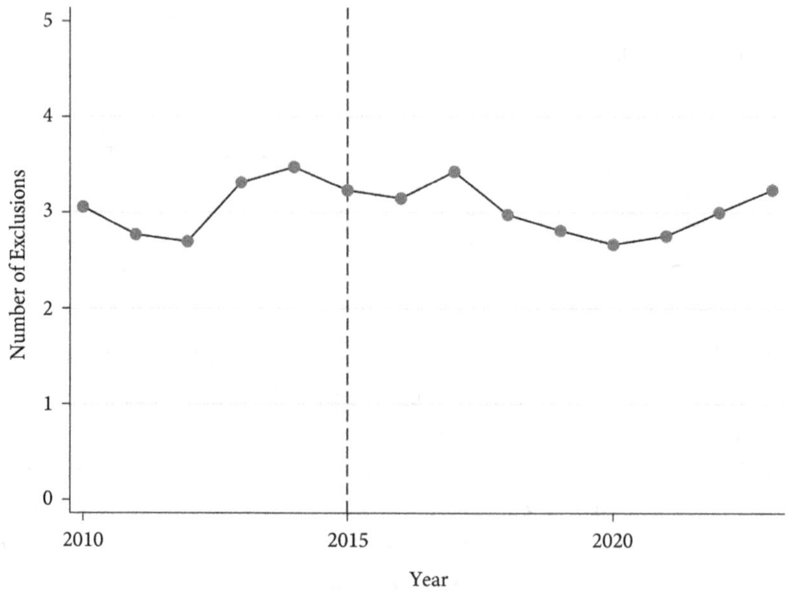

Figure 10.2 Mean number of ambiguous exclusions

and yet our data suggest that few if any parties are willing to expend the effort to define each term in light of the purpose and context of that particular contract. Given the uncertainty of different courts' determinations of what is and what is not meant by the terminology in NCD clauses, the standard term has become obsolete: the solution is to design a bespoke NCD clause by defining the terms more precisely. That drafters do not do so speaks to the dominance of production cost concerns over optimal contract design.

There is a nirvana image of contracting parties in a bespoke contract carefully tailoring each contract provision to realize the vigorously bargained for rights and obligations of each party. We think of bespoke contracts much like a bespoke suit—better fitting and thus superior in quality as compared to an off-the-rack counterpart. But bargaining over terms and then formulating the language to capture this bargain is costly. Rather than contract nirvana, drafting the bespoke contract can be a nightmare: parties constrained by resources and time are motivated to limit their tailoring of the contract to the key terms relevant to price and performance and pay less attention to those terms—like the troublesome NCD clause—that are only relevant in the event that the contract is breached.

The high cost of contracting for quasi-bespoke contracts can lead to greater contractual incompleteness. When parties then attempt to fill these contractual gaps, often by opting out of disfavored default rules, the bespoke contract setting produces a different kind of boilerplate problem. Here the resort to standardized terms is driven by the cost of contract production in a thin market. The high cost of production in this context stands in contrast to the efficiencies that drive the production of boilerplate in the thick market setting.

In theory, drafters can ask their clients to absorb the cost of formulating original terms. But since the overwhelming majority of contracts are performed and not breached and the incentives are to get the deal done quickly, clients undervalue the risk of breach. An agency problem arises when lawyers—familiar with cases such as *Biotronik*—are nonetheless deterred by the high cost of drafting an alternative and yet choose not to disclose their knowledge of the times the NCD clause has blown up in litigation. Instead, drafters in the quasi-bespoke context turn to artifacts: rote language widely used by others that only imperfectly describes the consequences of nonperformance. The choice is understandable: deals vary from one another, and the relevant pool of similar contracts is relatively small, so better formulations can't be borrowed from related transactions. Moreover, the one-off nature of contracting in this thin market means that there aren't many others from whom a drafting lawyer can learn how best to avoid landmine risk.

In the quasi-bespoke world of commercial agreements, contractual artifacts are both similar and dissimilar to the artifacts we observed in the highly liquid sovereign debt market. Artifacts are similar in both markets in the sense that meaning can get lost through obsolescence: a failure to update core terms following developments in the case law or in the underlying economic conditions. Fundamentally, however, the constraints on contract change are dissimilar in the two markets. In the sovereign debt market, artifacts arise from the expectations by the liquid, secondary market of a contract that looks "market" in its components. The "market" concept does allow for some variation in language, particularly for components such as a manifest error provision that are not central to the performance of the contract. But the more central a term to the market's concerns, the stricter are expectations for what constitutes "market." The degrees of freedom to change an interest payment term without running afoul of the expectations of "market" are smaller than for terms relevant only upon breach.

Lawyers drafting quasi-bespoke commercial agreements are only loosely constrained by "market." There is no need to create a contract that looks "market" and thus is amenable to wide resale. Instead, the notion of "market" is more limited in the bespoke context; many clients will not even look at the actual contract language. Instead, artifacts arise due to the high cost of change for lawyers untutored in the complexities of contract law. This high cost of change leads novice drafters to reuse prior contracts and turn to obsolete standard forms even if they are ill-fitting. This desire not to incur the cost of modification can turn much of the contract into an artifact. And that leads to a situation ripe for the creation of landmines.

We turn in Chapter Eleven to examine a different market-- private M&A contracting. The sophisticated practice environment of private equity M&A is a market where drafters can share information on how to combine highly standardized boilerplate clauses with important bespoke provisions. In that sense, the M&A market falls somewhere between the thick market extreme of sovereign debt and the thin market extreme of commercial agreements. As Chapter Eleven illustrates, this market and its landmines evolve differently from what we have seen so far.

Chapter Eleven

Fixing a Landmine: *M&A v. Corporate Bonds*

Introduction

Thus far, we have drawn the distinction between thin markets and thick markets more sharply than what we see in the world of commercial contracting. This stylization is designed to illustrate the differences in contracting practices that are our focus. Reality is less clear, however, and the lines between the two markets are blurred. If thin market bespoke contracting and thick market standardized contracting are poles of a continuum, many markets in between will exhibit features of both. This chapter and the next examine one such market. The merger and acquisition (M&A) market involves large sophisticated parties with the resources and, on occasion, the motivation to craft bespoke contracts: it includes a number of repeat players, including private equity sponsors, that both buy and sell companies for the funds they manage, and their law firms. Both private equity sponsors and their lawyers benefit from employing standardized terms across deals. Given the trade-off between efficient contract design and efficient production, we predict that in a world of agency costs the production benefits of standardization will lead to landmines even in the sophisticated M&A market. Perhaps there will not be as many landmines as in the sovereign bond world, and perhaps they will not be as sticky, but they should be there.

Tampering with the No Reliance Clause

One of us teaches several M&A opinions from the Delaware Chancery Court in his contracts class. Experts from the world of practice are frequently invited to provide the students with real world context. A few years ago, the guest was Pete Lyons, who we met in Chapter Three. Pete, formerly a senior

Contract Hazards. Stephen J. Choi, Mitu Gulati, and Robert E. Scott, Oxford University Press.
 DOI: 10.1093/9780197821770.003.0011

partner at Freshfields Bruckhaus Deringer, is now an adjunct lecturer at the University of Virginia. Pete agreed to join the class for the discussion of *ABRY Partners V, L.P. v. F & W Acquisition LLC*, a classic Delaware case that addresses the validity of an attempt by a seller to contractually forestall all claims for fraud that the buyer might bring.[1]

In setting the stage for the discussion of *ABRY Partners*, Pete described to the students the No Reliance clause, the primary contractual mechanism used to contract out of fraud liability. The No Reliance clause provides that the buyer has not relied on any statements made by the seller or its agents other than the explicit representations and warranties in the contract. Since reliance is an element of a fraud claim, a buyer unable to show reliance cannot claim that any of those extra-contractual representations were fraudulent.

From that prelude, Pete described a negotiation several years ago where he had nearly been snookered out of the No Reliance clause he thought he had negotiated for his client. Pete was representing the seller in a cross-border merger, one of the biggest deals he had done. No Reliance clauses were part of the standard package of terms, and Pete explicitly asked for the clause to be included in the contract. He thought that was the end of the matter since the buyer's counsel readily agreed. Pete explained that he might well not have paid any attention thereafter since he was not the one responsible for making sure the deal documents were in good order. But out of habit he skimmed the final package of documents when they came to him before closing. And there he noticed that in the No Reliance clause, there were the additional words, "except in the case of fraud." His head almost exploded.

To allow an exception for fraud in the No Reliance clause "makes it worthless as a protection against fraud claims," Pete explained to the students. The only reason to have a promise that the buyer did not rely on any statements made outside the contract is so the buyer cannot sue for fraud. But with an exception to the No Reliance clause for fraud, all such fraud claims are now available to the buyer. Asked whether his counterparty had deliberately inserted the "except in the case of fraud" language, Pete responded:

> Maybe. I don't know. Once I pointed out the flaw, and explained the problem, they took out the language. It is possible that was in their form document and it had contained that language in multiple deals and no seller's counsel

[1] 891 A.2d 1032 (Del. Ch. 2006). For discussion of ABRY Partners, *see, e.g.*, Glenn D. West, *Too Much Dynamite—The Non-Recourse and Survival Clauses Are Both Subject to Delaware's Built-in Fraud Carve-Out for Intentional Intra-Contractual Fraud*, Weil Private Equity Blog (Aug. 24, 2021).

had noticed. It is also possible that what they really meant to say was "except in the case of intentional fraud" which would have been a more reasonable ask. But that's not what they said. No one is reading the boilerplate at the very end when everyone is rushing to get the transaction done.

To us, this looked like a subversive accretion landmine on the buyer side. Along the way, a lawyer representing the buyer's interests had inserted the "except in the case of fraud" language in order to negate the effect of the No Reliance clause, and counsel on the seller side did not notice the additional qualifying phrase. Here we had a beginning: there was at least one instance of an M&A landmine.[2] Moreover, it appeared to be a subversive accretion, the most worrisome type of landmine that we had encountered.[3]

M&A and the Poles of the Continuum

In Chapter Ten, we told a story about contracts in thin markets where one should also expect landmines to arise and persist—albeit through a dynamic different from the sovereign bond context. Both situations are ripe for landmines because either a mutation or an obsolete formulation can be embedded in deal documents that have fossilized into artifacts. Once a landmine exists in such a document, it can migrate into the next deal and the next and so on. In a thin market, with few transactions, just as in a thick market with many, there is no obvious corrective mechanism until the deal blows up.

The question is whether M&A contracting is different. M&A is a large industry that has standard boilerplate provisions that are expected to be in every deal, and there are existing templates that lawyers draw from. But there are also deal-specific provisions in every contract. And M&A deals are,

[2] M&A guru, Wilson Chu, pointed out that the 2016 Deal Points Study found that 7% of No Reliance clauses contained these anomalous exceptions for fraud. Chu has been a key player in creating the Deal Points studies that are produced annually by the Mergers and Acquisitions section of the American Bar Association.

[3] As we were finishing the draft, we sent a copy of this chapter to Pete to make sure he approved of the version of the story we had in our notes from class. He said he was fine with the story, but added:

> I would mention that I got angry in this instance because I thought opposing counsel tried to pull a fast one. But in earlier years, when I was on the buy side, I would sometimes insert a "fraud exception" into a markup. If the seller objected, we would drop the comment pretty quickly. If, as sometimes happened, the seller didn't pick up on it, or they bought the argument that, "you're not really saying that you want to be able to commit FRAUD" we wouldn't discuss it further.

of course, not traded on a thick and active market, unlike sovereign or corporate bonds. The pressure to be "market" should be different, therefore, but even so it should translate into both the existence and persistence of landmines.

The presence of landmines in M&A is interesting given that private M&A deals tend to be high dollar transactions and the private equity sponsors are represented by elite law firms. Moreover, if we focus on those provisions that create a potential for individual liability, an issue of high salience to private equity sponsors, we would expect to see such clauses carefully scrutinized for landmines.

What, then, concerns private equity sponsors? Gurus of the private equity bar have consistently mentioned a single issue: protection against fraud claims is most concerning to the private equity sponsors of many M&A deals. When a transaction turns sour, unhappy counterparties may seek to use a fraud claim to reach the individual assets of the private equity sponsor, breaking through whatever legal barriers that might have been put in place to cordon off those private assets. One would predict that private equity lawyers, knowing this concern, would be careful to include provisions protecting their private equity clients against fraud suits to the maximum extent possible, and to remove any errors that undermined that goal.

This dynamic, where the client is focused on a particular issue, differs from the agency problems described in the sovereign bond context. There, neither of the true principals in the deal are present when the contracts are written. Nor do they have any direct oversight over their agents (government officials and underwriters) who are approving the original deal documents. Government officials may internalize some of the long-term consequences to the sovereign of a poorly drafted contract, but the government official will still be inadequately motivated. In contrast, a private equity fund will more fully internalize the cost of a potential fraud suit owing to a poorly drafted contract (since the fund and its executives will be defendants in such a suit). This dynamic also differs from the lack of attention to limitations on consequential damages that characterized quasi-bespoke commercial contracting. This difference between the private equity M&A context and both poles of our continuum should affect the lifecycle of the landmines in the contracts. Even if the imperatives of the production process lead to agency problems that produce landmines, these errors should get corrected more quickly in the private M&A context.

But how do things play out in reality? Would we find landmines buried in M&A boilerplate? As in the case of the two poles of the continuum, would those landmines be concentrated in standardized contract enforcement provisions? And, would we see that these landmines are corrected more rapidly in the private M&A market than in either thick or thin market settings? If so, how? We tested these propositions using two landmines that appear in both M&A and thick markets.[4]

Obsolete No Recourse Clauses

The No Recourse clause has its origins in bond indentures from the early twentieth century, when the shareholders of corporations faced unlimited liability in most US jurisdictions. The No Recourse clause was a contractual means of limiting shareholder liability: the bond contract would state explicitly that the shareholders were not liable to be sued personally. A typical clause read:

> *No recourse under or upon any obligation . . . of this indenture, or . . . because of the creation of any indebtedness hereby secured, shall be had against any incorporator, stockholder, officer, or director of the company or any successor corporation, either directly or through the company, by the enforcement of any assessment or by* ***any legal or equitable*** *proceeding by virtue of any statute or otherwise. This indenture [is] solely a corporate obligation, and no personal liability whatever shall attach to or be incurred by the incorporators, stockholders, officers, or directors of the company, or any successor corporation because of the incurring of the indebtedness hereby authorized, . . . , and any and all personal liability* ***either at common law or in equity****, or by statute or Constitution, of every such stockholder, officer, or director, is released and waived as a condition of and as part of the consideration for the execution of this indenture.* (emphasis added)

This version of the No Recourse clause was a feature of bond indentures from the turn of the century until the 1960s. Thereafter, with the move to

[4] The material for this chapter is drawn from two articles: Robert E. Scott, Stephen J. Choi, & Mitu Gulati, *Revising Boilerplate: A Comparison of Private and Public Company Transactions*, 2020 Wis. L. Rev. 629 (2020); Stephen J. Choi, Mitu Gulati, & Robert E. Scott, *Comparing Agency Costs in Contract Production: Private Equity M&A Versus Corporate and Sovereign Bonds*, 74 Case W. Res. L. Rev 47 (2023).

limited corporate liability in state legislatures as the default rule, the drafters of the Model Indenture Provisions revised the language of the original clause, reducing its length, first in 1983 and then in 2000. Importantly for our purposes, unlike the original clause, the new model clauses did not purport to limit liability for claims brought in equity:[5]

> *All liability described in the Securities of any director, officer, employee or stockholder as such, of the Company, is released.*[6] (1983 version)
>
> and
>
> *A director, officer, employee or stockholder, as such, of the Company shall not have any liability for any obligations of the Company under the Securities or the Indenture or for any claim based on, in respect of or by reason of such obligations or their creation.*[7] (2000 version)

We call these versions of the No Recourse clause the "Old" clause because they lack any reference to claims based in equity or fraud. The core of all variants of the Old clause is that the language does not explicitly bar veil piercing claims or other noncontractual claims against the principals and managers of the corporation.[8]

How did these No Recourse clauses migrate into the private equity M&A market? The private equity market is largely a modern creation, having grown in importance over the past two decades. The initial template for the private equity M&A contract was borrowed from generic M&A deals that did not take into account the particular needs of private equity sponsors. The No Recourse clauses in those contracts likely migrated from bond indentures. In the early years of private equity M&A deals, there was no impetus to revise the No Recourse clause because the sponsors of the deal would not agree to *any* liability whatsoever. The contracts would specify that the surviving private equity acquisition vehicle post-merger was the only relevant party involved in the purchase and sale agreement for purposes of liability. Here, the No Recourse provision, providing that the counterparty had contractually

[5] We suspect that the drafters of the revised model indentures assumed that equity claims were now barred by the background state law.

[6] *Model Simplified Indenture*, 38 BUS. LAW. 741, 772 (1983).

[7] *Revised Model Simplified Indenture*, 55 BUS. LAW. 1115, 1163 (2000).

[8] *E.g.*, *Simons v. Cogan*, 549 A.2d 300 (Del. 1988); *LaSalle Nat'l Bank v. Perelman*, 82 F. Supp. 2d 279 (D. Del. 2000).

promised not to seek recourse against the private equity sponsors, was superfluous.[9]

But in the mid-2000s, as the private equity market expanded and evolved, sponsors began to take more risks. In particular, they were increasingly prepared to put their own money at risk in the event the deal cratered. These funds came in the form of "termination" and "reverse termination" fees. In addition, courts were beginning to find gaps in the limited liability default rules, imposing liability on sponsors particularly where there was egregious conduct constituting fraud or its equivalent.[10] Since the sponsors were now bearing some financial responsibility, and courts were increasingly receptive to equitable claims, there was an impetus to update the obsolete Old versions of No Recourse provisions.

One way of determining whether deal lawyers were updating their contracts to take into account the new context is to see whether their No Recourse clauses barred equitable and fraud claims. Potential claims for fraud or other equitable relief were the most concerning because of the possibility of punitive damages attached to a finding of liability. Thus, the boilerplate clause was ripe for revisions once a number of courts expressed uncertainty about the reach of the Old style No Recourse clauses. The obvious answer was for drafters of bond indentures and M&A deals to revise the obsolete clause and explicitly exclude any personal liability of shareholders or sponsors for equitable or fraud claims arising out of the transaction.

The first publicly discussed version of the No Recourse clause that addressed equity and fraud claims was proposed by Glenn West and his co-author Natalie Smeltzer in a 2011 *Business Lawyer* article.[11] Having noticed that many deals were using obsolete versions of the clause, they proposed a new version of the No Recourse clause designed to exclude all potential sources of personal liability for principals and managers.[12] In our data, we coded instances of the West–Smeltzer clause as the "New" clause. It reads, in relevant part as follows:

> *[A]ll claims, obligations, liabilities, or causes of action* ***(whether in contract or in tort, in law or in equity, or granted by statute)*** *that may be*

[9] We take this history largely from, Glenn West & Natalie Smeltzer, *Protecting the Integrity of the Entity-Specific Contract: The "No Recourse Against Others" Clause—Missing or Ineffective Boilerplate*, 67 Bus. Law. 39, 40 (2011).

[10] Scott et al., *Revising Boilerplate*, *supra* note 4 (telling the story).

[11] West & Smeltzer, *supra* note 9 at 40.

[12] *Id.* at 71–72.

> *based upon . . . arise under. . . or be connected with . . . this Agreement may be made only against . . . the entities that are expressly identified as parties in the preamble to this Agreement ("Contracting Parties"). No Person who is not a Contracting Party, . . . and any financial advisor or lender to any Contracting Party, . . . and any financial advisor or lender to any of the foregoing ("Nonparty Affiliates"), shall have any liability* **(whether in contract or in tort, in law or in equity, or granted by statute)** *for any claims, causes of action, obligations, or liabilities arising under. . . or related in any manner to this Agreement . . . or its negotiation, execution, performance, or breach; and, to the maximum extent permitted by law, each Contracting Party hereby waives and releases all such liabilities, claims, causes of action, and obligations against any such Nonparty Affiliates.* ***Without limiting the foregoing, to the maximum extent permitted by law, (a) each Contracting Party hereby waives and releases any and all rights, claims, demands, or causes of action that may otherwise be available at law or in equity, or granted by statute, to avoid or disregard the entity form of a Contracting Party or otherwise impose liability of a Contracting Party on any Nonparty Affiliate, whether granted by statute or based on theories of equity, agency, control, instrumentality, alter ego, domination, sham, single business enterprise, piercing the veil, unfairness, undercapitalization, or otherwise;*** *and (b) each Contracting Party disclaims any reliance upon any Nonparty Affiliates with respect to the performance of this Agreement or any representation or warranty made in, in connection with, or as an inducement to this Agreement.*[13] (emphasis added)

There is a substantial amount of new language in the New clause. The important additional provisions are those in boldface—the waiver of rights language and the sentences that explicitly mention agency theory, alter ego, piercing the corporate veil, and so on. The New clause also specifies at the outset that liability—to the extent it is permitted—is only against those expressly named as contracting parties. This adds clarity to the older version that would designate those with liability as "the undersigned."

We also coded for other instances where the No Recourse clause was revised to address some of the new liability issues dealing with equity and fraud claims but not as extensively as the New version. We designated these

[13] *Id.*

as the "Modified" versions of the clause.[14] In contrast to the New clause, the Modified clauses lack explicit disclaimers with respect to veil piercing, alter ego, and the other versions of claims of that type. Given the tendency of courts, particularly in Delaware, to read these clauses narrowly and from a formalist perspective, the absence of a clear indication that the drafters wished for a different meaning supports the inference that this clause is less protective of the principals and managers than the New clause.

The No Recourse provision and the need to revise it in the modern era is relevant for our project for two reasons. First, the Old style No Recourse clause has elements of both the *historical holdover* and *obsolete* landmines that we found in sovereign bonds.[15] Second, because this clause was used both in thick market public company bond deals and in private M&A deals, it provides the opportunity to compare the evolution of a clause in different markets.[16] In a perfect contract design world, the drafters in both contexts would have updated the No Recourse clauses in order to clarify that there was no personal liability for fraud or other equitable claims.

To be sure, the two markets are different; in particular, individual liability is less likely in the public company bond context. Nonetheless, the revision is trivial to accomplish, as illustrated by the italicized language in the sample revised boilerplate. Assuming the drafting lawyers are focused on design, we would expect them to revise the clause in both contexts.

To test this conjecture, we collected data on over six hundred contracts that contained No Recourse clauses during the period from January 1, 2005

[14] An example of a Modified clause from a 2018 Stock Purchase agreement specifies that there is no liability in "contract, tort, equity or otherwise" but has no explicit disclaimers with respect to veil piercing, alter ego, etc.:

> *This Agreement may only be enforced against, and any action . . . or proceeding based upon, arising out of or related to this Agreement may only be brought against, the Persons that are expressly named as parties to this Agreement. Except to the extent named as a party to this Agreement, and then only to the extent of the specific obligations of such parties set forth in this Agreement, no past, present or future shareholder, member, partner, manager, director, officer, employee, Affiliate, agent or Advisor of any party to this Agreement or any Subsidiary of the Company will have any liability* ***(whether in contract, tort, equity or otherwise)*** *for any of the representations, warranties, covenants, agreements or other obligations or liabilities of any of the parties to this Agreement or for any action . . . or proceeding based upon, arising out of or related to this Agreement.*
>
> Stock Purchase Agreement Byland Among Leggett & Platt, Incorporated, Elite Comfort Solutions, Inc. and Elite Comfort Solutions LP, § 11.10 (November 6, 2018). (emphasis added)

[15] *See* Chapter Two, *supra*.

[16] Public company bond deals look similar to the sovereign bond contracting practices we have previously examined, with dispersed investors on the creditor side and dispersed shareholders on the debtor side.

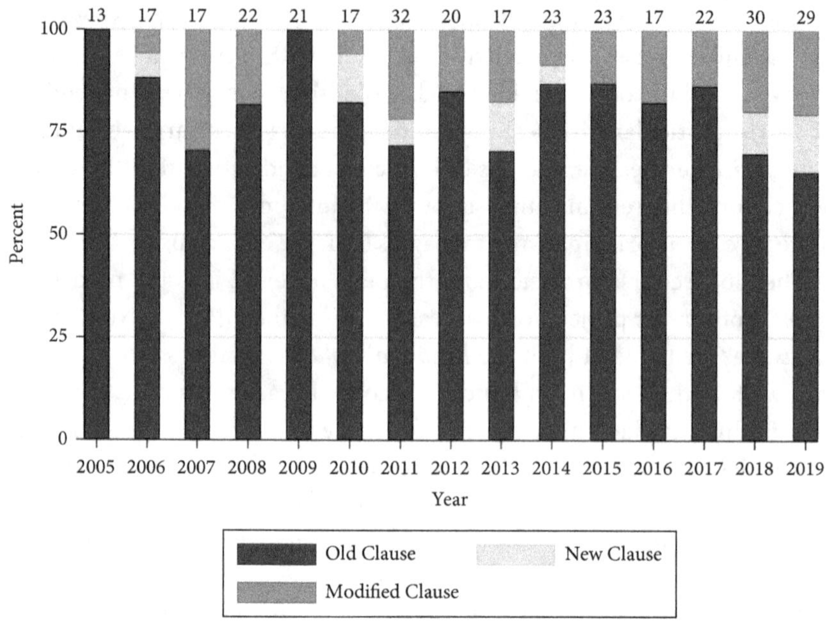

Total number of deals for the year at the top of each bar. Repeat transactions included.

Figure 11.1 Public bonds No Recourse clauses

to June 1, 2019 for both public company bond and private M&A deals.[17] As depicted in Figure 11.1, we found that the Old clause largely dominated the public company bond deals through the period from 2005 to mid-2019.[18] In short, public company bond documents kept using the outdated version of the clause.

In the public company bonds data, the percentage of contracts using either the New or Modified No Recourse clause is never greater than 35% in any year after 2005 (and there is no discernable trend). The Old clause remains in over a majority of public company bond deals in each year from 2005 to 2019. Now consider Figure 11.2 that depicts the No Recourse clause for private M&A deals.

In contrast with the public company bond market deals, there is a significant shift away from the Old clause and toward the Modified and New

[17] We assembled our dataset using two primary sources for the January 1, 2005 to June 1, 2019 period: (1) Westlaw's What's Market database that has compiled M&A deals from 2010 to 2019; (2) Bloomberg's SEC EDGAR database of exhibits attached to company 8-K filings that we used for the 2005–2010 period.

[18] There were some versions of the No Recourse clause in public deals that did address equity and fraud claims that we coded as "Modified" clauses and "New" clauses.

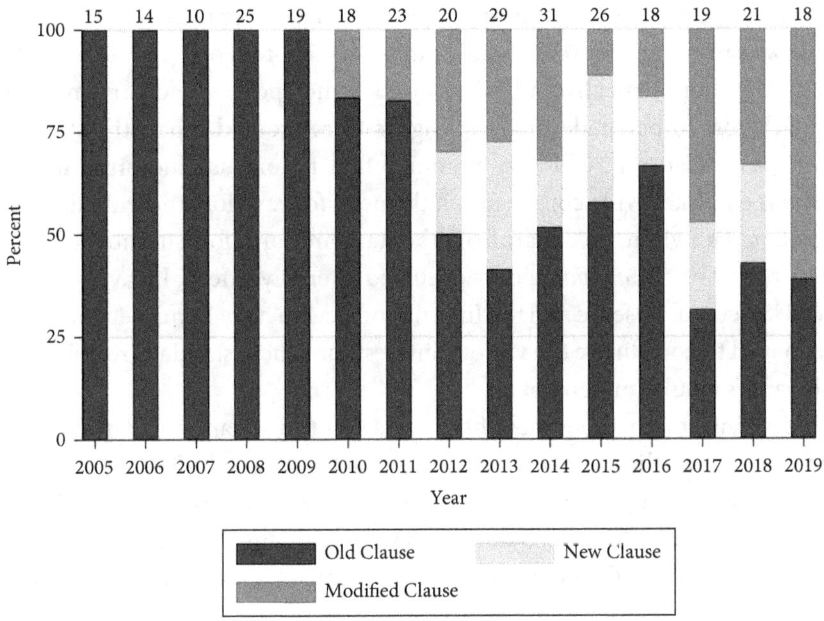

Total number of deals for the year at the top of each bar. Repeat transactions included.

Figure 11.2 Private M&A No Recourse clauses

clauses for private M&A deals. In 2010, we see the introduction of the Modified clause in private M&A deals. After 2012, we see both the introduction of the New clause and a rapid increase in the prevalence of both the New and Modified clauses, ultimately constituting a majority of the private M&A deals: the New or Modified clause is present in 52.5% of the private company transactions from 2012 to 2019.

Our conjecture is that the different patterns of landmine repair are the result of differences between the M&A and the public bond markets in the way expert opinion influences the actions of the drafting lawyers. There was a campaign by leading practitioners in the M&A world to alert parties in their cohort to the importance of updating the obsolete No Recourse clause. Through a combination of articles in prominent practitioner journals, blog posts, and presentations at practitioner conferences, this group of experts appears to have induced change. The revisions started occurring almost immediately after the efforts of the experts at educating their peers.[19]

[19] Not every participant in the market changed their clauses, however. At least 25% of the private deal contracts in every year after 2012 (until 2019) still used the Old No Recourse clause.

This dynamic stands in contrast with the drama over the *pari passu* clause that we saw in the sovereign bond context in Chapter Four. There, respected senior practitioners also published articles and spoke at industry meetings in an effort to persuade their colleagues to revise and repair the standard *pari passu* clause in order to eliminate that notorious landmine. Yet, despite the market-wide consensus on the need for revision, individual parties remained unwilling to depart from the standard form for a number of years. The revisions to *pari passu* only occurred after key external players such as the US Federal Reserve and the International Monetary Fund stepped in and managed to coordinate the various interests around a standard revision that all parties would implement.

Most intriguing about these findings is that the dynamics of landmine repair look quite different in different contracting markets. The same type of landmine (e.g., a historical holdover or obsolete clause) can occur in two different markets. But the dynamics of what happens thereafter, particularly after the experts in the field notice the problem and urge repair, are different.

Outdated Choice-of-Law Clauses

The choice-of-law provision is an ideal candidate for a landmine comparison across contexts. The clause is found in literally every modern commercial contract, regardless of subject matter. The clause is a key feature in any litigation where the applicable law can impact the outcome of the case.

Despite being crucially important whenever a contract is litigated, the clause receives little attention from drafting lawyers.[20] It is as boilerplate a clause as there is, and is often copied thoughtlessly from prior forms: this copying manifests itself in language that appears to have no function other than it has been used previously. Drawing largely from the work of John Coyle, the leading expert on these clauses, we can sketch out a simplified history of these clauses and how landmines have appeared.[21]

[20] We take this observation from the work of John Coyle. He has studied choice-of-law clauses in greater detail than any other scholar and is invited to law firms around the world to discuss problems with the drafting of these clauses. *See, e.g.*, John F. Coyle, *The Canons of Construction for Choice-of-Law Clauses*, 92 Wash. L. Rev. 631 (2017); John F. Coyle, *Choice of Law Clauses in U.S. Bond Indentures*, 13 Cap. Mkts. L. J. 152, 164–165 (2018) ("Since both the issuers and the underwriters generally view the ancillary language in the choice-of-law clause as unimportant, this language is virtually never discussed or negotiated").

[21] The history is detailed in John F. Coyle, *A Short History of the Choice-of-Law Clause*, 91 U. Colo. L. Rev. 1147 (2020).

Under early contract law doctrine, the state law that governed the interpretation and enforcement of a contract was decided by the courts and not the parties. The parties specified the substantive terms of their deal while the court decided what state's law applied as a function of factors such as the state where the contract was made. But in the modern era, courts across the United States began to view the choice-of-law question through a contractarian lens. Parties today can choose the state law they wish to have govern their contracts. Coyle explains why the drafting of these clauses rarely receives adequate attention:

> First, most lawyers lack the time to read hundreds of published cases about choice-of-law clauses to identify drafting pitfalls. These lawyers are busy and their clients don't want to pay for them to undertake this research and so the lawyers (rationally) choose not to undertake it.
>
> Second, most lawyers don't really understand conflict of laws. It's a famously complicated body of law and is a class that very few people take in law school. Without a sound doctrinal grounding in conflicts, most lawyers lack the ability to appreciate the significance of small wording changes in a choice-of-law clause.
>
> Third, the choice-of-law clause only really matters when the contract winds up in litigation and the contract touches on more than one jurisdiction and the law is different across the two jurisdictions. Since this constellation of factors is rare, most lawyers rationally devote little time to the intricacies of how to draft choice-of-law clauses.[22]

The simplest form of a governing law clause will state: "This agreement will be governed by the law of [State X]." And that clause will work for most purposes. But imagine a deal that is concluded in Massachusetts and the parties specify the governing law to be that of New York. Assume there is an allegation after the deal is done that some of the statements made in the contract were fraudulent and that there was fraud in the inducement to enter into the contract. If the party claiming fraud brings both contract and tort claims, what law governs? Would the contract claims be governed by

[22] Choi et al., *Comparing Agency Costs in Contract Production*, *supra* note 4 at n. 29 (quoting an email from Coyle).

New York law and the tort claims by Massachusetts law? This would at best cause inconvenience. But beyond that, what if the law of Massachusetts, unlike New York, looked with disfavor upon No Reliance provisions? What if it refused to enforce them altogether? That could change the outcome for the fraud claims because it potentially would make them more potent. Clients would not want to face this kind of uncertainty or, for that matter, the risk of a large tort judgment with punitive damages.

As Coyle describes the history of choice of law clauses, courts began in the 1970s to require parties to specify explicitly if they wished their contract claims and all tort and related matters arising out of that contract to be decided under the same law. Starting around 2009, and in response to the emerging case law, a chorus of eminent practitioners exhorted lawyers to draft their choice-of-law clauses more broadly to expressly include tort and related matters.[23] Numerous articles were written to the same effect and with the same urgency.[24] Then came more decisions, including a well-publicized case from Delaware in 2017 in which the court made clear that the wording of the choice-of-law clause mattered in determining whether tort and related issues arising out of the contract would fall under the same governing law.[25] And senior private equity lawyers, whose sell-side M&A clients were likely to care about this question, discussed this in their appeals to colleagues.[26]

Since the issue should have been important to transactional lawyers in both private M&A deals and public bond offerings, we assembled a data set of different types of public bond contracts (including sovereign, low-yield corporate, and high-yield corporate) to compare with private M&A contracts from 2010 to early 2020. For each deal type, we collected available information on approximately 25 to 30 deals in each year, selected at random.[27]

[23] *See, e.g.*, Glenn D. West & W. Benton Lewis, Jr., *Contracting to Avoid Extra-Contractual Liability—Can Your Contractual Deal Ever Really Be the "Entire" Deal?*, 64 Bus. Law. 999, 1002–1004, 1029–1031 (2009) (explaining tactics attorneys can use to draft effective choice-of-law provisions); *See also* Mitchell J. Geller, *Ensuring Choice-of-Law Provision Includes Non-Contractual Claims*, N.Y. L. J. (July 7, 2009) (expressing disbelief that "corporate attorneys continue to rely on 'standard' language used in prior agreements that do not contain [expansive choice-of-law clauses]").

[24] Choi et al., *Comparing Agency Costs in Contract Production, supra* note 4 at 59–61.

[25] Choi et al., *Comparing Agency Costs in Contract Production, supra* note 4 at 60 (citing *Reid v. Siniscalchi*, No. 2874-VCS (Del. Ch. May 3, 2017) (bench ruling)).

[26] The issue should be relevant to all deals that touch multiple jurisdictions (imagine an international bond offering where there are marketing road shows and sales occurring in a wide range of jurisdictions, and there are fraud claims regarding representations made at the time of the issuance).

[27] We collected information from Perfect Information and Westlaw's What's Market database on the governing law clause for the four types of deals. We focused only on deals governed by US law jurisdictions. For the sovereign, low-yield, and high-yield deals, the US jurisdiction was invariably New York. Most of the private equity deals chose Delaware law, but a small fraction used other

We then compared the contracts' choice-of-law clauses in the different markets to see which markets were more responsive to the calls for change during our study period.

We focused in particular on whether the choice-of-law clause had been updated to include an "extra-contractual" provision that applied the same governing law to tort and other matters arising from the contract. In particular, some choice-of-law clauses begin with the following: "*This Agreement, the rights of the parties hereunder and all* ***Actions arising in whole or in part under or in connection herewith****, will be governed by* . . . ." This extra-contractual term encompasses phrases that expand the application of the clause to "Actions arising . . . or in connection herewith" or its equivalents: "all extra-contractual matters arising out of"; "tort and statutory matters arising out of"; or any other similar phrases. Figure 11.3 displays the incidence of extra-contractual clauses by year for each of the four markets.

The graphs in Figure 11.3 speak for themselves. As with the No Recourse clauses, revisions that update the obsolete language to provide for extra-contractual matters in the choice-of-law clause appear to a much greater extent in the private M&A context than for corporate or sovereign bonds. In the former setting, we start in 2010 with about 15% of the contracts having the revised clause (leading lawyers in the M&A world had by then been recommending changes). By 2020, as the chorus of voices from within the industry grew louder, about 50% of the deals have updated clauses. In the sovereign bond market, however, there are only a few contracts with the improved version of the choice-of-law clause. Here, the percentage is between 0 and 10% of deals all through the period of our analysis, with no trends. In the corporate bond context, we see even fewer contracts with the improved language.

As with the No Recourse clause, these markets (sovereign bonds, private M&A, low-yield corporate bonds, and high-yield corporate bonds) differ across many dimensions. The likelihood of litigation will vary across markets as will the relative vulnerability of the primary clients to liability. But what is the same in both the thick public markets and the thinner M&A market is how the improvements to obsolete contract terms can be made at a minimal cost. Unlike some of the earlier examples of landmines we have discussed,

jurisdictions including New York. Given that the drafting advice in the practitioner literature invariably applies to contracts used in all US jurisdictions, we treat contracts drafted under different US jurisdictions as the same for purposes of our analysis.

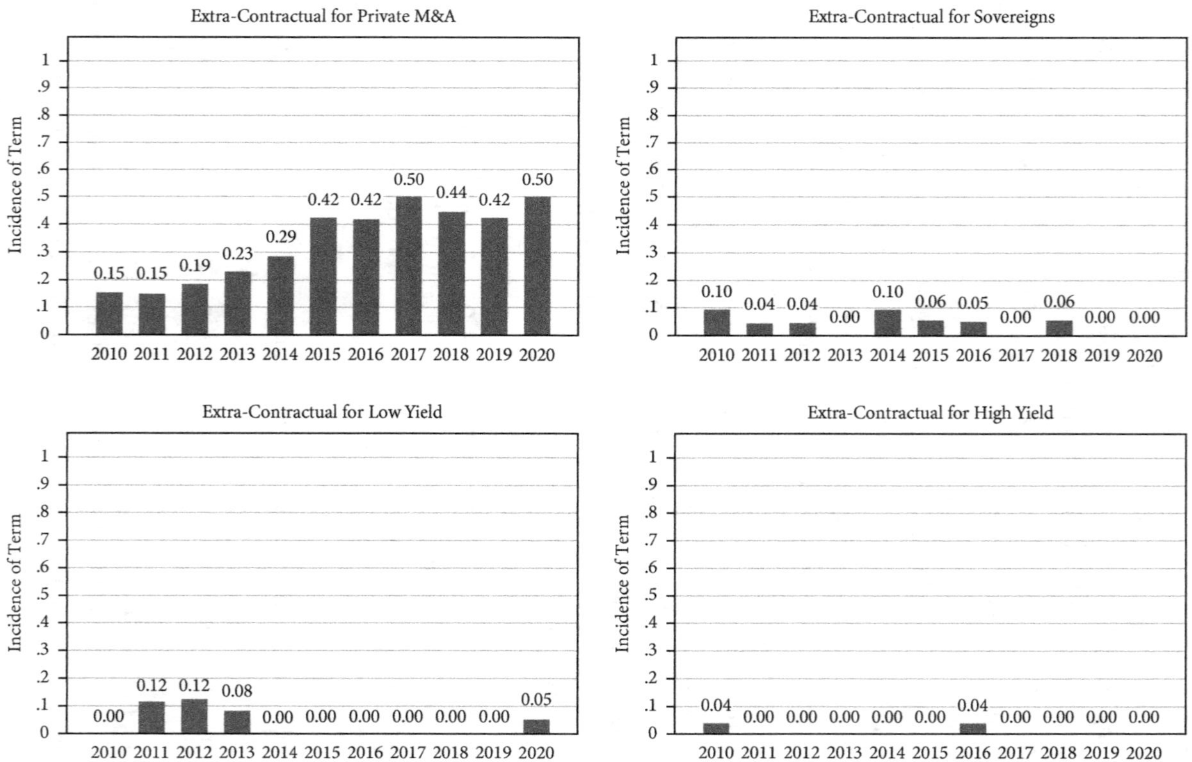

Figure 11.3 Incidence of an extra-contractual provision in the choice-of-law clause

where a lawyer must read the boilerplate carefully to discover a mutation to the standard form, in these cases all that is required to remove the landmine is to add a few clarifying words to a standard clause. These are changes that are trivial actions for anyone with a basic understanding of the issues.

Nevertheless, easy changes were not made in the vast majority of contracts in the public bond context. This is consistent with our earlier suggestion that barriers to innovation deter individual parties and their lawyers from effecting revisions to the historic boilerplate of sovereign and corporate bonds. In these markets, where the contract is artifact, there is a first mover disadvantage to making even low cost changes to the standard form. In contrast, a majority of the contracts in the private M&A context are revised. That tells us that different dynamics are at play. Further, when we analyzed the data, we found that the changes correlated with the protestations of eminent practitioners in the private M&A world.

Yet, further conversations with M&A lawyers suggested that the dynamics of landmine repair were not as simple as a prominent lawyer publishing an article in the *Business Lawyer* and drafters thereafter responding by revising their contracts. In Chapter Twelve, we look more closely into the precise dynamics of updating obsolete boilerplate in private M&A. We want to see if we can identify the mechanism that causes change to occur there where it does not in the public debt markets.

Chapter Twelve
Uncovering the M&A Network

Introduction

In our discussion of the No Recourse and Choice-of-Law landmines in Chapter Eleven, we saw that market participants in the world of private M&A contracting responded to the call from leading practitioners to address the problem of obsolete terms. This stands in contrast to our research into the sovereign debt market, and in particular the *pari passu* saga. In the *pari passu* case, Lee Buchheit and other leading sovereign debt practitioners had for years unsuccessfully urged a revision of the boilerplate clause. Eventually, there was a market-wide revision to the standard clause, but this change did not materialize until a giant shock roiled the market. Only then, and after considerable delay, did external agents such as the US Federal Reserve and the IMF respond to the shock by enforcing a coordinated solution.[1] By comparison, standard practice in the M&A world responded to the landmine threat even without a big shock to the market and without any external agents enforcing coordination. Here, the market response was not the "all at once" shift that occurred in the sovereign debt setting with *pari passu* and Collective Action clauses. Instead, efforts to repair landmines in the M&A world occurred gradually through a more organic process.

In this chapter, we investigate an additional set of M&A landmines and the processes by which they are both created and then repaired. Our goal is to use the differences in landmine creation and remediation between the M&A and the sovereign debt markets to shed further light on the contract production paradox.

[1] Stephen J. Choi, Mitu Gulati, & Robert E. Scott, *Variation in Boilerplate: Rational Design or Random Variation*, 20 Am. L. & Econ. Rev. 1 (2018).

Contract Hazards. Stephen J. Choi, Mitu Gulati, and Robert E. Scott, Oxford University Press.
 DOI: 10.1093/9780197821770.003.0012

Agency Costs Are Not the Full Story

In comparing landmines across different markets, two points of interest are how the landmines are created and what are the efforts at remediation. Our focus in this chapter is on remediation. We choose this focus because the dynamics of landmine creation are likely similar across different settings: deals have to be done quickly, and lawyers borrow from existing precedents even where the fit is imperfect. Remediation is where differences are likely to be found across markets.

At a surface level, an agency cost story can explain much of the difference in the speed of response to a perceived threat. M&A clients, and especially those in private equity deals, care about avoiding personal liability. And nowhere is that concern more manifest than when they are threatened with fraud claims. These big money clients are face to face with their lawyers. Those lawyers know who pays their bills and who they need to please to be retained on the next deal. And so, the lawyers are responsive to the needs of the clients. If M&A clients care about fraud claims, then their attorneys will focus on the boilerplate terms in their contracts that purportedly place limits on such claims.

In the sovereign bond context, by contrast, the real clients are distant from the actual transactions and the lawyers working on the legal terms. Even if litigation occurs years later, rarely are costs imposed on either the government representatives, the underwriters, or their attorneys. By the time a poorly drafted contract term becomes the focal point of litigation, it is virtually impossible to determine who drafted the original deal documents (especially if the term was copied from documentation used in prior deals). Quite literally, no one is directly on the hook if and when a contract term blows up.[2] In this setting, it makes sense that the task of repairing a landmine that has but a small chance of exploding in the future gets short shrift.

To be sure, the magnitude of agency costs is less on the sovereign side than for underwriters: government officials can have a longer-term horizon and often care about the welfare of the sovereign and its citizens. And the goal of the drafting lawyer is to facilitate those interests. Nonetheless, compared with private equity funds that fully internalize the risk of a fraud lawsuit,

[2] In the hundreds of hours of interviews we've conducted, there isn't a single instance where a respondent has suggested that "X associate or partner was responsible for this landmine in Y deal," let alone suggested that there was any value in determining who X was and why they did what they did.

sovereigns face appreciably greater agency costs than do private equity clients in the M&A context.

The differences in agency cost between private M&A and sovereign debt is, however, only a part of the story. It does not explain all the differences we see between these two markets. Even in the M&A market, change takes time. And it is not as if the diminished agency costs in the M&A setting results in landmine-free documents, even when the problems are readily apparent. Far from it. M&A deals tend to have multiple landmines. And there is variance in the shape of these landmines across deals, in contrast to the far more standardized sovereign debt documents. In short, there is more to say here than "the levels of agency costs differ across these settings."

The question that we investigate in this chapter is exactly how landmine revisions occur in the M&A market. In Chapter Eleven, we saw that several articles in the *Business Lawyer* had urged revision of certain obsolete clauses in the standard M&A contract. Publication in the most prominent practitioner journal in business law appeared to correlate with subsequent changes in the market. At first blush it appears that senior practitioners called for changes to the standard boilerplate and then revision occurred. One might then ask: Do M&A lawyers regularly read the *Business Lawyer* and promptly respond to the suggestions they find there?

When this question is posed to practicing lawyers, it usually induces laughter. Most M&A lawyers have neither the time nor inclination to read articles in the *Business Lawyer*. Many of them do not even read the important cases in their field. The *Business Lawyer* articles are not irrelevant to inducing landmine repair, but they are a small part of the story of how information dissemination induces market-wide changes.[3]

To better understand the dynamics of landmine repair in the M&A market, we focus on another M&A landmine, one that concerned efforts to limit fraud claims against private equity sponsors. Unlike the M&A landmines described and analyzed in Chapter Eleven, where our goal was to show the differences between sovereign and corporate bonds and private M&A, here we explore the world of M&A lawyers by adding interviews with

[3] We cannot help but recall our own experience with publishing in the *Business Lawyer* when the first surprising sovereign *pari passu* decision came down from a local court in Brussels in 2001. Imagining that a case from a commercial court in Brussels might not be noticed by leading practitioners in London and New York, one of us coauthored a note about the case and how it called for practitioners to revise their clauses. On the belief that every senior sovereign debt lawyer received the *Business Lawyer*, we sent the piece there and it was accepted. As best we know, hardly anyone read it—and not a single contract was revised based on it.

M&A gurus to our quantitative analyses. The story that emerges is one of spiders and webs.

Glenn West and the (Not So) Exogenous Shocks

Sometime in late 2022, we received an email from Glenn West, whom we didn't know personally at the time, stating that he had read an article of ours and found some "issues" that he would like to discuss. Every legal academic has stories of an eminent practitioner who feels compelled to tell them how wrong their academic theories are, and none of us particularly enjoys such scoldings. Nevertheless, on the theory that we might learn something from the conversation, we called Glenn. His concern was that legal academics doing empirical work on M&A often didn't understand the phenomena they were trying to study and usually drew incorrect inferences from their data. Glenn urged us to talk to lawyers on the ground to understand what was really going on.

Glenn's specific critique concerned a conjecture we had made that his articles on the No Recourse clause in the *Business Lawyer* had induced a change in drafting practices in the private M&A world. To Glenn, we had missed the forest for the trees. If we wanted to get a deeper understanding of the dynamics of contract term revision in the M&A market, we should investigate another instance of contract term evolution, the "fraud carve out" provision in the typical private M&A contract. In particular, Glenn suggested that we might benefit from going beyond the quantitative data and attending and observing American Bar Association gatherings of M&A lawyers. It was at those ABA gatherings, in particular sub committees, where the sausage of contract change was made. That's where there often were discussions among the gurus of the profession about problematic clauses and how to fix them. From there, information got disseminated to others in the M&A bar.

Glenn explained that he had written an article in 2014 in the *Business Lawyer* about the fraud carve out. He imagined that the data would show that the article was correlated with changes in market practice, but that it would nevertheless be an error to conclude the changes were caused by the article. That work was not the "shock" that caused the changes. In fact, he had written another article in the same journal five years earlier, making essentially the same point about the need to fix the same type of drafting blunder, but few had responded then by repairing their clauses.

Frustrated with the lack of a market response, Glenn and other M&A gurus began providing more information to the market on the need to update the obsolete fraud carve out. To be sure, one action was Glenn reissuing his earlier article in a shorter form in 2014. But this was but one of many actions undertaken by this group of lawyers, including having the ABA's Deal Points Study collect data on the clauses. That data built greater awareness and led to West's decision, in conjunction with the leadership of the M&A section of the ABA, to publish the new version of his article. Thereafter, in 2015, the group of lawyers went on the road giving Continuing Legal Education (CLE) presentations and conducting conference discussions and video chats with other M&A attorneys. And only then was discernable change visible. In short, landmine revision was not caused by a shock in the form of the 2014 article (as we had conjectured). The conditions for change had been put in place years before, and change only occurred when a confluence of pressures came to bear on deal lawyers.

We decided to try to better understand the conditions motivating landmine revision in M&A by exploring the fraud carve out provision.

Undefined Fraud

In what follows, we focus particularly on the responses by private M&A deal drafters to the evolving changes in the ability of parties to contract over fraud. First, we set out some background on developments in the industry.

No-Reliance to Fraud Carve Outs

At common law, efforts by commercial parties to contract over fraud were strictly policed. Courts routinely held that claims of fraud were an exception to the parol evidence rule. They did so even where the contract contained a merger clause that most common law courts otherwise held was conclusive evidence that the written agreement was fully integrated and contained all the terms of the parties contract.[4]

[4] Stephen F. Ross & Daniel Trannen, *The Modern Parol Evidence Rule and Its Implications for New Textualist Statutory Interpretation*, 87 Geo. L. J. 195 (1995) (discussing the history of the parol evidence rule).

The first crack on this bulwark occurred in New York in *Danann Realty v. Harris* in 1959.[5] The contract in *Danann* contained the following language:

> The Seller has not made and does not make any representations as to the physical condition, rents, leases, expenses, operation or any other matter or thing affecting or related to the aforesaid premises, except as herein specifically set forth, and the *Purchaser hereby expressly acknowledges . . . neither party is relying upon any statement or representation, not embodied in this contract,* made by the other.[6]

The New York Court of Appeals held that this clause, now commonly known as a "No-Reliance" clause, was enforceable to prevent the purchaser from claiming fraudulent misrepresentations made by agents of the seller regarding the expenses for maintaining the leased property.[7] Over time, the freedom of parties to contract over extra-contractual fraud was recognized in other jurisdictions as well, including the Delaware Chancery Court in *H-M Wexford LLC v. Encorp, Inc.*[8]

The question of how far parties to agreements governed by Delaware law could contract over fraud became even more salient when buyers in private equity acquisition agreements began in the early 2000s to insist on a "fraud carve out." The fraud carve out originated in response to private equity deals' growing use of indemnification provisions, which limit an acquirer's remedies in the event a seller breaches certain representations regarding the qualities of the target company (generally to 10%–20% of the contract price). While buyers came to accept those seller-friendly indemnification terms, they in turn negotiated for fraud carve outs as exceptions that retained a broader range of remedies for a buyer in the event the seller was found to have committed fraud in the transaction.[9]

The fraud carve out was one side of a swinging pendulum. Sellers' desire for finality and a clean break upon the sale of a company led to increasing use of indemnification provisions, which circumscribed buyers' remedies to

[5] Danann Realty Corp. v. Harris, 5 N.Y.2d 317, 157 N.E.2d 597, 598 (NY 1959) (denying a claim that the plaintiff was induced to enter into the contract based on false oral statements).

[6] *Id.*

[7] *Id.* at 600. The New York court emphasized that the clause was clear and specifically disclaimed any reliance on the representations at issue in the case. In the years following *Danann Realty*, courts in New York consistently affirmed the ability of contracting parties to deploy the No-Reliance clause to bar claims of fraud for extra-contractual representations by agents of the seller.

[8] 832 A.2d.129, 142.

[9] *Id.*

a certain percentage of the purchase price, among other limitations.[10] The fraud carve out was the buyers' reaction: they were willing to swallow the limitations the indemnification regime imposed on their potential recovery, but not when the seller was found to have defrauded them.[11]

The fraud carve out has now been used in acquisition agreements for at least two decades. These carve outs can appear in multiple places in a private equity acquisition contract, most commonly in the indemnification and damages cap provisions.[12] They have a simple structure. Whatever the primary clause provides (typically a limitation on the type or quantity of damages), the fraud carve out specifies that the limitation does not apply in the case the party in question (typically the seller) commits fraud.[13] But this ultimately led to the question: What do the parties mean by fraud given its numerous and varied meanings across jurisdictions?[14] If bound by the laws of a jurisdiction with an expansive view of fraud, sellers could be subject to a much greater liability than they had anticipated. Could sellers contract for a more limited fraud liability at the outset? The Delaware courts, responding to market concerns, said yes.[15]

ABRY Partners and the Emergence of Limited Fraud Clauses

The evolution of the fraud carve out accelerated when the Delaware Court of Chancery decided *ABRY Partners v. F&W Acquisition* in 2006.[16] The issue posed in *ABRY Partners* was whether the parties could contract out of fraud liability for statements made both *within* the contract (as part of the representations and warranties) and outside the contract (informal statements about the company made by the sellers or their agents in the course of negotiations or due diligence). Vice Chancellor Strine first held that the No-Reliance clause only applied to extra-contractual

[10] *Id.*
[11] *Id.*
[12] Sarah McLean & Sarah Nealis, *Fraud Carve-Out Provisions for M&A Agreements*, THE ENERGY LAW ADVISOR (October 2018).
[13] *Id.*
[14] Glenn West, *The Pesky Little Thing Called Fraud*, 69 BUS. LAW. 1, 1052 (2014).
[15] *See, e.g., H-M Wexford LLC v. Encorp, Inc.*, 832 A.2d 129, 140 (Del. Ch. 2003) (concluding the parties can contract around fraud).
[16] For the court decision, see *ABRY Partners V, L.P. v. F & W Acquisition LLC*, 891 A.2d 1032 (Del. Ch. 2006).

representations. The Vice Chancellor then explained that parties could not contract out of fraud liability for representations and warranties *in the contract*, but they could limit their liability for these intra-contractual misrepresentations by specifying that the fraud carve out applied only to deliberate or intentional misrepresentations. Such an exclusion would then be effective to eliminate claims based on reckless or negligent misstatements in the contract.

The question that interested us was whether the M&A market would respond to Strine's invitation to limit the fraud carve out to intentional fraud only. In short, we wanted to know the prevalence of contracts where the drafters used a fraud carve out but then *failed* to so limit the fraud carve out. From the seller's perspective, that would be a landmine: the seller remained vulnerable to a broad range of fraud claims by failing to define the fraud exception narrowly.[17] This failure to update a clause that was now obsolete in light of the opinion in *ABRY Partners* would be a blunder.

Our analysis, discussed below, finds a correlation between changes in the fraud carve out clause and the timing of Judge Strine's invitation. We found that pre-2015 there were many contracts that used the fraud carve out but failed to limit the fraud claim to intentional fraud. Starting in 2015, however, there was a distinct shift: the incidence of landmines resulting from the failure to limit fraud claims declined significantly. The question then is why? The obvious initial answer was that Glenn West's article from 2014 had stimulated the change. But Glenn had told us that the story was more complicated than the publication of his 2014 article in the *Business Lawyer*. So, we decided to look more closely at the question by gathering qualitative evidence to supplement our quantitative results.

[17] Even if drafters were able to coordinate on a Limited Fraud carve out, a further legal challenge emerged that should have motivated more revisions to the basic acquisition agreement. No Reliance clauses and Limited Fraud clauses are not universally enforceable. A number of states—particularly California and Massachusetts—decline to enforce provisions that purport to eliminate fraud claims by contract. Glenn D. West & W. Benton Lewis, Jr., *Contracting to Avoid Extra-Contractual Liability—Can Your Contractual Deal Ever Really Be the "Entire" Deal?* 100 Bus. Law. 1024–1025 (2009). In several cases, buyers had claimed that a governing law clause designating Delaware law as the basis for evaluating claims under the contract did not apply to claims for fraud that were grounded in tort rather than contract. A test then might be to examine how and when governing law clauses in acquisitions contracts are revised to designate Delaware law for both contract and tort claims arising out of the transaction in response to this concern. We described the data on this in Chapter Eleven, although we did not explore the nuances of the network there, as we do here. *See also* Robert E. Scott, Stephen J. Choi, & Mitu Gulati, *Comparing Agency Costs in Contract Production*, 74 Case Western L. Rev. 48 (2023).

Data

We began by compiling data from the SEC's EDGAR database on both public and private M&A deals for the period from 2000 to 2020.[18] We collected roughly two thousand contracts. The dataset was made up of a hundred randomly selected contracts per year; fifty private target deals and fifty public deals. We used the data to observe both the utilization of fraud carve out clauses in the marketplace and the related question of fraud carve outs that failed to limit the claim to intentional fraud. We coded each contract for both the presence of fraud carve out provisions and the landmine—the failure to limit the fraud claim.

The Fraud Carve Out

The fraud carve out clause emerged in the early 2000s, when our dataset begins, and it had become standard by the end of our dataset in 2020. To construct the variable reported in the figures below, we looked across each M&A agreement to identify the instances where a fraud carve out appears. Tracking the incidence of the fraud carve out clause is important because it gave us a measure of the incidence of the landmine risk (i.e., the carve outs that fail to limit fraud claims). These carve outs tend to be found in one of six different types of provisions—Indemnification, Exclusive Remedy, Survival, Financing, Termination, and No Additional Representations. We then tracked the incidence of fraud carve outs in those provisions in two ways.

Figure 12.1 shows that the prevalence of fraud carve outs steadily increased over the two decades for which we have data and that fraud carve outs were more prevalent in private as compared with public deals across our sample period.[19] For all private deals in our dataset, 57.8% have at least one fraud carve out compared with 46.0% for public deals.

[18] Our analysis in this chapter is based on our work with Matt Jennejohn. *See* Stephen J. Choi, Mitu Gulati, Matthew Jennejohn, & Robert E. Scott, *Contract Production in M&A Markets*, 171 U. PA. L. REV. 1881 (2023). The category of "private M&A" deals, in terms of the data we are able to collect from SEC filings by public companies, comprises deals where a public company is acquiring a private firm and the contract qualifies as "material" for the public company. This gives us only a partial window into the M&A world since many M&A deals do not involve a public company. Moreover, for public acquisitions, the company doing the acquisition is so large that most of its acquisition contracts do not qualify as "material" and, therefore, do not have to be disclosed. All that is to say that, roughly speaking, our data is a mid-market sample.

[19] Fraud carve out incidence is captured as a binary variable, which is set to one if a fraud carve out appears in any of the six provisions above (and zero, if not). Figure 12.1 depicts the percentage

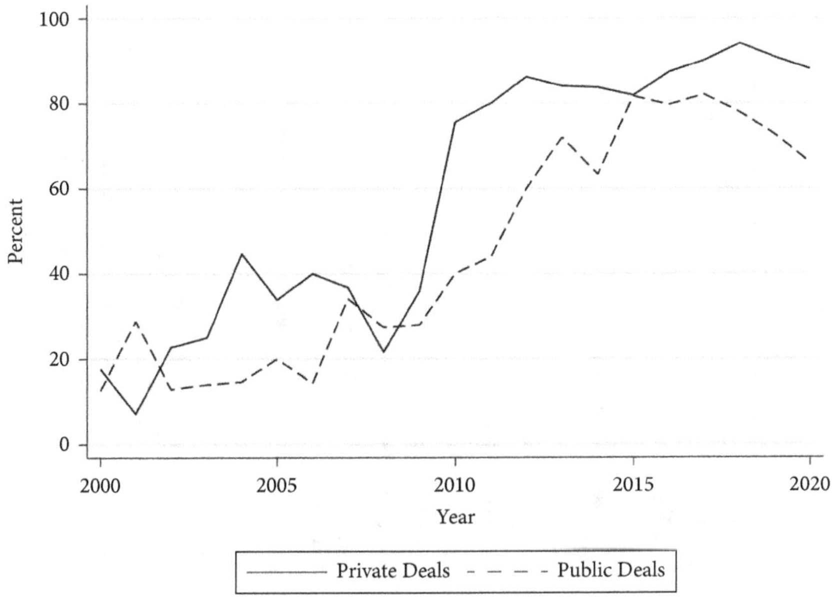

Figure 12.1 Fraction of deals with at least one fraud carve out

In Figure 12.2, we take a different tack. Here, we tallied the fraud carve out's incidence across all six of the provisions. This allowed us to track the mean number of fraud carve outs per agreement in our sample. Consistent with the trend in Figure 12.1, there is an upward trend in the number of fraud carve outs for both public and private deals. In the early 2000s, there was less than 0.5 instances of a fraud carve out on average in both public and private deals, corresponding to less than one fraud carve out in every two deals. By 2020, there were about two fraud carve outs on average in private deals and about one fraud carve out on average in public deals.[20]

of deals with at least one fraud carve out. The solid trend line depicts the percentage of private target transactions and the dashed line depicts public targets.

[20] In the public company world, there is less benefit to carving out fraud since parties cannot contract around whatever fraud standard the federal securities laws impose; nor is there much risk of stockholders being held liable for the misstatements of company managers. *See* Section 14, Securities Act of 1933 ("Any condition, stipulation, or provision binding any person acquiring any security to waive compliance with any provision of this subchapter or of the rules and regulations of the Commission shall be void"); Section 29(a), Securities Exchange Act of 1934 ("Any condition, stipulation, or provision binding any person to waive compliance with any provision of this title or of any rule or regulation thereunder, or of any rule of a self-regulatory organization, shall be void").

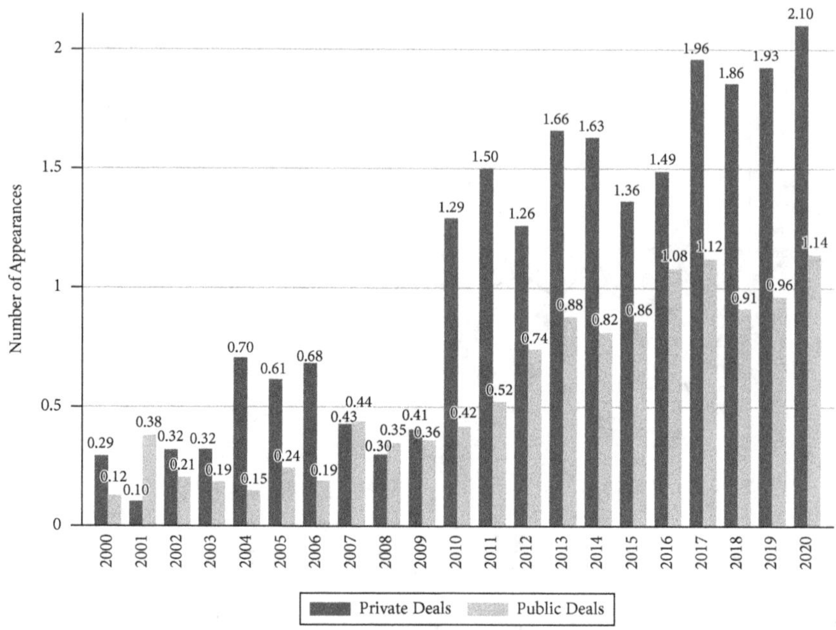

Figure 12.2 Frequency of fraud carve outs, private and public target deals

Now to the main event. The data tells us that fraud carve outs are pervasive in M&A deals, and we know from the discussion earlier that these clauses will be landmines should they lack the updated language limiting fraud claims. So we looked to see how the landmines in the fraud carve outs evolved. And, in particular, to see how the Limited Fraud addendum evolved as a function of the articles by Glenn West in the *Business Lawyer*, first in 2009 and then in 2014.

The Incidence of Limited Fraud Clauses

Over our sample period from 2000 to 2020, 17.3% of private deals with a fraud carve out also included a Limited Fraud clause that restricted the buyer's claims of fraud to intentional fraud. In comparison, only 3.7% of public deals with a fraud carve out contained a Limited Fraud provision.

Figure 12.3 shows the incidence of a Limited Fraud term in deals with at least one fraud carve out for both the public and private markets. For both markets, we see that only a few deals with a fraud carve out also included a

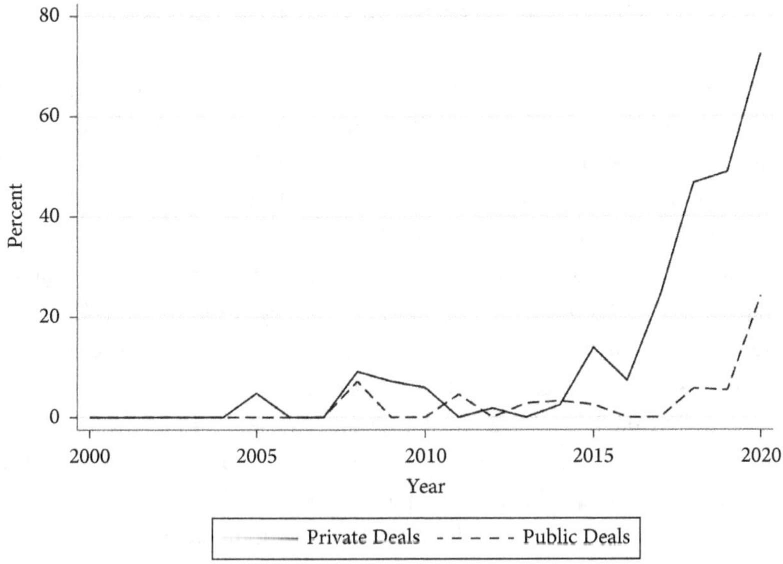

Figure 12.3 Percent of deals with a fraud carve out that include a Limited Fraud term

Limited Fraud term until around 2015. From then, coinciding with the publication of Glenn's 2014 *Business Lawyer* article, we see a steady growth to the end of the dataset particularly in the private deal market. The shift toward fixing the landmine begins about a decade after Judge Strine's *ABRY* decision (2006) and eight years after Glenn West's 2009 *Business Lawyer* article with Benton Lewis urging practitioners to narrowly define fraud.[21]

The fact that Glenn West's article was published in 2014 does not by itself tell us that it had anything to do with the shift in drafting practices. After all, this article was mostly a retread of the 2009 article, and not much changed in the data after that first article. In addition, Glenn had warned us at the outset of our inquiry that a lot more was going on, particularly in terms of information transfers across lawyer networks within the M&A community. To find out what happened at a ground level, therefore, we turned to interviews with the people who might have been inducing the information transfers—the gurus of the M&A bar.

[21] See Glenn D. West & W. Benton Lewis, Jr., *Contracting to Avoid Extra-Contractual Liability—Can Your Contractual Deal Ever Really Be the "Entire" Deal?* 100 Bus. Law. 1024–1025 (2009). For the court decision, see *ABRY Partners V*, *supra* note 16.

The Interviews: M&A Spiders and Their Network

Networks are mechanisms for coordination and cooperation between formally independent but functionally interdependent entities. They provide parties in multilateral markets with indispensable cognitive resources—knowledge about the world and its possibilities—and frameworks for addressing coordination problems that can reduce the costs of conventional forms of standardized contracting.[22] Parties in thick markets have limited information about the universe of possible partners. It follows that it is worthwhile to search for potential partners who know, or might quickly discover, solutions a single party could not reach alone.[23]

Contracting parties in the M&A market are members of such a network of commercial collaborators empowered to solve coordination and collective action problems. All the participants in the market stand to be harmed by the inefficiencies of standardization, yet no single party, not even a guru such as Glenn West, can easily update standard terms as conditions change. By participating in a network, the parties can address these inefficiencies collectively.

To evaluate the private M&A lawyers network, we interviewed thirty eminent practitioners. We first note the unique relationship this network has to the legal system in the M&A context studied here. Unlike other markets, where it is not unusual for there to be a disconnect between specialized market participants and generalist courts, the Delaware Court of Chancery is embedded within the M&A ecosystem.[24] One respondent explained:

> Unlike in other contexts, such as the federal courts in New York, things are different in Delaware. The judges in the Delaware courts are an integral

[22] *See* Lisa Bernstein, *Beyond Relational Contracts: Social Capital and Network Governance in Procurement Contracts*, 7 J. Legal Anal. 561, 563 (2016) (noting the power of "network governance" to empower the enforcement of contractual duties).

[23] Networks that form to obtain information about potential partners, including most famously the biotech collaborations in Silicon Valley, have been studied by organizational sociologists. *See, e.g.*, Walter W. Powell, Kenneth Koput, & Laurel Smith-Doerr, *Inter-Organizational Collaboration and the Locus of Innovation: Networks of Learning in Biotechnology*, 41 Admin. Sci. Q. 116, 119 (1996) ("We argue that when knowledge is broadly distributed and brings a competitive advantage, the locus of innovation is found in a network of interorganizational relationship"); Walter W. Powell, *Inter-Organizational Collaboration in the Biotechnology Industry*, 152 J. Inst. & Theoretical Econ. 197, 198 (1996) (analyzing the effects that institutional designs can have on increasing cooperation).

[24] *See* William Savitt, *The Genius of the Modern Chancery System*, 2012 Colum. B. L. Rev. 570, 570–571 (2012) (arguing that the Delaware Court of Chancery's circumscribed jurisdiction and deep connection to a specialized bar has allowed it to play a leading role in US corporate governance).

> part of the legal community. They listen to the concerns of the lawyers, go to their conferences, and answer questions about the direction of the law. Federal judges in New York do not do this. It is rare that you will get a real shock in a Delaware case—these judges are all experienced and careful lawyers. They think hard about what is best for the market. Judge Strine, who wrote ABRY, prided himself in understanding the bar and what was needed. I think that that's true of the other judges too.

The Court of Chancery is not the sole coordinating institution in the M&A market. Vice Chancellor Strine's opinion in *ABRY*, standing alone, was not sufficient to spark swift and comprehensive adoption of fraud carve outs with limited fraud definitions. Nor does the private bar operate wholly divorced from the bench, picking up the pieces, as it were, when periodic judicial interventions change previously optimal drafting practices. The judiciary and advisory network work hand-in-glove, the former seeking to anticipate the latter, and the latter translating the former's decisions into practice.

The Court of Chancery's place in that ecosystem is visible due to its public status, but the precise way that the network facilitates coordination among market participants is less clear. Our prior work on the revisions to the No Recourse clause suggested several different mechanisms that a private equity network could use to coordinate needed changes in the standard acquisition contract.[25] One possibility is the dominating influence of a single individual, such as a leading lawyer, who serves as the "spider in the web"—an agent of coordination who uses their voice to influence change. Another coordinating factor could be the capacity of the leading law firms in the industry to serve as the "spider."[26] A third avenue of coordination is the evolutionary process of learning. This process proceeds from the individual level of deal partners teaching each other during bespoke negotiations to the group level of collective engagement at conferences and bar meetings between drafters and the judges who rule on litigated cases.

To aid in identifying the likely pathway(s) to coordination, we explained to the M&A respondents that we were interested in understanding the evolution

[25] Robert E. Scott, Stephen J. Choi, & Mitu Gulati, *Revising Boilerplate: A Comparison of Private and Public Company Transactions*, 2020 Wisc. L. Rev. 630.

[26] This possibility is suggested by the evidence of the role of the five leading law firms in private equity in motivating coordination over changes to the No Recourse clause. *See* Scott et al., *id.* at 651–654. The conception of the spider in the network web was introduced in Ariel Porat & Robert E. Scott, *Can Restitution Save Fragile Spiderless Networks?*, 8 Harv. Bus. L. Rev. 1, 3 (2018) (contending that a controlling relationship in the center of a network dictates its success).

of standardized terms relevant to contracting over fraud. We asked: What impediments might explain the time lag between bespoke efforts to contract over fraud and the standardization of those changes in the market contract? And what factors were most likely to affect the speed of a successful coordination on new clauses?[27] Their responses follow.

The Individual Spider

In a pair of articles in the *Business Lawyer*, the first in 2009 and the second in 2014, Glenn West flagged the failure to limit fraud in fraud carve outs as a stubbornly persistent issue in private equity deals. Glenn's message was clear. Sell-side clients, in his experience, were willing to agree to fraud carve outs because they believed fraud was limited to intentional misbehavior. But in many jurisdictions, fraud was susceptible to a broader range of meanings, including reckless and negligent misstatements. Glenn proposed a solution: parties could specify in their contracts that "fraud" meant intentional fraud only.

It is plausible to ask whether Glenn's two publications in the *Business Lawyer* were the key factors motivating the market to coordinate on a standard term for contracting over fraud. Could it be that Glenn, regardless of his private views, was the spider in the web: Did his actions cause the network to coordinate around changes in fraud related terms? Many respondents flagged Glenn's writings as important. Multiple respondents, not knowing that our project had started with Glenn's articles, even urged us to read them to better understand the fraud carve out issue. That said, none of our respondents thought Glenn's articles on their own were capable of causing a broad-based move toward a new standardized clause. One respondent wryly observed:

> I don't know many senior lawyers who would actually sit down and read an academic article. Most don't even read the important Delaware cases. And

[27] Similar to the interviews reported in other chapters, the interviews were generally done over zoom and generally lasted between a half hour and an hour. At the start of each conversation, we assured our respondents that nothing they said would be attributed to them and their identities would be kept confidential. We then gave a short explanation of why we had found the fraud carve out provision and the process of defining it intriguing. In a handful of cases, we had follow-up conversations by email.

> make no mistake; Glenn [West] may be a senior partner at a big firm—but those articles are academic. You need much more than just a couple of such [academic] articles for change.

Glenn's academic writings alone were not the spider in the network. For change, there needed to be more.

Another respondent described the dynamic as follows:

> Glenn had been telling us to define fraud for years and we'd all nod our heads and then just copy the old provisions from the prior deals. But at some point, and probably after that [2014 Business Lawyer] article, the rhetoric got ramped up. He and others at the ABA's M&A meetings began telling us that we were essentially committing malpractice by failing to define fraud. That got people to listen. There may have been something else going on as well. There had always been the threat that opportunistic claims for fraud would be made. It might have then happened in a few cases like EMSI.

Law Firm Spiders

Our prior study of changes to the No Recourse clause found that coordination in the market occurred among the five leading law firms who had the largest share of the private equity acquisitions market.[28] This suggests that perhaps these law firms have assumed a special responsibility to function as the spider in the network web. Even if the private acquisition market lacks an obvious controlling entity, drafters in these leading law firms could work together to coordinate changes in response to need.[29] By acting as first movers, they could provide key information to others in the market regarding the efficiency benefits of the new contract terms. Moreover, by being the first drafters in the market to design new terms, the design costs for subsequent drafters would be reduced. But respondents rejected the prediction that

[28] *See* Scott et al., *Revising Boilerplate*, *supra* note 25, at 651–654.

[29] For a similar finding on the effect of leading law firms in coordinating innovation in the sovereign bond world, see Stephen J. Choi & Mitu Gulati, *Innovation in Boilerplate: An Empirical Examination of Sovereign Bonds*, 53 Emory L. J. 930, 948 (2004) (predicting that law firms experienced with a "large volume" of sovereign bonds can lead the path toward newer terms in bonds).

we would see particular law firms as leading the move to a new contractual standard. Sometimes law firms were involved, but that was not the key mechanism for change. To the extent we were seeing correlations in the data and jumping to conclusions, we were making the correlation/causation error.

Contract innovation, we were told, spread in a more disaggregated way in this market than we were imagining. Elite law firms, either individually or together, were unlikely to be the spiders spreading innovation. Contracting innovations were spread through a more organic process, via connections across individuals, at industry conferences, meetings, and other collective events.

The Influence of Multilevel, Collective Engagement

The evidence we've collected, both from the interviews and reports, on the actions of lawyers and judges in the private equity M&A bar suggests that the network lacks a single spider. In that respect, the M&A world, and particularly its private equity subset, more closely resembles the sovereign debt market than it does the trade association networks such as those studied by Lisa Bernstein.[30]

But unlike sovereign debt, there is a well-documented practice of both individual and collective information exchange among the leading players in the private equity M&A market.[31] For example, in 2009, the M&A Committee of the ABA's Business Law Section began sharing information about the fraud carve out issue with practitioners in two ways. First, the M&A Committee's Deal Points study,[32] which gives deal lawyers insight into the current state of market practice, began collecting and reporting data on what fraction of a sample of deals were limiting fraud to intentional actions in their fraud carve outs.[33] Practitioners could see in the study the initial uptake in Limited Fraud

[30] *See, e.g.*, Lisa Bernstein, *Private Commercial Law in the Cotton Industry: Creating Cooperation Through Rules, Norms, and Institutions*, 99 MICH. L. REV. 1724, 1725–1725 (2001) (describing the private legal systems that govern trade association dealings); Lisa Bernstein, *Merchant Law in a Modern Economy*, PHILOSOPHICAL FOUNDATIONS OF CONTRACT LAW 246–249 (Gregory Klass et al. eds., Oxford University Press, 2015) (illustrating the transactional practices used in merchant communities).

[31] For empirical evidence of this information exchange within the M&A network, see Kristina Bishop, Matthew Jennejohn, & Cree Jones, *The Diffusion of Deal Innovations in Complex Contractual Networks*, BYU Research Paper No. 23-22.

[32] https://www.americanbar.org/groups/business_law/committees/ma/deal_points/

[33] See Bishop et al., *supra* note 31 (providing evidence that the ABA Deal Points Study affects diffusion patterns of new deal terms in the M&A market).

provisions. And because this information on the market practice in narrowly defining fraud was reported by the Deal Points study every year since 2009, drafters could follow the evolution toward standardization of the new fraud definitions in the market over time.

Second, alongside the data reported in the Deal Points studies, the issue of limiting fraud was explicitly discussed in the programming provided at the M&A Committee annual meetings. Beginning roughly in 2010, Glenn West and a number of the other M&A gurus began presenting on fraud carve outs at industry gatherings of lawyers. They informed their audiences of the basic issues and staged mock negotiations to illustrate the bargaining dynamics that would often arise in the design of a fraud carve out.[34] These presentations contextualized the raw numbers provided in the Deal Points Studies.

The judiciary stayed involved throughout this time period, though it would not provide another paradigm shifting treatment of the issue like the original *ABRY* decision. The Chancery Court interpreted fraud carve outs and Limited Fraud clauses from time to time, applying *ABRY* with fidelity.[35] Finally, to close the circle, the Delaware Supreme Court explicitly affirmed Judge Strine's *ABRY* decision in 2021, citing Glenn West's 2014 *Business Lawyer* article for good measure.[36]

Taking those dynamics together, we see interventions by both the judiciary and leaders within the bar woven together. *ABRY*'s invitation to draft a Limited Fraud clause was taken up by a few first movers in bespoke transactions. Leading practitioners and, in particular, the ABA's M&A Committee, amplified Judge Strine's teaching, drawing attention to and also educating deal lawyers about the *ABRY* decision and the need to update the fraud carve out by carefully defining fraud. All the while, the Delaware judiciary sounded a steady drumbeat in support of respecting parties' freedom to contract over fraud. As one respondent noted, "this is about conversations in

[34] Interview 13, Dec. 4, 2022 ("At that point, I took the fraud carve out on the road. I felt like John the Baptist crying in the wilderness to the unconverted. . . . We created a script for a negotiation [to demonstrate the typical bargaining dynamic and how to address it]"); Interview 14, Oct. 16, 2021 ("I've certainly talked about 'fraud carve outs' at ABA meetings"); Interview 26, Oct. 5, 2022 (noting the discussion of fraud carve outs at ABA meetings and that "those were really well attended meetings" where there "were some wake up calls").

[35] *See, e.g.*, Fortis Advisors LLC v. Johnson & Johnson, No. CV 2020-0881-LWW, 2021 WL 5893997 (Del. Ch. Dec. 13, 2021); EMSI Acquisition, Inc. v. Contrarian Funds, LLC, No. CV 12648-VCS, 2017 WL 1732369 (Del. Ch. May 3, 2017); Prairie Cap. III, L.P. v. Double E Holding Corp., 132 A.3d 35 (Del. Ch. 2015).

[36] *See* Express Scripts, Inc. v. Bracket Holdings Corp., 248 A.3d 824 (2021).

the industry—among practitioners on how best to draft. These are discussed at the meetings and conferences."

This story is consistent with the hypothesis that, even in an environment such as the M&A acquisition market that lacks a controlling entity or "spider," coordination can proceed in a multilevel organic way through an informal network. The evolutionary process begins with individual drafters experimenting with bespoke Limited Fraud clauses but then the efficiency advantages of these revisions are transmitted between negotiating partners and ultimately through a well-integrated network of lawyers and judges. And eventually, through this process, a more standard product emerges.

Why Coordination in M&A and Not Sovereign Debt?

We can attribute the difference in how boilerplate terms responded to market shocks in the private M&A and sovereign markets to the presence (or absence) of spiders and other coordinating mechanisms such as conferences and market-attuned judges. But at least one question remains: Why do we see such spiders and other coordinating mechanisms in the private M&A market but not the sovereign market? Could it be that purely idiosyncratic factors determine the success of coordination in one market but not another? Perhaps if a young Glenn West had decided to focus his practice on sovereign bonds instead of private M&A, we would have observed a much different response to the landmines embedded in the *pari passu* clause. On the other hand, there are figures akin to Glenn West in the sovereign bond market. After all, we started our story with Lee Buchheit visiting one of our classes to talk about landmines in Greek sovereign bonds.

To be sure, idiosyncratic factors could explain why a spider arises in a given market or why participants in a particular market become accustomed to meeting regularly in conferences. Thereafter, a market may find itself in a self-sustaining equilibrium that supports spiders and the coordination they facilitate. Moreover, the differential-in agency-costs story we introduced at the beginning of this chapter may explain why spiders and other coordinating structures have an easier time taking root in markets like private M&A as compared with sovereign debt. Because attorneys in the private M&A market care more about specific contract terms that affect their clients, these attorneys will pay more attention to commentary on such terms and be willing to devote time to attending conferences to keep current on the latest legal "technology" relating to boilerplate terms used in M&A deals.

In Chapter Thirteen, we look at a different market, the one for syndicated leveraged loans. This market seems to lack effective coordination mechanisms, at least thus far. Indeed, it more closely resembles both the structure and resulting landmine problems that we have observed in sovereign debt than it does the world of M&A. In our final Chapter Fourteen, we will return to examine more carefully the question why coordination evolves differently in each of these different markets.

Chapter Thirteen
The Form Is the Form

Introduction

The market for syndicated leveraged loans is the final environment we examine for landmines and their lawyers. As of mid-2025, this is one of the fastest growing financial markets in the United States. And the growth is not just in the volume of these loans, but—and this is what interests us—in the sudden increase in a particular type of lawyer behavior. That behavior involves the pursuit of contract landmines through what has been referred to as "creditor on creditor violence" but now travels under the more respectable labels of liability management "transactions" or "exercises." Euphemisms can tell you a lot: "Lawyers playing whac-a-mole," "They've made these contracts into Swiss cheese," and "crazy schemes" by lawyers to engineer "creditor on creditor violence" seems on its face to describe activity that is unproductive and harmful.[1] One would expect rational clients, trying to do productive deals, to avoid this activity.

A system with more legal aggression tends to give a larger portion of the economic pie to just one set of actors: the lawyers. And giving lawyers more of the pie is not what clients typically prefer to do. But if these new types of transactions are seen instead as "liability management exercises" or better "transactions," then they appear to evoke a worthwhile effort to restructure the debt of a troubled firm. Staving off an impending bankruptcy seems useful and productive. With that tension in mind, we turn to the story.

Before introducing the "crazy schemes" that mark the current state of liability management transactions (LMTs) in the leveraged loan market,

[1] This chapter draws from research with Matt Jennejohn and a conference invitation from Elisabeth de Fontenay and Samir Parikh. *See* Stephen J. Choi, Mitu Gulati, Matthew Jennejohn, & Robert E. Scott, *Swiss Cheese Contracts: The Costs of Creative Lawyering* BYU Law School Working Paper (2025). We borrow the "crazy schemes" language from *Financial Times* reporter Sujeet Indap who described the explosion in liability management transactions in the leveraged loan market to Bloomberg's Odd Lots podcast as "Lawyers in Their Basement Laboratories, Cooking up Crazy Schemes." Tracey Alloway & Joe Weisenthal, *Sujeet Indap on Creditor-on-Creditor Violence: What It Is and Why It's Grown*, Bloomberg Odd Lots (Nov. 26, 2024).

Contract Hazards. Stephen J. Choi, Mitu Gulati, and Robert E. Scott, Oxford University Press.
 DOI: 10.1093/9780197821770.003.0013

we note a few differences between the domestic syndicated lending world and that of sovereign bonds.[2] Lending done through groups of creditors is characteristic of both sovereign bonds and US domestic syndicated loans. Syndicated lending is generally done on a smaller scale than when issuing bonds, and it is usually not subject to US federal securities regulation. In its original form, syndicated lending was an outgrowth of direct bank loans to clients. Syndicates were created when the projects needed ever larger lending facilities and no individual bank was able to bear all the risk. In the syndicate, multiple banks combine to provide credit and create a syndicated loan. The leveraged syndicated loan market where LMTs live is the higher risk segment of the larger syndicated lending market. The "Term Loan B" segment that we focus on refers to lending backed by collateral.[3]

This background is important to our study of landmines because this is a market where we would expect landmines to be less prominent than in the sovereign bond world that we focused on earlier. Among the key differentiating factors are that the trading volumes in the leveraged loan market are smaller (that's part of why they are not regulated by US securities laws) and contract provisions should be more important to the parties (these are high risk collateralized instruments where the underlying entity could easily go into bankruptcy).

In addition, the modern incarnation of this market is new relative to the other markets we've examined—dating to the financial crisis of 2008–2010 when something of a revolution occurred in the syndicated loan market. Once a quiet and clannish world dominated by banks with volumes in the low billions, this is now a multitrillion dollar market. Nonbank lenders dominate today, and the market continues to grow. Banks still play a role in originating these syndicated loans, but they are no longer the key long-term investors. There is a robust secondary market: the dominant players are funds known as collateralized loan obligations (CLOs), which bundle together and manage collateralized loans for below investment grade entities. Other players include hedge funds, pension funds, and insurance companies.[4]

The leveraged loan market falls on our continuum somewhere between the thick market of sovereign bonds and the much thinner market of M&A

[2] Some insiders also use the term LME (liability management exercise) for what we call "LMT." *See* Armen Panossian & Danielle Poli, *The LME Wave*, Oaktree Credit Quarterly (4th Quarter Report, 2024).

[3] Michael T. Reese, *Sources of Available Project Financing: Term Loan B Facilities*, Practical Law (available at PillsburyLaw.com).

[4] For a discussion of this evolution, *see* Douglas Baird, *Three Faces of Creditor on Creditor Aggression*, 97 Amer. Bnkr. L. J. 213 (2023).

contracts. That framework does not, however, help us predict the extent of the landmine phenomenon that we have discovered. This was nothing like what we had seen elsewhere, and it yielded some of the most interesting insights of this project.

* * *

Our attention was first drawn to the leveraged loan market when we noticed a spate of articles in the financial press about an "explosion in creditor on creditor violence schemes." We were skeptical about this characterization. Was it plausible that an army of lawyers were devising ever more creative ways to exploit loopholes in loan documents? In our experience, syndicated loans inhabited a sleepy world dominated by banker's norms where violations such as the transactions we described in Chapter Three would be quickly shut down. Moreover, there was a strong industry association, the LSTA, along with a half dozen private firms specializing in monitoring contract documentation, such as Covenant Review, Street Diligence, Octus, 9Fin, and Xtract Research. This setting is a far cry from the sovereign bond world where there are few such institutions to do covenant analysis and industry coordination. Here, we thought, there should be effective coordination of efforts to revise documentation and close down value reducing activities such as lawyers chasing loopholes.

The financial journalist, Anna Szymanski, persuaded us to take a deeper look at the contemporary world of leveraged loans.[5] We had sent Anna an early draft of the book, which had chapters on sovereign bonds and private equity M&A. Her advice in response was prescient:

> You might benefit from looking at the explosion in liability management deals. It is happening now and an integral part of these transactions is lawyers competing with each other to come up with yet more creative ways of exploiting contract language . . . Sovereign bonds are sleepy. This is where the action is.

[5] Anna had just switched to Reuters after working for a number of years at Oaktree Capital, one of the biggest players in the liability management business. We also read a revealing series of articles on these LMTs by Alexandra Scaggs, of *FT Alphaville. E.g.,* Alexandra Scaggs, *Pet Smart Gives Shares of Its Growth Engine to PE Sponsor*, FT ALPHAVILLE (June 5, 2018); Alexandra Scaggs, *Double Dipping: Not Just for Crudités: We Love a Bit of Internecine Creditor Brutality,* FT ALPHAVILLE (Oct. 26, 2023); Alexandra Scaggs, *Lenders Can Still Get J. Screwed: The J.Crew Blocker Has Some Problems,* FT ALPHAVILLE (Feb. 12, 2024).

We had previously seen the decline of reputational norms in the sovereign bond world; a decline that was largely driven by the entry of distressed debt hedge funds occasionally engaging in aggressive holdouts. Yet, in the world of LMTs there was nothing marginal about the apparent trampling of norms. Paraphrasing a former student of Bob's, who once worked at a bank that did old-style syndicates but now works on creating and blocking these deals: "A horde of wild beasts entered the arena, and they are eating contract rights for breakfast that many used to think were sacred."

Lawyers and Their LMTs

We begin the LMT story by recalling the Serta transaction described in Chapter Three. Serta Simmons was a giant mattress company in financial distress and the prospect of Chapter 11 bankruptcy loomed large. Two groups of creditors came to the private equity sponsors with proposals to buy Serta some additional "runway." Both sets of proposals used loopholes in the credit agreement to benefit themselves at the expense of the other creditors.

Both the proposals were using terms in the standard contract that had been borrowed from the public bond market and, after being slightly modified, were inserted into leveraged loan contracts in the early years of the new version of this market in 2008–2010. At first cut, these terms looked like a version of the historical holdover landmines we have seen earlier. Clauses that were originally intended to deal with the financial crisis of 2008–2010 were being repurposed for (arguably) more nefarious purposes by new and more aggressive players.

In the Serta transaction, two competing groups of creditors were proposing deals to the debtor. The first group proposed to circumvent restrictions in the credit contract by moving valuable assets out of the company into an "unrestricted subsidiary" using what is known as a "J.Crew trapdoor." The group could then effectively obtain priority for its loans over the other creditors by using the transferred assets as collateral. The second creditor group, fearing that they would be left in the cold, came up with a different loophole in the credit agreement. They proposed to exploit a term in the contract that allowed the debtor to purchase the interests of its creditors on the "open market," but failed to specify whether such offers to purchase had to be made to *all* creditors.[6]

[6] Those of our respondents who were around at the time of the inclusion of the "open market purchase" language insisted that the open market clause was not intended to allow the debtor to

Relying on the uncertainty about the meaning of the open market purchase language, the second creditor group used a version of a well-known technique from the bond context called the Exit Consent (permitting a simple majority to agree to subordinate the entire set of creditors) in order to leapfrog the first creditor group.[7] The assumption had been that this subordination provision would be used when the company was doing *new* borrowing and not to advantage a subset of existing creditors at the expense of their equally ranked colleagues. But the contract didn't prohibit such a transaction, and so it was done. And this deal was quickly named the "Up Tier."

The first creditor group, irate about what had been done, and putting aside the fact that it had planned a deal to disadvantage the second group, claimed foul and sued. Two other distressed companies, Boardriders and Trimark, having the same loophole in their contracts, quickly jumped on the bandwagon and did similar Up Tiers. More litigation ensued. The LMT world was up and running.

Five years later, the Fifth Circuit Court of Appeals rejected the use of the "open market" loophole in the Serta Up Tier.[8] But as of this writing, neither unhappy creditors nor court disapproval is dampening the enthusiasm of lawyers for devising new and clever ways for private equity sponsors to collaborate with subsets of creditors to buy space and time at the expense of other creditors. One respondent, who we spoke to a few months after the Fifth Circuit's decision, said:

> It took just three weeks for lawyers to come up with a way to do an Up Tier LMT that worked around the Fifth Circuit's decision. There had been an LMT in the works that planned to use the "open market" mechanism from Serta. After the decision came down, the lawyers were easily able to figure out a way to sidestep the constraint imposed by the Court and still do the Up Tier. The contracts are the equivalent of Swiss cheese. You can fill one hole, but there are going to be a half dozen other ones.[9]

exchange debts with a subset of creditors that would advantage them and disadvantage the others: it was intended to benefit all.

[7] Vincent S.J. Buccola & Marcel Kahan, *Getting to Yes: The Role of Coercion in Debt Exchanges*, University of Chicago Working Paper (2025).

[8] In re Serta Simmons Bedding, 125 F.4th 555 (5th Cir. 2025).

[9] Although the respondent didn't name the transaction, it was later discussed on an industry podcast. *See* Cloud 9Fin, *Jane's LME Addiction: Never Been in Better Health* (Apple Podcasts) (Feb. 13, 2025) (observing that enthusiasm for LMTs has not waned).

Our first encounter with the phrase "creditor-on-creditor violence" came even before the Serta transaction. An article in the *Institutional Investor* told of an allegedly "manufactured default" by a distressed debtor in order to benefit certain holders of credit default swaps (CDS).[10] The quid pro quo was that the CDS holders provided the firm with new financing at below market rates. The article described other transactions where some creditors had collaborated with a distressed debtor to the disadvantage of other creditors. What caught our attention was the highlighted role of lawyers searching the fine print of lending documents to devise ways to do these crafty deals. Industry insiders predicted that this behavior would be short-lived: contracts would be revised to constrain such behavior in the future.[11] That was not to be. A 2020 article, focusing solely on the leveraged loan market, described a series of transactions, including Serta, where groups of creditors had collaborated with distressed debtors to take value from other creditors who then challenged the majority in court.[12] Once again, lawyers exploiting the credit documents creatively was a key part of the story.[13] While partial repairs ("blockers") were thereafter inserted in many contracts, the underlying behavior rather than being constrained became even more common.

Two years later, the story had still not gone away. Lawyers took center stage again in an article by Sujeet Indap of the *Financial Times.* Skilled lawyers were supposedly weaponizing loopholes in loan contracts in order to pit groups of creditors against each other, all in service of private equity sponsors seeking to stave off Chapter 11 bankruptcy.[14] By 2024, reports of the new and clever

[10] Christine Idzelis, *The Rise of Creditor-on-Creditor Violence*, INSTITUTIONAL INVESTOR (May 30, 2018).

[11] *Id.*

[12] Alicia McElhaney, *'Creditor on Creditor Violence' Lands Big Managers in Court*, INSTITUTIONAL INVESTOR (Nov. 20, 2020).

[13] *Id.*

[14] Sujeet Indap, *Slick Lawyers Test the Limits in Distressed Debt Machinations*, FIN. TIMES (Oct. 31, 2022). The aggressive actions of these private equity lawyers echoed the theme of a book Indap and Max Frumes had published a year earlier describing a series of financial battles over the bankruptcy of Caesar's Casino. MAX FRUMES & SUJEET INDAP, THE CAESAR'S PALACE COUP: HOW A BILLIONAIRE BRAWL OVER A FAMOUS CASINO EXPOSED THE CORRUPTION OF THE PRIVATE EQUITY INDUSTRY (Diversion Press, 2021). Several years later, Indap summarized the changes in the lawyers behavior in an interview:

> [T]here was a sense [in the past] that these documents are standardized and there's some kind of template which you downloaded and they're all kind of the same, more or less. What's happened is there has been now this arms race amongst the law firms and the investment banks to read these documents really carefully. **And then in their laboratories in the basement come up with a crazy transaction structure.**
>
> . . .
>
> [T]he creativity that lawyers and bankers try to exploit has been accelerated and ratcheted up. And there's this idea that we are going to ask for forgiveness, not permission. We'll do the transaction. If someone wants to sue, we'll see them in court.

ways lawyers in the leveraged loan market were exploiting loopholes in the credit contracts were everywhere—the press, blogs, podcasts, and academic papers.

The story of lawyers finding creative ways of facilitating LMTs by exploiting landmines in the documents is at odds with conventional theory.[15] Contract theory understands the role of lawyers writing contracts as implementing an efficient design, one that maximizes the ex ante surplus from the parties' agreement. This task requires the lawyers to anticipate and allocate future contingencies so as to optimize contracting costs between the front end (the negotiation stage) and the back end (the enforcement stage).[16] On this account, parties to leveraged loans would expend more efforts on front-end design in order to reduce the substantial back-end costs resulting from transfers to lawyers both to find loopholes and then to litigate over them. As the author of one of the original LMTs admitted:

> The whole thing is strange. Business people hate giving money to lawyers unless they have to. Each of these LMTs costs millions in legal fees. And sometimes companies do them multiple times before they go into bankruptcy. The lawyers are making a killing and everyone knows that is going to happen at the outset of the deal.

But as we have emphasized through the book, contract theory fails to explain the world we see because it focuses solely on contract design and not on the companion task of contract production. Once production considerations become relevant, the theory can be harmonized with facts on the ground. In addition to making efficient design choices, parties must also optimize between efficient design and efficient production. Design considerations give way in a liquid market such as leveraged loans because the front-end costs

Tracey Alloway & Joe Weisenthal, *Sujeet Indap on Creditor-on-Creditor Violence: What it is and Why it's Grown*, Bloomberg Odd Lots (Apple Podcasts) (Nov. 26, 2024) (emphasis added)

[15] *Cf.* Kenneth Ayotte & Christina Scully, *J.Crew, Nine West, and the Complexities of Financial Distress*, 131 Yale L. J. F. 363 (2021). Ayotte and Scully focus on the contrast between the assumptions of contract theory and the imperfections of the contracts at the center of the J.Crew and Nine West deals. They suggest that the flaw in contract theory is the assumption that the complex contracts that these types of deals require can be perfectly designed. They suggest that a bounded rationality view of contract design is more appropriate.

[16] *See* Robert E. Scott & George G. Triantis, *Incomplete Contracts and the Theory of Contract Design*, 56 Case Western L. Rev. 1 (2005); Robert E. Scott & George G. Triantis, *Anticipating Litigation in Contract Design*, 115 Yale L. J. 815 (2006).

of production are substantially reduced by using historic standard forms in lieu of customized terms: the effect of the contract as artifact (which imposes a constraint on altering core terms other than by modest changes) is to shift contracting costs to the back end in the eventuality that the deal goes south.

One way then to understand the phenomenon of creditor-on-creditor violence is as a choice by contracting parties to optimize by reducing production costs at the front end and accepting the risk of higher renegotiation and litigation costs at the back end. Theory would then predict at least two ways in which parties who make this trade-off could still constrain back-end contracting costs when inadvertent errors or loopholes appeared in the formulation of the deal documents. First, norms of comity and reciprocity could be encouraged so as to constrain lawyers and their law firms, all repeat players, from exploiting these anomalies.[17] Second, once problems in the documents were identified, they could then be corrected by revising the standard contract terms.[18]

But neither of those tactics appear to have constrained creditor aggression in the LMT world. Instead of being constrained either by norms or redrafted contracts, LMTs have increased in prevalence. To be sure, there have been attempts to design "blocker" provisions for the different types of LMTs.[19] And some of these blockers have been adopted in subsequent transactions.[20] But while there are now more blockers in documents, it is not at all clear that the documents are getting tighter overall.[21] As we report below, 2024 was a blockbuster year for LMTs. Lawyers have turned to other loopholes to exploit, unconstrained by reputational norms or the fear of being penalized in future deals. Indeed, lawyers are even more aggressive in arguing for new

[17] Ronald J. Gilson, *Value Creation by Business Lawyers*, 94 Yale L. J. 239 (1984).

[18] Clifford W. Smith & Jerold B. Warner, *On Financial Contracting: An Analysis of Bond Covenants*, 7 J. Fin. Econ. 117 (1979).

[19] There are blockers named after the LMTs for Serta, J.Crew, Envision, Westco, At-Home, Chewy, Pluralsight, and more. For industry discussions of the rise in LMTs as of the end of 2024 and the prevalence of different blockers, see *Liability Management Exercises: What Are They and What They Mean for Market Participants*, Quinn Emmanuel Client Note (Jan. 15, 2025); Sergio Padilla, *Barclays: Creditor-on-Creditor Violence to Continue*, Private Debt Investor (Aug. 8, 2024); Komal Shahzad & Jonathan Kramer, *Should CLO Investors Be Concerned About Rising LMEs*, Pinebridge Investments Client Note (Dec. 9, 2024).

[20] For examinations of the prevalence of blockers, *see* Vincent S.J. Buccola & Gregory Nini, *The Loan Market Response to Dropdown and Uptier Transactions*, 53 J. Legal Studies 2 (2024); Octus, *Elimination of Material IP Transfer Prohibitions, Anti-PetSmart Guarantor Protections Could Be Next Frontier in Lender-on-Lender Violence* (Oct. 3, 2022); LSTA, *Loan Market Covenant Trends* 2Q24 (July 16, 2024); and Alastair Gillespie, *Comparing Anti LMT Provisions in European Versus U.S. Market High Yield Bonds*, Creditsights (Jan. 24, 2025).

[21] *Davis Polk's Tsiouris on the Next LME Act: State of Distressed Debt*, Bloomberg Distressed Debt Podcast (Apple Podcasts) (Apr. 16, 2025).

and creative meanings of terms in the contract, and many of the elite law firms that might have initially disapproved of this type of lawyering are setting up their own LMT departments. To be sure, an apparent change is that deals are becoming a bit more participatory. Not that all creditors are getting equal treatment, but that all are getting something, often in exchange for a promise not to sue.[22]

Profit maximizing clients would want their agents to design and produce deals that efficiently reduce the rents that otherwise go to lawyers. Yet, in the real world of LMTs, clients are willingly spending more and more on lawyers at the back end of deals to find and exploit loopholes and, if need be, litigate them. This is a phenomenon unlike any that we have seen elsewhere in our research on contract landmines. These parties are not expending efforts at the front end to produce cleaner contracts. Nor are they working to reestablish norms that might constrain those back-end expenditures. Understanding why parties have made these choices to stay with, as they say, Swiss cheese contracts and whac-a-mole lawyering is our focus. Why are the gaps in the documentation multiplying instead of being closed?

The Data: Blockers Proliferate and LMT's Explode

Given the volume of press rhetoric about creditor-on-creditor violence and active efforts to design and distribute blocker provisions by the industry group LSTA, we expected LMTs to be quickly shut down. And research from both academics and industry groups suggested that there was a quick and significant increase in contracts barring the subordination of creditors without unanimous approval of all the creditors in an agreement.[23]

This is what conventional theory would predict. If market actors are surprised by a transaction that uses standard form contract provisions in ways that had not previously been understood to be permissible, contract terms will be revised to prohibit that transaction.[24] And for documents where the contracts are not revised (e.g., credit deals that were done before the Serta transaction), we should see the market adjust to the higher risk of an Up Tier in the secondary market price.

[22] *Id.*

[23] Steve Miller, *Up-Tiering Liquidity Management Transactions, Recoveries and Broader Context: A Thought Experiment*, CreditSights (Oct. 19, 2023).

[24] Another example of the credit market adjusting quickly is examined in Eric Talley, *Discharging the Discharge for Value Defense*, 18 NYU J. L. & Bus. 147 (2021).

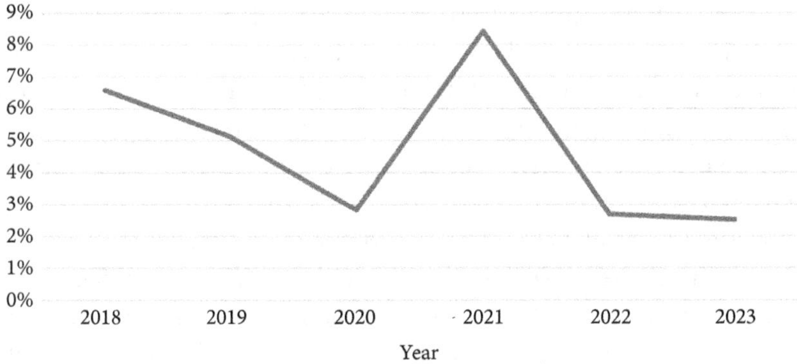

Figure 13.1 Borrower can only make open market purchases if offered to all equally

At first, the data seemed to show that conventional market theory was working. But as Mitu's grandmother would say, there was something black in the lentils. The Serta type Up Tier might be shut down, but had the loose language of the open market purchase provision been fixed? If not, that language potentially could allow for other types of disadvantaging transactions (after all, priority status was not the only important provision in the agreement that required less than unanimous approval to be altered).

To answer this question, we did our own cut at the data. We examined over two thousand credit agreements for leveraged syndicated loans for the 2018–2024 period. On the theory that changes to standard forms would be made regardless of whether the debtors in question had an 80% chance of default or a 5% chance, we looked beyond the subset of agreements most vulnerable to LMTs.[25] We focused in particular on whether the open market provision was modified to require the borrower to purchase bonds in offers made equally to *all* creditors. Figure 13.1 reports the result: there was little happening in terms of repairing the open market provision. There was a bit of an uptick from 2020 to 2021 (after the Serta, Trimark, and Boardriders transactions), when the percentage of credit agreements requiring an open market purchase be offered to *all* creditors increased from 3% to 9%. But in 2022 and 2023, the percentages went back to the 3% range. The open market purchase landmine was not being repaired in the contracts.

[25] In many industry reports and academic studies, the focus has been on the subset of deals most vulnerable to LMTs. *See* Buccola & Nini, *supra* note 20.

We also looked to see whether there were other, broader, attempts to solve the LMT issue in our credit agreement dataset. For example, did credit agreements include broad prohibitions on LMTs or provide for a mutual good faith duty among all the creditors?[26] As of the end of 2023, however, we found no evidence of these types of provisions in any of the agreements in our dataset.

What was going on? On the one hand, the subordination risk was being reduced with the Serta blockers, but that was only a partial solution. There remained a wide range of ways the open market purchase provision could still be used to do non pro rata deals. And more broadly, there were other ways to do LMTs that weren't being fully closed, including the J.Crew type trapdoor transaction.[27] Conversations with lawyers in the LMT market suggested that they didn't think Up Tiers, or LMTs more broadly, had been shut down. They were still finding clever ways to do what they called "non pro rata" transactions, including synthetic Up Tiers, Up Tiers combined with Trapdoors, Double Dips, Up Tiers with Consent Payments to minority creditors to ensure no lawsuits, Up Tiers added to new lending, and so on. Finally, there was chatter that a number of the existing blockers didn't even block what they claimed to be blocking or did so imperfectly.[28]

To explore further, we needed to get a better sense of the number of LMTs. Unfortunately, the extent of LMTs in the market is difficult to observe. LMTs exist because aggressive private equity sponsors together with one set of creditors use a loophole or gap in the contract as leverage to extract concessions from other creditors. We only find out about LMTs if the negotiations break down between the private equity sponsor and both

[26] A few refinanced deals in 2025 have adopted such provisions, but it is rare. Sabrina Fox, *Time for Lenders to Insist on More Protection in Finance Deals*, Fin. Times (May 1, 2025); Prudence Ho, *Rare LME Blocker Emerges as Investors Bolster Protections*, LoanConnector.com (Feb. 20, 2025).

[27] *See* Buccola & Nini, *supra* note 20. If the market was as clear in rejecting the Serta Up Tier transactions, we should also see a pricing impact, in particular, for deals where the contracts were done prior to the Serta Up Tier. Academic work, however, fails to find evidence of such fine-grained deal-by-deal pricing impact. *See* Adam Badawi, Vince Buccola, & Greg Nini, *Price Discipline for Non-Price Terms*, University of Chicago Working Paper (2024). Other research is skeptical that the contracts are finely tuned to balance opportunism and flexibility. *See* Vincent Buccola & Marcel Kahan, *Getting to Yes: The Role of Coercion in Debt Negotiations*, University of Chicago Working Paper (2025).

[28] Scaggs, *Lenders Can Still Get J. Screwed*, *supra* note 5. As an illustration of the conflicting stories we were told, consider the report from Oaktree, one of the pioneers in this market, that focused on the continuing vulnerability to LMTs despite the many blockers being devised. Figure 6 of the Oaktree 2024 report shows loopholes remaining in a large fraction of credit agreements for every type of LMTs. The report further explains that the blockers examined were often "imperfect" and "inconsistently applied." Oaktree Credit Quarterly, *The LME Wave* (Q4, 2024).

creditor groups and the new type of LMT gets reported to industry observers such as Covenant Review or S&P. We've been told by our respondents that the most effective LMTs do not get reported, in part because their designers would like to use them again and in part because nondisclosure agreements may cover certain deals.[29]

With the caveat that we are surely underreporting the number of transactions, we focused on LMTs used in restructurings where public data exists. We obtained data from CreditSights and S&P Global.[30] Some of the law firms designing cutting-edge LMTs also shared their internal data, but we only used that data to make sure that we were on the right track in our reporting.

Most observers point to the J.Crew "drop down" or "trapdoor" transaction as the first LMT to garner attention. Here, a landmine in the contract allowed the debtor to move valuable assets of the parent into an unrestricted subsidiary through permissive "investment baskets" that supported the parent's existing debt. A variation on the drop down transaction is the "double dip." In the double dip, the distressed debtor gives the favored lenders two different and additional repayment protections. Typically, the debtor creates a new subsidiary that borrows money that is guaranteed by various entities related to the parent that also guarantee the parent's debt. This guarantee is the first dip. The new subsidiary then lends the borrowed funds to the parent debtor through an intercompany loan. If the parent defaults on this loan, the new subsidiary can enforce the loan against the parent for the benefit of the creditors of the new subsidiary, leading to the second dip. Both the guarantee and the potential claim of the new subsidiary on the parent for the intercompany loan will be structured to be *pari passu* with the parent's existing debt.[31]

[29] Another indicator of the rise in LMTs that we are not able to capture in our data is the increase in cooperation agreements among subsets of creditors. The popularity of these cooperation agreements shows the concern about LMTs, but they also can enable LMTs when a creditor subgroup where the participants have contractually agreed to cooperate is formed before the LMT is even proposed.

[30] *See, e.g.*, Liability Management Transactions: Quarterly Update Through Q3 2023, CreditSights (Dec. 12, 2023); Credit FAQ: Demystifying Loan Liability Management Transactions and Their Impact on First-Lien Lenders, S&P Global (Oct. 30, 2024); Oaktree, *The LME Wave*, *supra* note 28.

[31] In another variation, the *pari*-plus double dip, the guarantee of the new subsidiary's debt comes from entities outside of the existing credit group such as a nonguarantor subsidiary of the parent company. Because the nonguarantor subsidiary does not guarantee the parent's existing debt and only guarantees the debt of the new subsidiary, the creditors of the new subsidiary enjoy more protection compared with the preexisting creditors of the parent. There are myriad other drop down LMTs. In a Chewy transaction, the debtor engineers a transaction where a portion of the previously wholly owned subsidiary that was excluded from guarantee requirements is transferred to another party. The transaction results in the debtor's release of a restricted subsidiary guarantor of the parent's debt from the guarantee obligations. In the case of PetSmart and Chewy, PetSmart transferred a portion

The next set of transactions are the Up Tiers where the distressed debtor gets new financing from a subgroup of creditors by promising higher priority over the other creditors in the event of default. The precise design of the Up Tier is always a function of the underlying credit agreement. Some agreements readily permit an Up Tier, while others require more creative ways to argue that the provisions of the credit agreement allow the deal. Variations of Up Tiering include "vote rigging" where the debtor incurs additional debt (placed in the hands of friendly parties) to achieve sufficient votes to meet the amendment voting consent threshold.

There are also LMTs that mix and match elements of the different transaction types. For example, Envision in 2022 engineered both a drop down of assets into an unrestricted subsidiary and an Up Tier exchange offer to its preexisting lenders. Yet another variation is to do the LMT and then offer the excluded creditors consent payments or participation rights at a lower level than the favored creditors in exchange for waivers of the right to raise legal challenges to the LMT. And as of this writing in mid-2025, we learned about yet more types of LMTs, including ones making use of third-party financing (the "deal away") and one named the Hunter Gatherer.[32]

Using the publicly available data on LMTs, Figure 13.2 depicts the main categories of LMTs used in restructurings and their rise over the past decade. From Figure 13.2, note that the overall use of LMTs in restructurings appears to be increasing at an increasing rate. Further, the diversity of LMTs also increased.

Respondents from the LMT Trenches

The market is not constraining LMTs and instead appears to have evolved to accepting a growing number and variety of these transactions.[33] Note that what we report is a rough measure: we don't try to measure the degree of minority creditor oppression or anything like that. Our interest is in the

of the Chewy equity to another unrestricted subsidiary of PetSmart and another portion of Chewy's equity to PetSmart's private equity sponsor.

[32] Kartikeya Dar, *iHeart Media Discloses Agreement with Creditor Group on Dual-Track LME*, 9Fin.com (Nov. 7, 2024); *Davis Polk's Tsiouris on Next LME Act: State of Distressed Debt* (Apple Podcasts) (Apr. 15, 2025); *Simpson Thacher's Liability Management Expresso*, Stblaw.com (Feb. 2025).

[33] We are by no means confident that, as of this writing, the situation has reached a stable equilibrium.

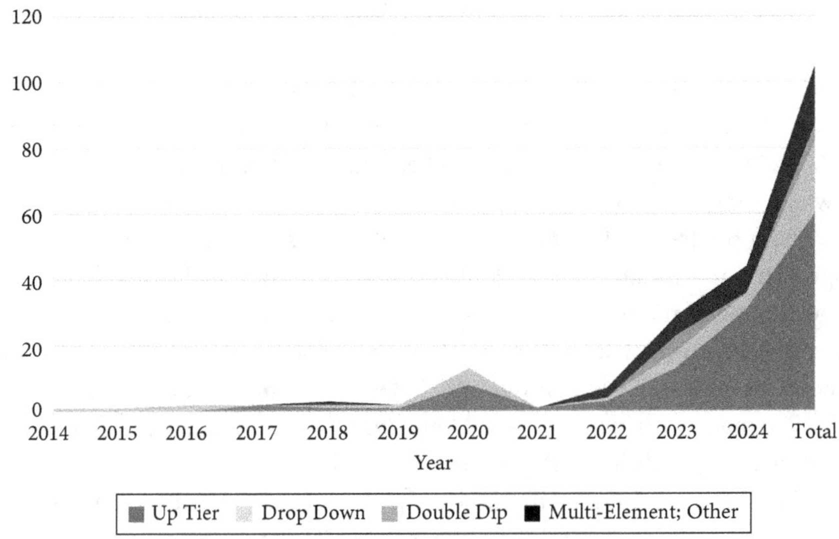

Figure 13.2 LMTs used in restructurings from 2014 to 2025

increase in popularity of LMTs as that term is understood in the market. To understand that, we reached out to lawyers knowledgeable about the leveraged loan markets. Using the same methodology we've described in prior chapters, we interviewed over sixty lawyers at the level of partner or equivalent at their firms.

To provide context, we explained to the respondents that we were coming to this project having studied the sovereign debt world. The infamous instance there of creditor-on-creditor violence occurred in the context of the Iran hostage crisis in the 1970s. After the United States imposed a freeze on Iranian assets and Iran was forced into default, Citibank argued that the fine print of the sharing clauses in its syndicated loan entitled it to set off its claims against Iranian deposits in its bank without having to share proportionately with other members of the syndicate. In response to Citi's action, which was viewed as having violated long-standing bankers' norms, syndicated loan contracts were quickly revised to protect against such self-interested behavior in the future.[34] And that seemed to have worked. Why then are contemporary syndicated loans different?

Below are the key responses from the interviews.

[34] *See* Lee C. Buchheit, How to Negotiate Eurocurrency Loan Agreements 76–78 (Euromoney, 2000).

Too Much Money Chasing Too Few Deals

We started each of our interviews the same way. We told respondents we were seeing the proliferation of blockers and, nevertheless, a seeming explosion in LMTs. One of the terms we had been hearing even before our interviews was "whac-a-mole." What was going on?

The most frequent response in our interviews—from literally every respondent and usually among the first things that they said—was that there was too much money chasing too few deals. That, we were told repeatedly, was the product of fifteen years of low interest rates and, despite recent increases in rates, it was continuing. That excess demand for deals resulted in CLO managers caring more about being part of the syndicate than ensuring that their contracts had airtight protection against LMTs.

This story was perplexing on a couple of fronts.[35] If all the bargaining power was with the debtor because there were "too many lenders chasing too few deals," then why didn't the debtor use that power to maximize the size of the contractual pie and then take a bigger slice? It may be that giving the debtor greater ex post flexibility allows for restructurings that increase the economic value of the contract. But if this is the case, then why wouldn't the debtor insist on a document that clearly allows the debtor flexibility to restructure. Or, it may be that economic value is greater if debtors do not have such ex post flexibility. In this case, why wouldn't the debtor put in place clear and effective blockers and then use its bargaining power simply to ask for a lower yield (thereby taking a bigger piece of the economic value from the deal)? Why is the present equilibrium a Swiss cheese contract that results in lawyers on both sides charging fees to find loopholes and ways to block them?

We asked this question repeatedly. None of the responses directly answered our question. But we can recount what else we heard, and then try to piece together an answer to our puzzle from those responses.

Some Deals Are Airtight

Perhaps seeing our puzzlement at their responses, many of our respondents added a caveat to their answers. The creditors were able to negotiate for better

[35] In a project complimentary to ours, David Hoffman and Vince Buccola explore a version of what puzzled us. They ask why adjustments to terms such as blockers (called "flex terms") are constrained in terms of both the degree of adjustment permitted and the pricing of the adjustment. *See* Vince Buccola & David Hoffman, *Precedent Terms*, University of Chicago Working Paper (2025).

terms in the post-LMT or post Chapter 11 contexts. Once a deal blew up and a LMT was used to restructure the debt, the resulting new arrangement among the debtors and creditors would typically contain new documentation that implemented airtight blockers that prevented any subsequent LMTs. One LMT proponent explained:

> It isn't that the technology to design air tight blockers does not exist. Creditor counsel know how to do that. They put them into post-LMT deals—those doing the LMT don't want it done to them. But those are different. There is a negotiation. It is a different type of agreement.

The explanation was that in these post-LMT deals, creditors were at the table (as opposed to just the arrangers), there wasn't the same time pressure, the distress level was even higher, and these contracts were not the standard forms used in initial offering deals. Despite the market's ability to implement airtight blockers in post-LMT restructured deals, our respondents also told us that new deals, fully aware of these post-LMT airtight blockers, would not use the language from the post-LMT deals: in these new loan deals, airtight blockers were nowhere to be found. Instead, the existing forms contained the standard "market" terms with open market purchase clauses among the other ambiguities continued to be used in new deals.

The Form Has a History

One explanation for the persistence of contracts with open market purchase clauses and other ambiguities that make leveraged loan contracts vulnerable to litigation-intensive LMTs is that the form has a history. A number of our respondents told us that we needed to understand how these documents had evolved over the past decade and a half.

The story almost always began with the 2008–2010 financial crisis where contract terms were amended to adjust to the new needs of the market. Banks were exiting as syndicate participants and CLOs and other similar nonbank entities had entered. And then there was the crisis. Crucially, a number of terms were borrowed from public bonds and were subsequently weaponized in ways that were not anticipated at the outset.[36] The two initial categories

[36] Some respondents provided graphs from industry observers such as S&P showing the increase in cov-lite lending over time.

of LMTs (Drop downs and Up Tiers), in particular, came from the drafting changes made during the crisis.[37] In the old days, open market purchase transactions required the unanimous approval of all the syndicate members. The modified terms no longer did.

In the following years, these "cov-lite" provisions became embedded as "historical holdovers" in the standard loan contract. Then in time some lawyers recognized that the open market purchase clause exception was a loophole that could be exploited. One respondent reported giving a client presentation at a private equity firm "at least four or five years prior to Serta on how this clause could be used." At that point, he reported, "they didn't seem to take this option seriously."[38] Other respondents emphasized how COVID-19's impact on the economy forced innovation. But some noted that the seeds for change had already been planted. A respondent who had a career as an inhouse bank lawyer before moving to a law firm clarified:

> Necessity is the mother of invention. The open market purchase provision that allowed buybacks from individual lenders came from the 2008 crisis. And then about a decade later, COVID hit. And a number of private equity sponsors who had bought otherwise thriving companies were now in trouble. And they began to listen to lawyers who claimed they had strategies to buy them breathing room before declaring bankruptcy. It is not surprising they found the "open market purchase" clause. Anyone who had given it thought for two seconds would have known it was a loophole. In fact, it was used before Serta in 2020—at least in one or two transactions. Then COVID hit and it got used . . . brutally.[39]

In time, this new use of the open market purchase provision gained traction because it provided a way to potentially delay bankruptcy. And to the extent there was an anti-subordination provision in the credit agreement, the key was to have the size of the participating group of creditors large enough

[37] The drafting changes would also typically allow "Dutch auctions," but our story focuses on the open market purchases.

[38] A handful of respondents also pointed to a transaction that had been attempted in 2017 for the clothing company, Not Your Daughter's Jeans. *See* Diane Lourdes Dick, *Hostile Restructurings*, 96 Wash. L. Rev. 1333 (2021). But minority creditors expressed displeasure, and a judge, while not ruling against the transaction, seemed to share the displeasure. In the end the transaction structure was modified to include all creditors pro rata. *See* Buccola & Nini, *supra* note 20.

[39] *See also* Buccola & Nini, *id.*

to vote to remove the anti-subordination provisions protecting the lenders in the old debt instruments.[40]

Why were respondents telling us these stories about the historical evolution of the credit agreements? The stories were an attempt to explain how the landmines in the document arose in the first place and why the standard terms found in the historical form were not revised. Responding to the question why didn't you revise the contract once LMTs exploded, one respondent who specializes in trying to coordinate creditors at later stages via so-called co-op agreements, replied:

> I can't revise the credit agreement. The big private equity shops all have their forms. They don't deviate and they don't need to. The form is the form.[41]

These deals are done on short timelines owing to market conditions, and favorable market windows may close. No debtor is hiring lawyers to change the core terms of the agreement: documents are made as close to the previous deal as possible. Initial deal documents are prepared by sponsors who have their own forms and law firms who watch over those forms. But these forms fit the general market expectation of the standard leveraged loan document.[42] And when it comes to the deal, the sponsors don't want valuable time spent dickering over basic legal terms.

Contracting parties' unwillingness to deviate from a standard form contract that is accepted as "market" is a story we heard in the interviews described in prior chapters, both in sovereign bonds and M&A. The gravitational force of history and what participants consider as "market"—sufficient for resale in the liquid secondary market—results in a contractual structure that is difficult to change—a contract artifact. Contract as artifact does not

[40] Assuming that 51% of the principal amount of the original loan was required to give priority to new lending, a participating lender group larger than 51% could exchange their old debt instruments for new, higher priority debt instruments, while also removing the anti-subordination protections. We suspect the reason that the anti-subordination provisions often only required a majority vote was the assumption that new financing would come from a new lender, and the approval of 51% of the creditors would be an indication that this emergency funding would benefit all. The twist here was that there was no new lender. An existing creditor was buying its way into a priority position at the expense of those left behind.

[41] For a discussion along these lines, see 9Fin, *Scott Greenberg Wants Your Cooperation* (Apple Podcasts) (Mar. 5, 2025). On these Co-op agreements, *see also* Samir D. Parikh, *Creditors Strike Back: The Return of the Cooperative Agreement*, 73 Duke L. J. Online 1 (2023).

[42] This dynamic is described in detail in Buccola & Hoffman, *supra* note 35, who focus particularly on the puzzle that there is flex, but the flex is not priced.

mean that the basic contract structure cannot be changed. Doing so is costly, however, and no single set of contracting parties will willingly incur the cost, including the cost of the negative signal and the corresponding reluctance in the secondary market to buy such instruments.

Jurassic Park

One puzzle is why the historical form favors the debtor side, bringing with it numerous LMT possibilities that favor the debtor in the event of a restructuring. It could be mere happenstance that the historical form is light on protections for creditors. An alternative explanation is that market conditions have changed. Respondents told us that in the past the market norm was for participants not to utilize the contract language in unexpected ways to gain an advantage in restructuring. This norm possibly derived from the culture among law firms and their clients that emphasized collegiality and long-term relationships more so than today, or from the nature of the market participants themselves, including more long-term focused investors compared with the CLOs of the present. Because of this extra-contractual norm that protected the creditor side, the actual documentation in leveraged loan deals could survive with loose language without objection from creditors.

But then norms and culture shifted, particularly following COVID, exposing creditors to the loose documentation without the benefit of extra-contractual layers of protection. One respondent, now the head of the LMT department at an old-line firm, said:

> I remember after the Serta deal, a client called to ask whether we might do something like that. I told him that the fallout was likely to be bad. Today, it is expected that I'd have a menu of LMT options ready for clients. Law firms compete to come up with new types of LMTs, and others compete in figuring out ways creditors can block them: there are now creditor co-op agreements that can be used to force transactions or block them.

One of our former students, now an LMT guru, gave the following explanation:

> Between the GFC and COVID, things changed. It's like Jurassic Park. What happens when carnivorous wild beasts enter an arena that was previously

> populated by peaceful vegans? I remember the moment when it struck me that things had changed. It was more than a decade ago and [X]—[legendary private equity figure]—was in my office. One of his companies was in distress and needed financing to stave off Chapter 11. He had the 200-page indenture and he was aggressively flipping the pages. Periodically, in his almost maniacal flipping, he would come to a clause and ask: "What about this? Can we use this?" I'd explain why not and he'd flip again and ask the same question about some other clause. Today, X is not going to be in my office, flipping pages. The lawyers . . . go to clients having already researched their documents. [N]o sacred rights anymore—not if you can find a creative way in the docs to get around it.

To understand how the world had changed, we were told to look at those white shoe firms that initially might have found LMT transactions unseemly. Now, they are hiring their own LMT groups by poaching senior associates and young partners from firms such as Kirkland and Weil who were pioneers in the LMT game. Stripped of norms and cultural protections, creditors are now left with the language of the standard form contract and what is "market" allowing for the possibility of LMTs in the case of a restructuring.

To Price or Not to Price

In theory, if creditors priced the value of a contract with ambiguous language that may lead to an LMT compared with a contract with an airtight blocker (or alternatively a contract with an clear right on the part of the debtor to restructure the debt), then with enough collective action participants in the market could overcome the inertia of a contractual artifact. If creditors value an airtight blocker more than the cost to the debtor of inhibiting a restructuring, then including such a blocker would increase the contractual surplus. Creditors could then compensate the debtor for the loss of potential LMTs from the surplus created by increasing the overall economic value of their bargain, to the benefit of all parties.

However, many respondents questioned whether the potential for LMTs in a leveraged loan contract is in fact priced or at least priced accurately. In particular, we asked whether price was a consideration in having potential LMTs lurking in the standard form contract. We heard that there might be some pricing adjustment for the presence (or absence) of blockers, but not the kind of fine-tuned pricing we had imagined or that theory predicts. While no one believed there was any fine-tuned pricing of blockers, respondents did think that the general risk of an LMT was understood and probably priced in:

> LMTs are part of the architecture now. We cannot predict exactly what form the LMT will take, but something will be done. There are so many ways to do them. I have a deal I'm looking at on my table today that uses a technique I remember thinking was possible a year or so ago, but thought was too aggressive. And today, here it is.

We also heard from a few respondents that, in the early days of LMTs, there might have been a pricing penalty imposed on loans to certain sponsors. But not any longer.

> I remember hearing talk of how lenders would ask for a premium after Caesars if Apollo or one of the other four horsemen [Aries, Blackstone and Oaktree] was the sponsor or the big lender. If Apollo was there, you knew there was a risk of getting squeezed. That might have been true for a short while. There is no such premium now.

What explains the lack of any (or possibly only crude) pricing of blockers? One explanation pointed us to the nature of the ultimate purchasers of interests in leveraged loans. In a typical leveraged loan deal, arrangers facilitate the sale of interests in the loan to numerous CLOs. Many of these CLOs only hold the debt for a short-term before reselling into the secondary market. We surmise that the managers of the CLOs, themselves agents for the investors in the CLOs, care mostly about getting into scarce loan deals and the nominal return from the deal. And to the extent these managers do focus on contract terms, they care only that the contract is "market"—containing the basic features of the standard form irrespective of the specific contract language. The single-minded focus on "market" terms underscores the value the CLO managers derive from having a secondary liquid market into which they can sell their loan interests.

If language giving rise to potential LMTs is in the standard "market" contract and pricing responds only sluggishly to the presence of blockers, what is there left in the contract language for market participants to bargain over? Despite the artifact nature of the standard leveraged loan contract, we heard from respondents that some modifications at the margins were open for negotiations. Our respondents told of two new concepts: "flex terms" and the "bargain grid."

As explained, every deal has its core standard terms that are "market" but there are also supplemental or peripheral legal terms that are more flexible. We've seen the idea of core and peripheral terms in other markets such as M&A and sovereign bonds, but the difference in the LMT market is that there is an explicit concept of "flex." Deals set up by the arrangers often, if not always, have a grid with key terms—as many as a hundred in some cases. And many of these terms have some "flex": the arranger has a little room to adjust them depending on what the CLOs or other purchasers want.[43]

In the LMT world, blockers are part of the flex terms, and they show up on a grid when lenders, such as CLOs, are seeking participation interests. These flex terms are the provisions that the original "arranger" (typically banks that will resell their participation interests) is able to negotiate with the issuing sponsor. The banks are not acting on their own, however; they are simultaneously in contact with CLO institutions about their preferences for matters such as blockers.

In any given deal, the private equity sponsor may not be sure of its bargaining power vis-à-vis the universe of prospective lenders. Typically, the private equity sponsor will offer prospective lenders a menu of the blockers as "flex" terms. If the private equity sponsor (through the arranger) is unable to secure sufficient interest among lenders for its debt, it might sweeten the deal by including several blockers (Serta, J.Crew etc.). But where demand for the debt is strong, the sponsor may not offer any blocker. A creditor-side lawyer explained:

> Flex terms have become common in the marketplace. The initial deal document probably will not contain blockers. Instead, we will provide a grid of possible blockers as part of the flex terms. The understanding is that if there is enough demand for the deal then flex terms are off the table. However, if we need a blocker to close the deal, we will add them [as part of the flex] on the grid to the credit agreement. None of this changes the price. That's set before the flex comes into play.

[43] *Id.*

Importantly, while some contracts have more flex term blockers than others, our respondents were ultimately skeptical of the value of these flex term blockers. What seems to be happening is the creditor side asks for blockers on individual deals and sometimes gets a few, but the debtor-side lawyers, in cooperation with some creditor collaborators, can always come up with new ways to do LMTs. And further, sponsor-side lawyers are also modifying the contracts in small ways. One respondent told the following story:

> Blockers are included, but changes get made from the sponsor side. There were a few deals, after Serta, where "open market purchase" got changed to "purchase." It wasn't rocket science to see that striking the words "open market" would enable an easier use of that loophole. And this was even on financial twitter. I think that one of the Covenant Review guys even did a redline that got a bunch of comments. But the deal went through without objection. The term was still "market." And now, in hindsight, after *Mitel*, that was a big pro debtor change.[44]

Asymmetric Agency Costs

On multiple occasions, we heard stories that suggested agency problems on the creditors' side might explain the prevalence of blockers that failed to prevent a future LMT. Lawyers who had worked on the creditor side (including for CLOs) told us that the creditors seeking to buy into a syndicate had a mostly superficial concern about LMTs: the lawyers know that their clients wanted some protection from LMTs, but they were not willing to risk being excluded from the deal.[45] A creditor-side specialist explained:

[44] As Buccola and Hoffman explain in their study of these same contracts, we should (and do) see a shift in terms in the direction of the sponsors since they have more leverage in the drafting. But it is a constrained leverage because terms cannot be changed too much—they have to remain within the "market" paradigm. Buccola & Hoffman, *supra* note 35.

[45] In a different version of this story, respondents said that the participants in loan syndicates were mostly "term takers." The debtor or private equity sponsor would contact the arranger bank to raise money. The arranger would ask investors, such as CLOs, for interest in participating in the syndicate. And from there, things moved quickly. There was no real negotiation over a deal document. If there was high demand from lenders to participate in a particular syndicated loan, then the number of blockers would be fewer, or maybe even zero. Less demand and greater supply, by contrast, would mean more blockers. In some interviews, we were told that this dynamic might be different if "anchor lenders" demanded blockers. But these lenders, who expected to be in the driver's seat in an LMT, did not care as much about being excluded in a future LMT.

> The folks asking for the blockers know that they don't actually block Up Tiers or moving key assets into subsidiaries from which additional borrowing can be done. Having a blocker that stops the movement of IP into a sub is useless if the company doesn't actually have valuable IP but instead have valuable O&G rights. I have seen blockers that restrict IP movement when the company in question had no IP to move. Not sure that was a mistake: the agents want to be able to tell their clients they got a couple of the key blockers. Do they care if the blockers are effective? Maybe not? Look at the Open Market Purchase provision: that's key for the non pro rata Up Tiers. And one can design a way to close that pathway. But no one does.

Lenders seeking to participate in a syndicate often do not even see the terms of the credit agreement until they have bought into the deal: they only see a term sheet that lists the blockers in the deal. But the term sheet lacks details about the precise wording of any blocker, which would be crucial in determining whether the term would in fact block an LMT and in making requests for modifications of the contract language. Indeed, one respondent told us:

> Lenders who ask for too many blockers face the risk that they might get excluded from the deal altogether. No lender wants that. The risk of an LMT at the front end is too small to justify raising a ruckus and getting excluded.

CLO clients were not paying close attention to how the blockers were combined. If they had heard of the Serta or J.Crew transactions, it might reassure them that there were such blockers in their deal. But given how fast the deals were done, it was unlikely that anyone on the lender side was scrutinizing the precise wording of the blockers. Plus, many of the creditors did not expect to be left holding the bag if the debtor went into distress; they expected to have resold the credit by then.[46]

[46] One respondent reported:

> Look, you can put in a blocker for Serta, but searching for other vulnerabilities in a contract has now become institutionalized in the market. Many law firms have groups that specialize in uncovering new LMTs and these groups pitch the potential LMTs to private equity sponsors. LMTs and their use in restructurings have become so commonplace that they are now an expected part of the market.

Several respondents suggested that an additional structural feature might be in play as well: as in sovereign debt, the creditors' lawyers were often designated by the debtor (i.e., selected and paid for by the debtor).[47] These lawyers are motivated to avoid delays at the front end of the deals, and in any event, would not be retained in any subsequent litigation.

These stories together suggest that the dynamic between gurus and novices that we found in sovereign debt exists as well in the market for syndicated leveraged loans. We see a similar asymmetry in agency costs as between debtors and the various creditors. As in sovereign debt, arrangers (the equivalent of the underwriters in sovereign bonds) act as intermediaries on behalf of dispersed creditors. The result is an acute focus on the short term by lawyers for the arrangers/underwriters (and indirectly the creditors). These short-term focused lawyers do not have the time nor the incentive to master the terms in the leveraged loan documentation that may affect the use of LMTs. As a result, the lawyers on the creditors' side are relative "novices" with respect to the documentation relevant to LMT risk. In contrast, the lawyers for the private equity sponsors of debtor companies internalize the sponsors' longer-term focus on the possibility of a future restructuring. These debtor-side lawyers have an incentive to master the terms in the documentation that relate to restructurings: they are able to develop the necessary expertise to become "gurus" with respect to the LMT risk.

How does this asymmetric and acute focus on the short term on the part of creditors and creditor-side lawyers express itself in leveraged loan contracts? So long as the document looks "market," creditors take a pass on the existing template of contract terms. Thus, even if the first-best for debtors and creditors is a contract that eliminated all LMTs, debtors are unlikely to put in place airtight blockers because the change will not be priced by creditors (and so there is no compensation for the debtor's concession). While the resulting landmines may lead to inefficient legal costs at the back end, the debtor will accept this inefficiency as a second-best if the possibility of an ex post LMT results in the debtor getting a bigger portion of the now smaller contractual surplus.

There are several features that give us pause about the creditor agency cost story, however. While the creditors in this market face pressures to

[47] For more on this, *see* Trevor Clark, *The Pendulum Swing in Leveraged Finance Loan Terms: The Role of Designation*, 38 J. INT'L BANKING L. & REG. 45 (2023); Cathy Hwang & Andrew Tuch, *Lend Me Your Counsel*, S. CAL. L. REV. (forthcoming 2025).

make quick decisions without scrutinizing documents, and the lawyers for the arrangers are conflicted because they owe allegiance to the debtors who select them, this market, unlike the sovereign bond market, has many intermediaries (Covenant Review, 9Fin, Octus, Reorg, etc.). These firms specialize in reading contract provisions and, sometimes ahead of deals being closed, flag potential gaps in the documentation for the CLOs. Moreover, there are industry groups such as the LSTA and the LMA. To be sure, some of our respondents were dismissive of these organizations: "I'd never use an LSTA clause" and "Do you see who attends those meetings? It isn't the A team from any top law firm." Maybe so. But there are industry organizations and numerous intermediaries who, in theory, could coordinate to secure the value to be gained from improving the credit agreement. But that is not happening.

While industry associations in theory could act as a collectivizing force, the presence of asymmetric agency costs limit the effectiveness of industry associations in the leveraged loan market. While creditors as a group may benefit from the removal of LMTs (or alternatively, implement clear ways for borrowers to restructure without wasteful legal fees), the dispersed and short-term focus of most CLO creditors inhibits such collective action. In addition, all creditors are not treated the same in an LMT. Some creditors may have a sense of whether they will be on the winning side if creditor-on-creditor violence occurs: those creditors will not push for any blockers that might remove the LMT. In addition, to the extent LMTs systematically favor debtors and the debtor side has more concentrated and involved principals, there will be a corresponding systematic incentive in the market to maintain LMTs.

Put another way, it is hard to collectivize the industry to move in a particular direction when a large (and more motivated) portion of the industry does not want to change course. In such a world, the LSTA and other industry groups will find it less profitable to develop and promote effective LMT blockers.

The Story So Far

The interviews yield five insights about the process of drafting and restructuring leveraged loan contracts: (i) the source document that evolved from historical syndicated loans and corporate bonds has a canonical status as artifact that deters a full-scale rewriting of the document; changes are made at the periphery in the form of patches; (ii) cultural norms that may have deterred aggressive strategies to exploit landmines in the past have dissolved; (iii) bargaining over the price of potential LMTs does not generally occur: instead supplemental and peripheral terms such as blockers are bargained for but they do not prevent LMTs from succeeding (although they may increase the cost to the debtor of securing the LMT); (iv) guru lawyers who work on restructurings largely work on the debtor side and are motivated to master the intricacies of the artifact contract, while agency problems result in novice attorneys with an acute short-term focus representing dispersed creditors; (v) time constraints for initial financings impose costs on attempts to revise the standard form.

The challenge is to organize these observations in a coherent way. Our respondents left us with insights into the lawyers who work in this market and their role in the drafting and restructuring of leveraged loans. In what follows, we attempt to harmonize those insights with the assumptions of contract theory.

Contract as Artifact

What we learned from the interviews about asymmetric agency costs, the canonical status of the standard form, and the concept of flex terms poses a puzzle for conventional understandings of contract design. It helps to recall what theory would tell us to expect if rational parties bargained with a clean contractual slate. In such a world, we would expect that parties would choose those contractual terms that maximized the economic pie—the expected surplus from their agreement. If allowing for ex post restructuring of their agreement in times of financial distress provided debtors the breathing room necessary to escape distress and increase value, we should see a clear, unambiguous term in the contract allowing for such restructuring under well-defined conditions.

Next, we would expect the parties to divide the surplus from their agreement depending on bargaining power. Since these are sophisticated parties with equal access to the capital markets, their share of the surplus will be determined by their next best option, and that option largely turns on the relative supply and demand for credit.[48] We should then see the party with the

[48] Alan Schwartz & Robert E. Scott, *Contract Theory and the Limits of Contract Law*, 113 Yale L. J. 541, 551–554 (2003).

stronger bargaining power negotiate for a price giving it a greater share of the expected surplus from the deal.

But we do not see this dynamic in the market for leveraged loans and the demand for LMTs. Suppose that it is optimal for parties to contract for a future value-increasing restructuring. If this is the case, why implement this shared preference with an LMT that relies on landmines embedded in the contract? What is the benefit of putting in place imperfectly designed contract terms that may, with less than 100% certainty, give the debtor the ability to restructure its debt in times of distress? And why make the ability to restructure contingent on persuading other creditors and ultimately a court that the debtor's reading of ambiguous contract terms is correct? Relying on imperfect contract terms that are challenged in litigation introduces uncertainty and transaction costs to the restructuring process. Costs increase as LMT specialist law firms work to uncover and exploit contractual landmines and then litigate over these landmines once found. Litigation has an opportunity cost as well: it may delay value increasing restructurings, exposing the debtor to additional costs of financial distress.

The puzzle of a thriving LMT market burdened by these additional costs can be solved by challenging the assumption that parties are able to produce a perfectly designed contract that resolves each of the known significant contingencies. The evidence from the respondents teaches that debtors and creditors face a constraint: the parties must work with and within the existing market standard for the leveraged loan agreement.[49] Contracting parties in these large liquid markets do not design and produce their own contracts—even when there are sponsors who have their own forms. These forms still fit within the bounds of the recognized historical standard form contract that has evolved over time in the market. Only slight deviations from the form can be made (within the flex, in the case of the blockers). Why? Our conjecture is that doing otherwise would substantially increase the learning costs of other market actors, delay deals, introduce uncertainty, and send a negative signal to the secondary market that something is amiss. Contracting parties thus must take a large portion of the contract as a given.

This is the "artifact" that we've seen in other settings. It manifests in a somewhat different form in each market. Here, we have supplemental flex terms and grids—which is a greater degree of flexibility than, say, in the sovereign bond context, but the phenomenon constraining contract design is a

[49] *See also* Buccola & Hoffman, *supra* note 35.

common one. Just as *pari passu* is embedded in the sovereign debt contract, the cov-lite landmines are historical holdovers embedded in the standard leveraged loan contract. The artifact, however defined, constrains all parties. Due to the myriad costs of changing the artifact, contracting parties in any particular deal are limited to tinkering around the periphery of the contract while accepting as predetermined the core terms in the artifact.[50]

The divergence of interests between the creditor-side attorneys and their ultimate clients—the investors who purchase interests in leveraged loans—reinforces the artifact nature of the documentation. The ultimate investors are dispersed, focused on the short term, and do not accurately price the possibility of an LMT. Even without time pressure to complete a deal, this divergence in interests means creditor-side lawyers do not internalize the benefit to the investors from bargaining over language that may block an LMT.In a theoretical world, debtors and creditors could benefit by fixing the documentation. The greater economic surplus that results would allow creditors to compensate debtors for the loss of a potential restructuring advantage from having the possibility of an LMT. However, in reality the dispersed and short-term interests of the investors coupled with resulting agency costs make it unlikely that debtors will receive compensation for revising the contract. Thus, the sponsor is constrained by an inability to receive a price adjustment from creditors. Debtors are in a second-best world where their best strategy is to maintain the ambiguous language in the standard form contract that allows for the possibility of LMTs, despite the high ex post transactional costs.

Sponsors and creditors for now must make do in a market where the core of the standard leveraged loan agreement contains artifacts that lead to an uncertain number of LMTs. To be sure, the evidence from the great financial crisis and the creation of cov-lite agreements suggests that a similar shock to the system can motivate the parties to coordinate around a more efficient solution to the need for more runway to escape Chapter 11 bankruptcy. Until then, evidence from the sovereign bond world suggests that successful coordination in a large liquid market is a daunting prospect. Despite the presence

[50] This is not to say that contract terms cannot ever change in significant ways. The artifact in the leveraged loan market did change in the wake of the 2008 crisis with the borrowing of terms from the bond markets and the move to more covenant lite terms overall. But parties are limited to tinkering at the margins until there is a big shock such as a major crisis that causes the market to coordinate on a standard solution. *See* Stephen J. Choi, Mitu Gulati, & Eric A. Posner, *The Evolution of Contract Terms in Sovereign Bonds*, 4 J. Legal Anal.131 (2012).

of spiders such as the LSTA in the leveraged loan market, coordination may be difficult in a market where creditors are dispersed and do not accurately price important contract terms. Moreover, a large segment of creditors expect to come out ahead in any creditor-on-creditor transaction, further inhibiting coordination among the creditors to address LMTs.

These constraints affect the behavior of the lawyers charged with drafting syndicated loan agreements in different ways. Lawyers who principally represent either the debtors who wish to utilize LMTs or coalitions of creditors seeking either to prevent or profit from LMTs are more closely monitored by their principals. As we saw in sovereign debt, these lawyers are motivated to represent their clients faithfully: they become gurus, experts in the contract documentation, and skilled at exploiting or combatting landmines in cov-lite agreements. The lawyers representing dispersed creditors are more loosely monitored and thus have fewer incentives to master terms that their representation provides little opportunity to revise or exploit. They are novices: perhaps skilled in many areas but largely untutored in the intricacies of the documentation.

Conventional theory has a dry and soulless understanding of contract provisions in large commercial markets: they are modeled as the optimal set of provisions that rational actors would design in order to maximize expected surplus. In that world, the primary role of the drafting lawyer is to implement the contract's design by formulating terms that optimize total contracting costs between the front and back ends. The LMT world could not be more different. Few production costs are expended at the front end: the contract as artifact rules. The costs are mostly incurred at the back end with lawyers competing to search the standard forms for loopholes and landmines in order to restructure the contract.

In an earlier era, the inevitable errors and mutations resulting from the continued use of a fossilized artifact were likely remedied by a culture of comity. Lawyers who together formed a "reputation market" would bond their clients to norms of trust and reciprocity, and the detritus that developed on the artifact was largely ignored. But as those norms have eroded, the back-end costs have increased. Understanding why parties are seemingly incapable of avoiding these costs is a first step in the realization that, in many markets, contracts are not optimally designed instruments. Instead, they are historical artifacts where, to understand them, we must not only know the history of how the contract has evolved but the legal culture as well.

Chapter Fourteen
We Have Met the Enemy and They Are Us

Introduction

The claim of this book is that landmines are ubiquitous in all commercial markets in which transactions are concluded using standardized terms. Yet while landmines persist in all markets, all markets are not the same. On the one hand, landmines are more persistent and costly in the large liquid markets such as sovereign debt and leveraged loans. Here, we find a surprising imbalance favoring front-end production efficiencies at the expense of efficient contract design. The result is substantial costs incurred in back-end disputes over the restructuring of bonds and creditor priorities, costs that could be avoided more cheaply by the ex ante repair of landmine-infected contracts. On the other hand, the M&A market is different; there is no active secondary market to transform standard form contracts into full on artifacts. Here, problems are identified more readily by landmine entrepreneurs like Glenn West and some of his colleagues at the ABA. They do good by researching defective clauses and coordinating efforts to repair them. And perhaps they get rewarded for their efforts with new clients.

The puzzle, then, is why are landmines so persistent in the large financial markets? A key culprit is agency costs—the costs that result from drafters' failure to meet the markets' demand for *both* speed and accurate documentation. To meet that demand, drafters rely excessively on the core of the artifact contract in both the sovereign debt and leveraged loan markets. This inevitably leads to strategic manipulations, blunders, and obsolescence—deviations from the optimal form that give one side an advantage they didn't bargain or pay for.

The term "agency costs" is itself a bland generalization that must be unpacked if we are to understand better contemporary commercial deals. Why is it that many lawyers who draft financial contracts in these large liquid markets do not know either the precise content of the clauses that they certify to their clients as "market" or the case law that highlights the riskiness of particular contract provisions? What explains the common refrain of more

Contract Hazards. Stephen J. Choi, Mitu Gulati, and Robert E. Scott, Oxford University Press.
 DOI: 10.1093/9780197821770.003.0014

experienced lawyers who shake their heads at the novices in big law and say "when I was negotiating those deals I would read every word in the document before it went out." To be sure, in the sovereign debt market, the distance between the true parties in interest and the drafting lawyers is so great that it is easy to see why a norm has developed that gives unilateral drafting responsibility to the sovereign debtor. But for deals in the leveraged loan market, the parties are sophisticated and care a great deal about the terms of the contracts that their lawyers draft. Yet here as well landmines have exploded with regularity in recent years and costly LMT contests continue to proliferate. Why and why now? Are the answers as simple as drafters are novices and back-end specialists are gurus?

At the risk of oversimplification, our interviews with over two hundred deal lawyers for the various portions of this project point to a story that answers some, if not all, of the preceding questions. Landmines have been around in these large markets ever since contracts as artifacts with highly standardized historical clauses interacted with modern, technologically complex, financial transactions that enabled big money to chase one deal after the other with increasing speed. A historian might date that period sometime after the Second World War, and for sure by the 1980s when junk bonds and other leveraged mechanics became widely available. For a considerable period—say from the 1970s to circa 2000—those landmines were largely unexploited because this world was dominated by a "reputation market"—a normative culture of trust and reciprocity that was widely shared by the transactional lawyers and their bankers doing the deals. In that world, it was accepted that neither side would exploit a linguistic anomaly that undermined the understood and shared intent of the deal. That norm has deteriorated.

The first blow was struck by the activist hedge funds—Elliott Associates was an early poster child—who purchased debt on the secondary market and then used a tough litigation strategy to hold up bankruptcy reorganizations and sovereign bond restructurings. From there, it was a small step to the contemporary wild west of leveraged loan syndications where creditors maneuver against each other to conclude, or prevent a majority from concluding, an LMT.

The back end maneuvering that has burst forth in the leveraged loan market is being fueled by young lawyers who have devised strategies for creating super priority debt (or, depending on the client, defending against this attack on "sacred rights") by exploiting the historical holdover landmines embedded in the "cov-lite" contract during the great financial crisis. As we found in the sovereign debt market, this market, too, is divided between the gurus who engage in a contest at the back end to "restructure" core contract terms and the contract novices who draft the initial documentation. The gurus study the documentation carefully, read the case law and exploit language in the documentation that has remained unchanged even as the cultural norms of comity have eroded. Novice lawyers issuing the leveraged financial contracts rely naively on a check list of blocking strategies derived from past cases that only partially deters up tiering and related maneuvers. Meanwhile, the gurus understand that in a restructuring contest the entire contract is open to manipulation by a majority seeking to create an LMT.

The end result is that the lawyers in these restructuring contests have been transformed from Ron Gilson's "transaction cost engineers," who aimed to create value into "transaction cost creators" that systematically destroy it. It may be that no one in the leveraged loan world is surprised any longer by the ongoing contests to create super-priority loans. Nevertheless, the rents from the maneuvering over efforts to restructure sacred rights has led to the emergence of specialists in landmine discovery and exploitation whose efforts generate substantial and unnecessary social costs. We are reminded of the line from Commodore Perry in the War of 1812 (as modified in Walt Kelly's *Pogo*): "we have met the enemy and they are us."

This strategy succeeds because the documentation has become embalmed. To preserve the returns from the secondary market, the financial contract is treated as a complex and static entity tethered to its historical origins. This is contract as historical artifact. Exploitation of loopholes in the documentation is now a cottage industry, especially in the leveraged loan market where lawyers and their firms market teams of restructuring specialists expert in finding new ways of engineering an LMT. It seems undeniable that social welfare would be improved if the contract could be redesigned either to prohibit or to permit an LMT under clearly specified conditions, thus saving the back-end costs caused by creative contract manipulation. But in the current leveraged loan market, the speed of the transactions and the robust secondary market deters any individual lawyer, or even law firm, from attempting substantial adjustments to the contract on the fly.

No doubt the preceding story misses a number of important elements, but this much comes through consistently from our interviews. Norms have eroded in the large liquid markets of sovereign debt and leveraged loans, financial transactions have measurably increased in dollar volume, complexity and speed, the contracts have become ossified, and deal lawyers in big law are handsomely compensated so long as they keep the deals going and profits increasing.

In one plausible equilibrium in these markets, the principals simply view landmines as the inevitable costs of participating in markets where novice lawyers and reliance on historic contract terms are a necessary but imperfect means of translating the agreements into the language of the law. But accepting landmines and their social cost as part of doing business obscures the fact that there are losers in this equilibrium. The parties exploiting the majority of the landmines in sovereign debt and leveraged loans are, respectively, the debtors (whether sovereign or sponsor) and activist creditors. These are the entities who hire the specialists at the back end who can exploit landmines. But, if there is back end exploitation, in theory there should be incentives for someone to reduce the risks of back end costs by hiring gurus to improve drafting at the front end. That this does not happen is evidence that most of the costs of these landmines are not borne by these principals but by the passive investors in the secondary market, the very parties who are poorly represented in the drafting process.

Without adequate internalization of the costs of landmines, there is no incentive for novice drafters in these large markets to guard against creating (either inadvertently or purposefully) the landmines that invite ex post exploitation. And to the extent agency costs are systematically lower for one side of a transaction, for example, for the sovereign in sovereign debt deals, then one can expect guru lawyers adding (and not removing) landmines that favor the debtor. Given the divide between novices and gurus and the asymmetry in agency costs, landmines will predictably arise: they will be the product of errors, obsolescence, misguided borrowings from other contexts, and from actions by gurus representing clients faithfully. Thereafter, despite the axioms of efficient contracting theory, most of them will persist in the absence of a means by which parties can coordinate on ways to identify and remove them.

We now turn to the normative question: What, if anything, can or should be done to defuse the landmines that are an inevitable byproduct of modern financial markets that use historic documentation that is impervious to significant change?

Can Landmines Be Removed?

The previous chapters asked: Do landmines exist and persist? And although at various points we have characterized the landmines that we have found and cataloged as "harmful" and "dangerous," we have not focused on the welfare effects of the landmines. We have claimed that the presence of landmines, and the rents that can be obtained by using them to renegotiate transactions, have led to the rise of socially wasteful specialists in landmine discovery and exploitation. But we have not offered any solutions to the harms that these mutations and loopholes cause. As suggested above, a plausible response to this neglect is to accept landmines as the inevitable cost of participating in markets where the speed and complexity of transactions and the demands of a robust secondary market require contracts to be historical artifacts.

The problem with a "cost of doing business" approach is that the landmine problem, at least in the large market context, seems resistant to the capacity of *any* of the contracting parties, whether debtor or creditor, to monitor the efforts of their lawyers effectively. There are several reasons for this impediment to successful monitoring. First, the market for lawyers is separated by practice specialties in ways that make monitoring the actions of individual lawyers difficult, if not impossible. Many landmines, as we have seen, arise either from historic terms that are borrowed from other contexts and fit imperfectly in the current market or from mutations to standard form contract terms. These anomalies appear innocuous until subsequently weaponized when default looms. The drafting lawyer who failed to identify and correct the problem at the time of contract formation will no longer be engaged with the issue once a dispute arises and restructuring counsel or litigators (often lawyers from an entirely separate law firm) are retained. Documenting the evolution of a landmine in order to uncover the source of the problem and then to assign responsibility for its persistence requires a costly excavation of the many transactions that have occurred since the landmine first appeared. We have never seen this done.

Second, as we have noted, even if monitoring is successful and landmines are discovered, there are strong disincentives for the affected contracting parties to fix the problem in future contracts by introducing new language that removes the litigation threat going forward. The market resists changes to the historic and standard documentation. In addition, changing terms is risky and requires skill and understanding—whereas sticking to the standard form is safe, even when the standard is imperfect. This is not to say that corrections can't happen. We have suggested that some of the subversive accretions in the sovereign bond market occur because of the asymmetric incentives for gurus to correct errors that disfavor the debtor. Yet, in both the sovereign bond and leveraged loan markets, neither the debtors nor the activist creditors have the incentive to repair any landmines whose costs are largely borne by passive investors.

But before we engage with institutional responses to landmine problems, we must first turn to a discovery that intrigued us from the very beginning: not all landmines are the same.

Local Versus Market-Wide Effects

Not all of the landmines that we have cataloged in our search across different markets require a broad-based institutional response. Subversive accretions and random errors that we find prominently in sovereign bonds have only a local effect: they are mutations from the standard form that only impair the contract rights of the particular parties who agree to contracts that contain the anomalous terms. The creditors in Chapter Two who agreed to a bond with a prescription clause that undermined their expectation of a five-year statute of limitations are justifiably aggrieved as are the Piccinini family in the Save Mart case who lost $100 million when their counterparty knowingly exploited their drafting error. Affected parties seeking solutions to problems like these can appeal to standard contract law doctrines for redress.

There are several contract law doctrines potentially available to respond to sharp practices that create these localized landmines. Depending on the circumstances in the particular case, a creditor who has been victimized by a subversive insertion in the standard form can invoke the doctrine of *contra proferentem*: if a contract clause is ambiguous or vague, it should be read in a way that disfavors the party who originally drafted, introduced, or demanded the inclusion of that specific clause.[1] Similarly, the Save Mart sellers can turn

[1] The idea is that the drafting party is intentionally using ambiguity to create or provide for results that favor their own interests. A *contra proferentem* argument for rejecting a subversive accretion faces hurdles, however. A court must find that the passive investor in a sovereign bond has the same drafting disadvantage as an ordinary consumer. In addition, courts will be loath to invite a *contra proferentem* review based solely on the assertion of the creditor that this phrase is a subversive accretion. A court might require the creditor to make an initial proffer establishing the standard market version of the contested clause. For more on *contra proferentem*, see Tim Dodsworth, Maggie Hemsworth, & Severine Saintier, *Transocean Drilling v. Providence Resources*, Unpacking Contract Law (Apple Podcasts) (July 17, 2024).

(as they did) to the doctrine of good faith and fair dealing that mandates reasonable commercial behavior in the performance and enforcement of a contract. But the ruling against the Piccinini family in the Save Mart case signals the difficulty facing sophisticated parties who rely on either of these doctrines: each has been developed primarily to protect unsophisticated parties and ordinary consumers from exploitation. When the issue turns on the plain language in the contract, commercial parties are under the legal duty to read the terms they have agreed to in their contract. This obligation presents a high hurdle to a *contra proferentem* or good faith claim.

While stories of subversive actions or the knowing exploitation of counterparty errors are deplorable on normative grounds, they are not the type of landmines that justify a market-wide institutional response. Worthy of more attention are the market-wide landmines that we have characterized as historical holdovers and obsolete terms. These landmines are embedded in the core of the artifact contract, apply generally to all the parties in the market, and, as we have seen, are resistant to individual efforts to change them. These are problems that may justify an institutional response.

Any useful response to the problems posed by embedded terms that are obsolete or holdovers from historic documents needs to occur through collective action. There are two collective mechanisms that have the capacity and potential to reduce or ameliorate market-wide landmine costs. The first is the common law courts who, in the process of exercising the judicial duty of contract interpretation, are charged with adapting contract law to contemporary realities.

Reconceiving Contract Interpretation Doctrine

The Durability of Textualist Modes of Interpretation

Textualist theories undergird the New York and Delaware courts' doctrines of contractual interpretation designed to uncover the objectively reasonable, ex ante intent of the parties.[2] Textualist jurisdictions use a "hard" parol

[2] The standard interpretive principle courts are instructed to use in ascertaining the meaning of a contract term to which both parties have manifested assent is to look for the shared intent of the contracting parties. Intent is determined both objectively and prospectively: A party is taken to mean what its contract partner could plausibly believe it meant when the parties contracted. Alan Schwartz & Robert E. Scott, *Contract Theory and the Limits of Contract Law*, 113 Yale L. J. 541, 568–569 (2003).

evidence rule that gives presumptively conclusive effect to merger or integration clauses, and, in the same spirit, bars context evidence suggesting that parties intended to impart nonstandard meaning to contract language that, read alone, is unambiguous.

There is a justification for giving boilerplate terms in commercial contracts their plain or standard dictionary meaning: creating standard vocabularies for the conduct of commercial transactions is a valuable state function. When a phrase has a set, easily discoverable meaning, parties who use it will know what the phrase requires of them and what courts will say the phrase requires. By insulating the standard meaning of terms from deviant interpretations, this strategy preserves a collective good, namely a set of terms with meanings that are already understood by the majority of commercial parties.

Commercial parties seem to agree with the courts' textualist stance. They choose textualist jurisdictions in their choice of law clauses, we suspect, because the courts' interpretive rules exclude any evidence in court of the surrounding context of the transaction from legal consideration.[3] There are prudential reasons why commercial parties appear to prefer modes of interpretation that truncate the evidence available to the court in deciding the merits of the dispute. Textualist interpretation permits a court to resolve disputes on summary judgment, thus avoiding the punishing costs of a trial. Parties stand to gain ex ante if they can avoid an intrusive discovery of the firm's records together with compelled depositions of affected employees.

To be sure, there are circumstances under which a full trial is necessary. Should the court find that the relevant text is inherently ambiguous—where it reasonably admits of differing plain language interpretations—the only recourse is to conduct a full trial and consider the surrounding context in an effort to resolve the ambiguity. In this circumstance, an aggrieved party could argue that the interpretation favored by the counterparty was based on an obsolete or embedded term. But having that option will typically be a pyrrhic victory. The principal leverage of a party exploiting a landmine is to interpose their novel interpretation of the disputed clause. Providing the disadvantaged party the option of a trial, if that trial is costly and the evidence

[3] A textualist court will resolve any dispute as to the meaning of the contract by relying on the plain meaning of the contract terms, together with the lawyers' briefs outlining the nature and purpose of the transaction and the judges' own knowledge of transactional practice. *Id.* For a discussion of the different parol evidence and interpretation rules and their effect on contract drafting, see generally Alan Schwartz & Robert E. Scott, *Contract Interpretation Redux*, 119 YALE L. J. 926 (2010).

about landmines is not conclusive, will not deter landmine exploitation. If contract doctrine is to be deployed in deactivating historically embedded or obsolete terms, the doctrinal tools must be revised with those costs in mind.

Given the preference of commercial parties for summary judgment adjudications, efforts to reconceive contract interpretation in order to defuse market-wide landmines should attend to the cost concerns that motivate this preference. There are at least two different doctrinal routes that would permit an aggrieved party to argue at summary judgment that the text in question was infected by a landmine. Each one faces difficulties in implementation.

Historical Holdovers as Black Holes

Courts confront a dilemma when applying a plain meaning analysis to landmines that are historical holdovers in which the plain words of the text are clear but where meaning is *ambiguous in context*. We call these terms "black holes" because they are empty of meaning in the current market. This category includes negative pledge clauses and the *pari passu* provision in sovereign bonds, the "open market purchase," and other cov-lite provisions in leveraged loans. Here, the interpreter must somehow distinguish between meaningful language and hazardous boilerplate.

One solution to this problem is for a court to adopt a more contextualist analysis under the guise of interpreting the plain meaning of the text. This is the route taken by the 5th Circuit in *In re Serta Simmons Bedding, LLC.*[4] The 5th Circuit panel used a purported plain language interpretation but relied on conventional market understandings to conclude that "an open market purchase occurs on the specific market for the product that is being purchased" and because the product at issue was "first-lien debt issued under the 2016 Credit Agreement," the "market for that product is the secondary market for syndicated loans." The 5th circuit decision may be the canary in the mine suggesting that courts may be reluctant to approve LMTs whenever historic contract language has been weaponized. But it is unclear that courts more committed to textualism will concur with this sleight-of-hand approach. On the same day as the *Serta* decision, the New York Supreme Court's First Appellate Division in *Ocean Trails CLO VII v. MLN Topco Ltd,*[5]

[4] 125 F.4th, 555 (5th Cir. 2024).
[5] Case No. 2024-00169 (N.Y. App. Div., 1st Dep't, Dec. 31, 2024).

permitted a cashless LMT to go forward where the relevant version of the same contract term permitted the debtor to "purchase loans" at any time. It is an open question whether the outcome would have been different had the contract used the words "open market."

In any case, this problem is not solved simply by arguing that courts should instead adopt a variation of a contextualist interpretive style. Historical provisions such as the open market purchase clause are acontextual: the variations in language among different version of the clause are essentially random and thus contemporary context evidence may not aid in determining plausible meanings. Both textualist and contextualist courts are well advised to interpose a further step when interpreting these historical holdover landmines.

In theory, courts should be open to arguments that, as a matter of law, the embedded clause has been emptied of meaning in context and functions as a black hole in the boilerplate. To be sure, the moral hazard risk of false claims by a party who has been disadvantaged by fate argues for a strong presumption against the existence of a black hole. But there should at least be an opportunity to admit evidence sufficient to overcome the initial presumption of linguistic clarity.

Parties alleging that an historic holdover such as the open market purchase provision is a black hole might proffer the following evidence: Has the clause been repeated for years as part of the historic documentation without having been tested in litigation and where repetition has robbed the term of any obvious conventional meaning in the relevant market? Is a historic or original meaning of the term accessible in a fashion that makes sense in the contemporary context and are contemporary commercial actors aware of that meaning? Is there credible evidence that the meaning claimed for the particular provision was not priced at the original issue stage?

If a court were to find evidence of a historical holdover landmine in the standard boilerplate, the presumption of shared meaning is no longer apt: when no party has reason to know of a different meaning attached to the clause by another party, the clause has become a legal black hole. A court intent on deactivating these market-wide landmines could adopt the presumption that the evidence of a historical holdover implies that the parties attached different meanings to the term in question. This presumption invokes the common law rule that if parties have attached different meanings to a term, neither party is bound by the meaning of the other *unless* at the time of contracting one party did know or have reason to know the meaning of its counterparty who in turn did not know or have reason to know the other's meaning.[6] Reading the clause out of the contract in this way permits textualist courts to maintain their commitment to plain language interpretation.

The problem is that this "black hole exception" offers only a narrow route to defusing the landmine. The necessary evidence is sufficiently hard to obtain that even if this exception is adopted by a court, the rule is likely to be infrequently applied.

Good Faith as Anti-Opportunism

Then there is good faith and fair dealing. Traditionally, the duty of good faith in standard contract doctrine is only an interpretive principle, a means of divining the shared intentions of the parties.[7] The duty commands contracting parties to observe the standards of fair dealing in the relevant market, but the obligation only applies to the performance and enforcement of the contract and (by implication) not to the negotiation and drafting of an agreement.[8] For those reasons, U.S. courts traditionally have been reluctant to apply the doctrine to disputes over the meaning of the terms in a contested agreement.

In view of the increasing use of seemingly opportunistic readings of the contract's text in the recent leveraged loan disputes, some have suggested that courts could apply a more robust version of the duty of good faith and fair dealing than they typically have. Arguably, such a reconception of the duty of good faith in commercial contracting was proposed by Judge Ralph Winter in *Sharon Steel v. Chase Manhattan Bank*.[9] In refusing to interpret commercial boilerplate language literally where it would have undermined the joint value of the contract to the parties, Winter proposed:

> Where contractual language seems designed to protect the interests of both parties and where conflicting interpretations are argued, the contract should be construed to sacrifice the principal interests of each party as little

[6] *See* RESTATEMENT (SECOND) CONTRACTS § 201(3) (American Law Institute, 1981). In the case where one party does not know the meaning of the other and the other *does know or have reason to know* the meaning of the first party, the term is interpreted in accordance with the meaning asserted by the first party. *See id.* § 201(2).

[7] Uniform Commercial Code, Section 1-203. The Comment states: "The doctrine of good faith merely directs a court towards interpreting contracts within the commercial context in which they are created . . . and does not create a separate duty of fairness and reasonableness."

[8] *See, e.g.,* UCC 1-304.

[9] Eric Talley & Sneha Pandya, *Debt Textualism and Creditor-on-Creditor Violence: A Modest Plea to Keep the Faith*, 171 PENN. L. REV. 1975 (2023).

> as possible. An interpretation which sacrifices a major interest of one of the parties while furthering only a marginal interest of the other should be rejected in favor of an interpretation which sacrifices marginal interests of both parties in order to protect their major concerns.[10]

If understood to be a robust version of good faith, the foregoing could be an effective deterrent against opportunistic behavior in financial contracting. By protecting the joint value of the contract, the court would be enacting a result that the parties would have agreed to ex ante. Eric Talley and Sneha Pandya explain that:

> At its core, Judge Winter's proposal deemphasized the parties' *actual* intent in contracting and replaced it with an imputed common purpose that commercial parties are presumed to share: maximizing the expected joint economic surplus available to the parties. Such a purpose makes considerable sense regardless of how the surplus is distributed because the parties can reallocate the now-maximized pie by adjusting pricing formulas. Contracting parties pursuing this goal would jointly favor a rule that deems a discretionary act by a party . . . to be consistent with good faith so long as it passes muster under a cost-benefit calculus.[11]

An enhanced version of the good faith duty along these lines would grant courts a wider discretion to reject a proposed interpretation of the terms in the leveraged loan contract that would have allowed an LMT. But in the recent spate of litigation in the leveraged loan context, courts have mostly declined to adopt a more robust version of what one might call "interpretive good faith." Excluded creditors have challenged numerous proposed LMTs as violative of good faith duties owed by the contracting parties to each other. Most of the litigation has not progressed to final judgment, but in the cases that have been decided, the courts have declined to apply the doctrine of good faith and fair dealing to the maneuverings over LMTs. Even the 5th circuit in *Serta* based its decision to reject the proposed LMT on an interpretation of contract text and declined to rule on the good faith claim that the plaintiffs had advanced.

[10] Sharon Steel v. Chase Manhattan Bank, 691 F.2d 1039, 1051 (2d Cir. 1982). Note that Judge Winter does not claim that his interpretive technique creates a new good faith standard. And other courts have not taken up the implicit message.

[11] Talley & Pandya, *supra* note 9 at 1989.

Parties themselves could overcome the reluctance of the courts to imply an enhanced duty of good faith by contracting explicitly for enhanced good faith duties. Yet, we have found no evidence of parties explicitly contracting for good faith duties in the credit agreements themselves. Nor have we found any inclination by market participants doing these deals to include such a provision.

* * *

Urging courts to modify well-established interpretation rules to deter landmines requires the patience to wait for litigation over a contested clause and then to argue successfully to the court that one or more of the proposed changes to interpretation doctrine is necessary in order to reduce wasteful social costs. It is helpful to that enterprise that the action most likely would occur in federal court in New York or in the Delaware Court of Chancery. Both these bodies have in the past created new doctrine when the occasion required it. Nevertheless, the probability in the near term of a successful ex ante deterrent or an ex post repair of landmines through judicial innovation seems low. This is especially so where judges are not themselves steeped in the intricacies of the market in question and are unfamiliar with the doctrinal preferences of the parties. In this latter context, doctrinal innovation by the judges is unlikely.

In Delaware, judges do have familiarity with high-end corporate transactions. And Chancery judges are sometimes prepared to move the common law forward in line with the preferences of the contracting parties. But they have shown a limited willingness to police opportunistic assertions of a meaning that is otherwise supported by the plain text. Our sense is that they believe sophisticated contracting parties prefer that the courts only do plain meaning textual interpretation.

If that somewhat pessimistic conclusion is warranted, then we should turn to the other collective solution to the landmine problem: Can markets that currently lack a coordinating structure create a means to eliminate landmines as they arise?

A Spider for the Network

The second collective mechanism for general landmine repair are robust networks within particular markets that can create the structure (what we have called the "spider" in the web) that will motivate parties in the market to remove the landmine collectively.

The landmine problem exists as a significant social cost because many (most) of the markets in which hazards are caused by historical holdovers or obsolete clauses seem unable readily to coordinate on solutions to the landmine problem. Yet, notwithstanding the familiar impediments to coordination, networks to remove these market-wide landmines do exist in some markets. What makes these markets different from those where coordination fails?[12] Some successful networks deploy standard mechanisms—whether in the form of a master contract as in the case of the derivatives market or a bureaucratic contractual structure as in the case of some trade associations—that support the collaboration needed to update obsolete terms and scrub improperly borrowed clauses.[13] These relationships have a spider—a controlling entity or hierarchy at the center of the network that facilitates network formation and maintains stability. In addition to these formal regimes, we have seen in the M&A context that an informal network of lawyers can have several spiders weaving webs through the collaboration of key lawyers and judges who belong to a high-status interest group. Networks such as these appear to emerge and form organically.

The leveraged loan market might benefit from an entity such as the International Swaps and Derivatives Association that centralizes contract terms. But unless the adverse reaction to "creditor on creditor violence" is sufficiently disruptive, there are few incentives for the market as an entity to create a similar mechanism. An obvious solution in the case of sovereign debt would be to enable one of the existing industry associations such as the International Capital Markets Association or the Emerging Markets Trade Association to play such a role. But here again there has been no appetite among the actors on the ground to fund this effort.

[12] The question of why some networks are durable and others are fragile has been largely ignored by legal scholars. Some exceptions are Alan Schwartz & Robert E. Scott, *Third Party Beneficiaries and Contractual Networks*, 7 J. Legal Analysis 325 (2015), and Lisa Bernstein, *Private Ordering, Social Capital, and Network Governance in Procurement Contracts: A Preliminary Exploration* 7 J. Legal Anal. 561 (2015).

[13] The derivatives market is an example of a thick market that was able to develop a coordinating structure largely because it is subject to regulatory oversight. The International Swaps and Derivatives Association (ISDA) updates derivative contract terms in light of changed conditions. The terms are voluntary, but the ISDA also makes binding determinations regarding what constitutes a credit or succession "event" (such as a merger), either of which may trigger obligations under a credit default swap contract.

The question then is whether an *informal* network such as what exists in the M&A market could emerge in the large liquid markets as well. Could the lawyers, the gurus of sovereign debt and leveraged loans, form networks that work to defuse the hazards caused by historical holdovers and obsolete terms? Would they want to? There are fewer mechanisms to control free riding risks in these large markets, but there is still significant information exchange, especially among the groups of gurus. The lawyers already form a network of sorts: they know each other, and the group is embedded relationally. There appears to be an environment where trust can develop and mechanisms for inter-lawyer collaboration can begin.

This dynamic may be playing out now in the leveraged loan market. There is evidence that investors who fear being in the minority when an LMT is organized are forming cooperative networks to guard against exploitation—although these "coops" among subsets of creditors can also be used to bargain with debtors to do LMTs even more effectively. Another more interesting development in the leveraged loan market is the dramatic growth of "private credit." These are nonbank loans by small groups of private investors to selected sponsors. While landmine repair is not the primary motivation for this development, a significant result has been the reestablishment of reputational norms in the private credit portion of the market, norms that may offer an effective deterrent against exploitation of some lenders by others in the network.

In theory, there are incentives for prominent law firms in the sovereign debt and leveraged loan markets to act as a spider by identifying landmine risks and proposing industry wide repairs. Playing the role of a spider holds the promise of increasing the law firms' importance and reputation in the market. A virtuous cycle then becomes possible: the law firms are rewarded with rents based on their increased reputation in the market, further motivating them to continue to act as fulcrums of coordination. But as yet we see no lawyers or law firms developing as spiders in either the sovereign debt or leveraged loan markets. Rather than coordination, the bargaining power of debtors in both markets only results in temporary repairs to localized landmines. In truth, our review of the possible ways that the social costs of landmines can be mitigated offers only some hope for progress but little certainty.

Concluding Thoughts

Our primary motivation has been to shine a light on a central feature of the contracting process long ignored by scholars who write in contract law and theory as well as by the empiricists who study contracting behaviors. Contract production matters, and no one can confidently make predictions about the relative efficiency of commercial contracts without taking account of how and by whom those contracts are produced. Once we take the production process seriously, we can see how landmines arise and persist as significant flaws in the design of highly standardized contracts, flaws that are largely unnoticed at the drafting stage but create significant opportunities for strategic behavior should the contract be disputed thereafter.

We find these landmines in both thick and thin markets. But there are yet more markets to study. We do believe we have identified the villains in our story: Agency costs separate the design and production phases of contracting.

The design phase is where much of contract theory lives: parties design their deal to perfectly allocate the risks and rewards of their transaction. The problems endemic to the production of that perfectly designed contract is where almost all real world contracts live. Here, we find drafters who both lack the expertise and have insufficient skin in the game to effectively oversee the production process.

The result of this separation of design and production is the crystallizing of contract terms intended to be individually designed into a fixed and unyielding whole. This is the version of the artifact contract that governs in large, liquid markets. Because drafting lawyers are disabled from addressing the structure of the contract's design, they become passive actors in the contracting process. Unable, or unwilling, to adopt the designer's role that they were (or could be) trained for, they fail to find the inevitable landmines that standardization creates. Yet, breaking the commercial contract into constituent parts so that drafters can ply their trade more successfully seems a bridge too far. Institutions do adapt over time and cultures change as well. But substantial relief from the hazards of commercial contracts will most likely occur when the markets experience even more highly publicized events analogous to the Argentine debacle. The sober conclusion is that high profile litigation outcomes that threaten to destabilize a market remain the most likely stimulus for changes that can reduce the costs of landmines.

Appendix

A. Subversive Accretions

1. Payments Subject to Fiscal Laws (Fiscal Laws landmine). Almost every international sovereign bond is listed on an exchange in a foreign jurisdiction, and typically that is also where payments to investors are made through a financial institution. The bonds often contain a provision that investors bear the risk of local taxes. The typical "fiscal laws" clause, therefore, makes clear that the issuer will protect bond investors from any issuer imposed taxes, but not any taxes imposed by the location of payment. And it will state the following: *All payments are subject in all cases to any applicable fiscal or other laws, regulations and directives* ***in the place of payment,*** *but without prejudice to the provisions of the tax gross-up clause.* In some bonds, however, the drafter omits the words "in the place of payment," causing the clause to read: *All payments are subject in all cases to any applicable fiscal or other laws, regulations and directives, but without prejudice to the provisions of the tax gross-up clause.* This latter version of the clause leaves open the interpretation that the "applicable fiscal or other laws, regulations and directives" might be those of the sovereign issuer itself. The omitted language creates a risk that this seeming innocuous change that is meant to cover only taxes imposed at the location of payment can be weaponized against a debtor. For example, a sovereign debtor needing to restructure the obligation might be tempted to argue that, per the fiscal laws clause, it is entitled to pass a variety of "laws, regulations and directives" imposing costs on bondholders.

2. Correcting a Manifest Error—Who Decides (Manifest Error landmine)? At the end of the standard "modification" clause is typically a subsidiary clause, the "manifest error" provision. The clause is generally understood to deal with trivial errors. Typically, the manifest error provision provides something like: *The Republic and the trustee may, without the vote or consent of any holder of debt securities.... amend the [debt securities] for the purpose of... correcting a manifest error of a formal, minor or technical nature.* Some bonds, however, state: ***The Issuer may agree,*** *without the consent of the Noteholders, to any modification of any of these Conditions...* either (i) for the purpose of curing any ambiguity or of curing, correcting or supplementing any manifest or proven error or any other defective provision contained herein or therein or (ii) *in any other manner which is,* ***in the sole opinion of the Issuer,*** *not materially prejudicial to the interests of the Noteholders. Any modification shall be binding on the Noteholders.* The clause, read on its own, appears to permit the Issuer to override the holdouts by claiming that, given the approval of the majority of creditors and the IMF, the modification is not "materially prejudicial to the interests of the Noteholders." The determination is delegated to the "sole discretion" of the issuer and that determination is to be binding on all the creditors.

3. Pari Passu—But for Provisions of Mandatory Law (pari passu Mandatory Law landmine). The basic sovereign *pari passu* clause provides: *The Notes rank* pari passu *with all other present and future unsecured and unsubordinated External Indebtedness of the Republic.* A possible purpose of this clause was to protect against the possibility that sovereigns might have domestic laws that could inadvertently subordinate creditors who didn't know to take certain actions required by domestic law. The *pari passu* clause thus contracts around the possibility that the sovereign might have such a domestic law. The landmine is found in the version of the clause that has the following additional language: *The Notes rank pari passu with all other present and future unsecured and unsubordinated External Indebtedness of the Republic,* ***save only for such obligations as may be preferred by mandatory provisions of applicable law.*** Adding this provision could arguably mean the sovereign issuer's domestic law directly contradicts the apparent purpose of the provision. The debtor arguably has the authority to pass a local law that subordinates the creditors.

4. Waiver of Sovereign Immunity—But for Applicable Law (Sovereign Immunity by Law landmine). A standard condition in international sovereign bonds is that the issuer waives immunity from suit, execution, and attachment. Given the foregoing, the typical waiver of sovereign immunity provides that the sovereign waives all immunities that it might have from suit, execution, and attachment, subject to the constraints on that waiver imposed by the law of the enforcing jurisdiction. Along these lines, the clause will typically state: *To the extent that the Issuer may in any jurisdiction claim . . . [immunity] from suit, execution, [or] attachment . . . the Issuer agrees not to claim and irrevocably waives such immunity* ***to the full extent permitted by the laws of such jurisdiction.*** In some bonds, however, the waiver reads differently: *To the extent that the Issuer may in any jurisdiction claim immunity from suit, execution or attachment, the Issuer agrees not to claim and irrevocably waives such immunity* ***to the full extent permitted by applicable law.*** If the provision is read literally, it appears to allow the retraction of the waiver since the law of the sovereign debtor is, in theory, one of the applicable laws. That interpretation essentially transforms the waiver into an option for the sovereign debtor: it can waive immunity until it decides not to.

5. Prescription—As Provided by Local Law (Prescription landmine). The "prescription" clause is largely unmentioned in the literature on sovereign debt clauses even though it is found in most international sovereign bonds. Venezuela in 2020 was the initial source of new relevance for the prescription clause. Venezuela had been in default since 2016 and was trying to negotiate with creditors to forestall litigation. In exchange for creditors deferring litigation, Venezuela offered to refrain from exercising its rights under the prescription clause. That clause, it argued, voided claims on interest that were more than three years old. Venezuela's prescription clause reads: *Claims in respect of principal and interest will become void unless presentation for payment is made within a period of ten years in the case of principal and three years in the case of interest from the Relevant Date,* ***to the extent permitted by applicable law.*** This argument was undermined by other provisions in the contract but the prescription clause continues to be included in the new offerings of the majority of sovereigns. Some bonds have the subversive form that Venezuela had asserted was in its bond. An example of an especially treacherous version of a prescription clause was in a 2017 Argentine issuance: *Claims against the Republic for the payment of principal, interest, if any, or other amounts due on the Bonds will be prescribed unless made within five years, with respect to principal,* ***and two years,*** *with respect to interest, premium, if any, or other amounts due on the Bonds,* ***in each case from the date on which such payment first became due, or a shorter period if provided by Argentine law.*** In the Argentine formulation, prescription functions precisely like a contractual reduction of the statute of limitations. Claims are extinguished two years after they are due. The Argentine formulation clause also appears to grant Argentina the option to enact a law that makes the prescription period even shorter.

6. Governing Law—Authorization and Execution Under Local Law (Governing Law Authorization and Execution landmine). Every international sovereign bond has a governing law clause that specifies what system of laws applies. The basic clause states: *The Notes are governed and construed by the law of the State of New York.* On occasion, however, there is a second sentence that carves out matters of authorization and execution of the bonds to be governed by the issuing sovereign's local law. For example: *The Notes are governed and construed by the law of the State of New York, provided, however,* ***that the laws of Ruritania will govern all matters concerning authorization and execution of the Notes.*** It looks as if challenges that are brought to the validity of the bond issuance (e.g., whether the legislature property authorized the debt) are to be governed by Ruritania's local laws. Could this mean that the New York court has to defer to the Supreme Court of Ruritania on this matter?

7. Sovereign Immunity Exclusions—Unless Necessary to the Sovereign's Proper Functioning (Sovereign Immunity Exclusions landmine). Most sovereign immunity waiver provisions are broad, initially waiving all of the sovereign's immunities from suit and execution. The broad waiver will be followed by exceptions where the sovereign excludes a few of its assets from its immunity waiver. On occasion, however, the exceptions swallow the waiver. For example, an exemption from execution "*of all property related to essential public functioning" and are "not for commercial" purposes.*" Exceptions such as these give the sovereign debtor a great deal more freedom to argue that the property the creditor is trying to attach is both "essential" for the public functioning of the state and is not used for commercial purposes. There are other exclusions as well in this family of landmines that may be even more potent than "necessary for proper functioning." These include exclusions for "public property," property that provides an "essential public service," and "noncommercial" property.

8. The Local Jurisdiction Option (Jurisdiction landmine). Some sovereign bonds are drafted to contain a "non-exclusive" jurisdictional clause, where the sovereign submits to jurisdiction in both the jurisdiction whose law governs (e.g., New York) and the sovereign's own courts. The clause does not generally say anything about the jurisdiction the creditors are agreeing to use. Can the sovereign bring that claim in its local courts? Or what if there are creditors whose interests are aligned with the sovereign? Can they take advantage of the sovereign's local courts to disadvantage other creditors? Consider, for example, this clause that states: "*Mexico and the Trustee*"... "*submit to the jurisdiction of these courts,*" where "these courts" include both the courts of New York and Mexico. In such a case, the argument is stronger that the creditors, through the trustee, their representative, have consented to jurisdiction in Mexico.

B. Random Errors (aka Blunders)

1. *Pari Passu—All Other Unsecured Indebtedness (pari passu Scope landmine)*
2. *Negative Pledge—All Other Unsecured Indebtedness (Negative Pledge Scope landmine)*
3. *Cross Default—All Other Unsecured Indebtedness (Cross Default Scope landmine)*

Sovereign bonds typically have negative pledge, *pari passu*, and cross default clauses that constrain the debtor from taking actions with respect to other outstanding debt that would impact the bond in question. A key question is: What debt does the clause cover? The solution in most international sovereign bonds is to define a term "External Indebtedness" narrowly to cover only those debts in a foreign currency, that has a maturity greater than a year, and is listed on an international exchange. Periodically, however, instruments will fail to define External or Public Debt narrowly. Instead, these bonds provide that clauses are triggered by "*all of* the sovereign's unsecured or public debt." This creates a risk that the sovereign's entire external debt stock could be accelerated because of a local action that led to a default on a state obligation (e.g., failing to pay the local firefighters in Buenos Aires on time). The erroneous, broad scope language could grant an advantage to activist creditors seeking a means to threaten the disruption of upcoming restructuring negotiations.

4. Reverse Acceleration—What Constitutes Cure? (Reverse Acceleration landmine) In a typical sovereign bond, the occurrence of an Event of Default generally gives a certain fraction of the holders of the bond (typically 25% in principal amount) the right to accelerate payment if the default event is not cured within a specified time. On occasion, though, there may be circumstances where a minority asks for acceleration but the majority is in the process of working out a deal with the debtor. To protect this circumstance, bonds typically contain a *reverse* acceleration provision where the majority can reverse the acceleration that a minority have requested. Italy's 2021 provision, for example, reads: *The holders of more than 50 percent of the aggregate principal amount outstanding of the debt securities may rescind or annul a notice of acceleration.* Some bonds, however, appear to subject the reversal to a condition precedent. Uruguay's 2021 reverse acceleration clause that reads: *Holders of debt securities representing . . . more than 50% of the principal amount of the [debt securities of that series] may waive any existing defaults, and their consequences, on behalf of the holders of all of the debt securities of that series,* ***if that event of default] has been . . . cured, remedied or waived.*** Requiring the sovereign to cure the Event of Default by paying the full amount of a debt that it was previously unable to pay defeats the purpose of the reverse acceleration clause. One could easily conclude that the waiver must come from the minority who exercised the right to accelerate in the first place. That interpretation gives a minority of creditors the textual basis for asserting a meaning that undermines the essential purpose of the reverse acceleration clause.

5. Enhanced CACs—No Provision Preventing Debtor from Modifying Disclosure Requirement (CAC Strategy Disclosure landmine). The most recent standard clause in sovereign bonds is the "enhanced" collective action clause (CAC). The prior generations of CACs did not allow for restructurings to occur unless a certain vote threshold was satisfied in each individual series of bonds. The rationale for these aggregation (enhanced CAC) provisions was to ameliorate the risks posed by holdouts. The point was to structure the aggregation provision so that, if holdout creditors had clustered into a particular series of bonds, the holdouts would not be able to undermine the whole restructuring process. The concern of the creditors was that once substantial relief was obtained from the cooperative creditors, the debtor would be tempted to pay the holdouts in full to get rid of them. To constrain such behavior, a condition of the enhanced CACs is that the debtor has to disclose to the creditors—before they vote—what its plans are with respect to those series being left out of the deal. Given the foregoing logic, the disclosure requirement is an indelible part of the apparatus that cannot be altered by the debtor colluding with a subset of creditors to disadvantage the others. However, nowhere does the contract say that this disclosure cannot be altered. This means that this protection can be changed with the same vote required to change ordinary matters in the contract (often no more than a simple majority vote).

6. Conflict Between the Modification Clause and Governing Law Clause (Governing Law Always landmine). Important provisions are usually specified to be "reserved matters." The modification provision of the bond provides that altering reserved matters requires a super majority vote. In some bonds, however, there is additional language in the governing law provision after the phrase stating that the notes are governed by the law of the State of New York. This additional language provides: *"notwithstanding . . . any reserved matter modification,* ***all matters related to the consent of the holders and modifications of the indenture*** **or the notes will** ***always be governed by . . . the law of New York.*** The modification provision specifies that the governing law provisions and all other reserved matters may be changed with a specific supermajority vote. But the governing law clause states that modifications of the indenture will "always" be governed by the law of New York. So, the governing law applying to changes to the vote requirements cannot be ever changed even though the contract also says that it can be changed with a certain pre-specified vote requirement. The contradictory provisions provide dissenting creditors with an opportunity for mischief.

C. Historical Holdovers

1. Buybacks—What Does It Mean (Buy Back landmine)? International sovereign bonds commonly contain a buyback provision. For example, Panama's 2018 repurchase provision reads: *Panama may at any time purchase debt securities in any manner and for any price.* But there is no general legal constraint on sovereigns purchasing their bonds on the open market that this clause is modifying. In other words, the clause is pointless. Yet a court is likely to assume clauses are in contracts because they have a purpose. That allows an opportunistic debtor or creditor to assert its meaning for the clause. A sovereign debtor might argue that the broad provision allowing repurchases indicates that the debtor has carte blanche to do any repurchases, including sending negative information about the bonds to the market and then repurchasing bonds after the market price drops.

2. Negative Pledge—What Does the Promise to Secure Equally and Ratably Mean (Negative Pledge landmine). The standard negative pledge clause states: *So long as the Bonds remain outstanding, the issuer shall not incur any lien* ***without at the same time securing the Bonds equally and ratably.*** The notion of bonds ranking equally and ratably is hard to understand in the context of a sovereign that cannot go into liquidation. Sovereigns almost never have assets outside their borders that they use to secure debts, and assets within their borders cannot be seized and liquidated by external creditors. That raises the question of what the negative pledge clause means within the context of domestic assets over which the creditor has granted a security interest. Assume a distressed sovereign, seeking emergency financing to stave off a crisis, grants a security interest to China to obtain the financing. The debtor defaults on its external creditors but continues to pay China because it received the Chinese lending on favorable terms. The question the negative pledge clause poses is whether the violation of the promise to secure the external debt equally and ratably gives these creditors an ability to interfere with the payments being made to China. Could they, for example, obtain an injunction from a foreign court barring the sovereign from paying China on its secured debt?

3. Pari Passu—Revised, Yet Still Mysterious (pari passu landmine). The *pari passu* clause may have had a purpose once, but it is not clear what that purpose is. Holdout creditors in Brussels (2001) and New York (2011–2012) persuaded courts that the *pari passu* clause entitled them to be paid pro rata with other creditors. Crucially, this included creditors who had already agreed to take significant write downs on their debt. In the end, the holdouts won. This caused consternation in the markets and, in 2014 key parties in the market coordinated to revise the standard *pari passu* clause. The basic clause was retained, but a sentence was added providing: *The Notes rank and will rank pari passu with all other unsubordinated External Indebtedness of the Republic.* ***It is understood that this provision shall not be construed so as to require the Republic to make payments under the debt securities ratably with payments being made under any other External Indebtedness.*** The revised clause reduces the likelihood of a court providing a holdout creditor with a right to pro rata *payments*, but what remains is a clause whose meaning is still unclear. Retention of the ambiguous *pari passu* terminology provides activist creditors opportunities to advance strategic claims.

Index

For the benefit of digital users, indexed terms that span two pages (e.g., 52–53) may, on occasion, appear on only one of those pages.

Figures and tables are indicated by "f" and "t" following page numbers.

www.ingramcontent.com/pod-product-compliance
Lightning Source LLC
Chambersburg PA
CBHW061652090526
44820CB00003B/220
9780197821749